The 180-Days of Communing with God Daily Devotional

LaRose Angela Richardson

Copyright © 2021 by **LaRose Angela Richardson**

All rights reserved. No part of this publication may be reproduced, distributed or transmitted in any form or by any means, including photocopying, recording, or other electronic or mechanical methods, without the prior written permission of the publisher, except in the case of brief quotations embodied in critical reviews and certain other noncommercial uses permitted by copyright law. For permission requests, write to the publisher, addressed "Attention: Permissions Coordinator," at the address below.

LaRose Angela Richardson/Rejoice Essential Publishing
PO BOX 512
Effingham, SC 29541
www.republishing.org

Unless otherwise indicated, scripture is taken from the King James Version.'

"Scripture quotations taken from the Amplified® Bible (AMP), Copyright © 2015 by The Lockman Foundation. Used by permission. www.lockman.org"

"Scripture quotations taken from the Amplified® Bible Classic, Copyright © 1954, 1958, 1962, 1964, 1965, 1987 by The Lockman Foundation. Used by permission." (www.Lockman.org)

Scripture quotations marked (NLT) are taken from the Holy Bible, New Living Translation, copyright © 1996, 2004, 2007 by Tyndale House Foundation. Used by permission of Tyndale House Publishers, Inc., Carol Stream, IL 60188. All rights reserved.

Scripture taken from the HOLY BIBLE, NEW INTERNATIONAL VERSION®. Copyright © 1973, 1978, 1984 Biblica. Used by permission of Zondervan. All rights reserved.The "NIV" and "New International Version" trademarks are registered in the United States Patent and Trademark Office by Biblica. Use of either trademark requires the permission of Biblica

Scripture quotations marked (GNT) are taken from the Good News Translation in Today's English Version- Second Edition Copyright © 1992 by American Bible Society. Used by Permission.

Scripture taken from the New King James Version®. Copyright © 1982 by Thomas Nelson. Used by permission. All rights reserved.

The 180-Days of Communing with God Daily Devotional/ LaRose Angela Richardson

ISBN-13: 978-1-952312-51-9
Library of Congress Control: 2021901413

Contents

ACKNOWLEDGMENTS...xi
INTRODUCTION..1
January 1st...3
January 2nd..5
January 3rd...7
January 4th...9
January 5th...11
January 6th...13
January 7th...15
January 8th...18
January 9th...20
January 10th...22
January 11th...24
January 12th...26
January 13th...29
January 14th...31
January 15th...33
January 16th...35
January 17th...37
January 18th...39
January 19th...42
January 20th...44
January 21st...46
January 22nd..48
January 23rd...51
January 24th...53
January 25th...55

January 26th..57
January 27th..59
January 28th..61
January 29th..63
January 30th..65
January 31st...67
February 1st..69
February 2nd...71
February 3rd..73
February 4th..75
February 5th..78
February 6th..81
February 7th..83
February 8th..86
February 9th..89
February 10th..91
February 11th..93
February 12th..96
February 13th..98
February 14th..100
February 15th..102
February 16th..104
February 17th..106
February 18th..109
February 19th..112
February 20th..114
February 21st...116
February 22nd...118
February 23rd..120
February 24th..122
February 25th..124

February 26th	126
February 27th	128
February 28th	130
February 29th	132
March 1st	134
March 2nd	136
March 3rd	138
March 4th	140
March 5th	142
March 6th	144
March 7th	147
March 8th	149
March 9th	151
March 10th	153
March 11th	155
March 12th	157
March 13th	159
March 14th	161
March 15th	163
March 16th	165
March 17th	167
March 18th	169
March 19th	171
March 20th	173
March 21st	175
March 22nd	177
March 23rd	179
March 24th	181
March 25th	183
March 26th	185
March 27th	187
March 28th	189

March 29th	191
March 30th	194
March 31st	196
April 1st	198
April 2nd	200
April 3rd	202
April 4th	205
April 5th	207
April 6th	210
April 7th	213
April 8th	215
April 9th	217
April 10th	220
April 11nd	222
April 12th	225
April 13th	227
April 14th	229
April 15th	231
April 16th	233
April 17th	235
April 18th	237
April 19th	239
April 20th	241
April 21st	243
April 22nd	245
April 23rd	247
April 24th	249
April 25th	252
April 26th	255
April 27th	257
April 28th	259
April 29th	261

April 30th	263
May 1st	266
May 2nd	268
May 3rd	270
May 4th	272
May 5th	274
May 6th	276
May 7th	278
May 8th	280
May 9th	282
May 10th	284
May 11th	286
May 12th	289
May 13th	291
May 14th	293
May 15th	295
May 16th	297
May 17th	299
May 18th	301
May 19th	303
May 20th	305
May 21st	307
May 22nd	309
May 23rd	312
May 24th	314
May 25th	317
May 26th	319
May 27th	321
May 28th	323
May 29th	327
May 30th	329
May 31st	333

June 1st..335
June 2nd...337
June 3rd..340
June 4th..343
June 5th..345
June 6th..347
June 7th..349
June 8th..351
June 9th..353
June 10th..355
June 11th..357
June 12th..360
June 13th..362
June 14th..364
June 15th..366
June 16th..368
June 17th..370
June 18th..372
June 19th..375
June 20th..378
June 21st..380
June 22nd...382
June 23rd...384
June 24th..387
June 25th..389
June 26th..391
June 27th..393
June 28th..395
June 29th..398
June 30th..400
ABOUT THE AUTHOR..402
REFERENCES...403

Acknowledgments

I would like to thank God, who is the head of my life, for giving me the ability to write my 3rd book, 180 Days of Empowerment Daily Devotional. I welcome the Holy Spirit to go into every page to transform every reader while studying this book in Jesus' name.

"Lord, I am asking that you send Your Shekinah Glory to make them a new creature in Christ Jesus."

It is so important to walk through our journey empowered with the Word of God having it in our hearts and spirits. While reading this book daily throughout the first six months of the year, the person will be challenged to believe God's Word. The best way to get in touch with God is through His Word, so come with me on a journey through these six months and feast on the Word of God to help you mature in your walk with Him.

I would like to thank my husband Richard Richardson for being the man of God that he is. Without his total support, I wouldn't be able to write the books that I have already written. I thank him for supporting me even to the point of taking my books with him to his business and selling them. I thank him for being my number one fan. He has stood by me from day one, encouraging me to keep going regardless of the warfare. Someone bound and in need of being empowered by the Word of God needs to see and read my books.

I want to thank my Pastors, Apostle Troy Williams & Pastor Carmela Williams, for the exhortation they have spoken over my life. I would like to thank Apostle Troy for seeing the gifts and calling that are on my life. He is always encouraging and pushing me toward destiny in God. I thank him for calling me out and giving me the opportunity to speak what God is saying in this hour. I want to thank Pastor Carmella for all the Boot Camp classes that she does to help me get to my next business venture and showing me about marketing my ministry for success. She teaches me how to market my book on social media websites, which is very useful so I can be successful in the business and spiritual side of ministry.

I want to thank Prophetess Kimberly Moses for being obedient to God to offer the School of the Prophets. I am grateful to God for giving me the go ahead and take the class to help push me to the next level in God. God has used her to get me out of my comfort zone and to get me out of the cave, so I can do what God is calling me to do in this season.

I would like to thank God for all my leaders and all covenant people that He has put into my life up until this present time to get me to my next level in Him.

Introduction

THE DEFINITION OF DEVOTIONAL by Merriam-Webster is of or used in religious worship.[1] The Greek word for devotional is "proskartereo" and the meaning is to attend constantly.[2] So this is a 180 daily devotional designed to help you get in touch with God on a daily basis. It will also help you get more of the Word of God into your heart. As you read each day, you will begin to build up your spirit man so you can continue to walk out the victorious Christian lifestyle that God has intended for all His children to walk in.

You will find Scriptures that will empower you, and the meaning of them are already broken down, so you can get a deeper revelation of what you are reading and studying for that day. All the days will end with the prayer of faith or declarations, so you can go about your day feeling renewed by the Word of God. Each subject will help you to meditate on the goodness of God each day. Knowledge is power and the more

---

1. "Devotional" Merriam-Webster. Com 2019. https://www.merriam-webster.com Accessed July 2020.
2. "proskartereo" The Greek word for devotional. https://www.biblehub.com accessed July 2020

we study, read, and meditate on the Word of God, the better off that we will all be. If you are going in the wrong direction, you will have at least 180 days to get back into the right alignment with the Word of God. So, you can be pleasing in God's sight and stay in His will for your lives. Let's embark on this journey together to start being a better creature in Christ. We need to be good stewards over His Word every day of our lives, and we will start at the beginning of the year and work our way down to the middle of the year.

We have to train our mouths to speak what we want to happen in our lives. Proverbs 18:21(AMP) says, "Death and life are in the power of the tongue, and those, who love it and indulge it will eat its fruit and bear the consequences of their words." So, it is very important about the words that are coming out of our mouths. We must speak life over ourselves when we are going through trials, tribulations, and storms. God's Word is life and it will bring life into any dead situation. The Word of God is a resuscitation to you from the storms that you are facing in life.

January 1st

Proverbs 3:6 (AMP) states, "In all your ways know and acknowledge and recognize Him, And He will make your paths straight and smooth (removing obstacles that block your way)."

In this verse, God said that we should always acknowledge Him, not just during crises but with all things. We are not just to acknowledge Him during worship but during every aspect of our lives.[3] The Hebrew word for acknowledge is "Yada" which signifies to know and recognize.[4] So, we must acknowledge God in all our dealings and relationships. When we acknowledge God, He will give us direction to get back in alignment. If we have traveled too far from God to the right or the left, God will help us get back on the right path for our lives. God will remove anything that is hindering our progress in Him. So when He removes it, do not go back and get into it again.

PRAYER:

---

3. "Acknowledgement" https://www.biblehub.com accessed July 2020
4. "Yada" Hebrew word https://www.biblehub.com accessed July 2020.

Father God, in the name of Jesus, I come before You today to acknowledge You as my Lord and Savior and to ask that You order my steps from this day forward in Jesus' name. Lord, I desire to stay on the right path that You have for my life in Jesus' name. I want to walk the way You want me to walk so I can walk into the destiny that You have set for my life. Lord, You said in Proverbs 3:6 (AMP), "In all your ways know and acknowledge and recognize Him, and He will make your paths straight, and smooth (removing obstacles that block your way)." Thank You for watching over and after me in Jesus' name. Thank You for getting me back on the right track so I can come into perfect alignment with You in Jesus' name. Amen.

January 2nd

*P*ROVERBS 3:7 (AMP) SAYS, "Do not be wise in your own eyes, fear the Lord, (with relevant, awe, and obedience) and turn (entirely) away from evil."

Merriam-Webster's definition of the word wise is characterized by wisdom, marked by deep understanding, or keen discernment.[5] The Greek word for wise is "sophos," which means skilled, wise, learned, or clever.[6] In this verse, it is talking about not leaning to your understanding of things, and we don't need to be operating in self-sufficiency, self-conceit, or self-reliance. We must put our trust in the Lord only and not in ourselves. To have the wisdom of God, we must put our total trust in Him. When you are wise in your own eyes, you tell God that you don't need Him and that you can do it by yourself. Walking in the spirit of pride, puts you in an awful place. We must repent if we find ourselves walking in pride. We must depart for anything evil and stay in right standing with God.

---

5. "Wise" Merriam-Webster.com 2019. https://www.merriam-webster.com July 2020
6. "Sophos" Greek word https://www.biblehub.com accessed July 2020.

PRAYER:

Father God, in the name of Jesus, I come before You today to repent for all the times that I have walked in pride. Lord, I know that You are the one that has gotten me this far in my life, and it wasn't anything that I could have done for myself. Lord, thank You for forgiving and restoring me to my rightful place in You in Jesus' name. I bind the spirit of pride and all the symptoms that come with it. I release the spirit of humility to come upon and live within me right now in Jesus' name. Lord, thank You for setting me back on the right path for my life in Jesus' name. Amen.

January 3rd

REVELATION 3:20 (AMP) SAYS, "Behold I stand at the door (of the church) and continually knock. If anyone hears my voice and opens the door, I will come in and eat with him (restore him), and he with me."

According to Merriam-Webster, knock is to strike something with a sharp blow.[7] In the Greek, knock is "krouo," which means to knock, beat at the door with a stick, or gain admittance.[8] God is standing at the door of our hearts, wanting to gain entrance and live there. God wants to be our friend and commune with us daily. He wants to be there for us when we have a problem so we can tell our troubles to Him. But God doesn't force Himself on anyone. We must go to Him willingly and unafraid. It must be our choice to go to Him, and when we do it sincerely, He will come to live inside our hearts. Invite God into your lives if you haven't already because it will be the best decision you can ever make in this world. But if we reject Him again, sometimes He leaves and comes back again later to

---
7. "Knock" Merriam-Webster.com 2019. https://www.merriam-webster.com accessed July 2020.
8. "Krouo" Greek word https://www.biblehub.com accessed July 2020.

draw you closer to Him. So, it is so important to seek the Lord while He can be found. Don't ever wait too late to give your life to Christ because dying without Him is the worst thing in life that you can do. After death, there are no second chances. Since you rejected Him on earth, He will reject you before the Father in heaven. So, the rejection of Christ will have your fate forever sealed, to a place of torment forever and ever. Jesus seeks to come into the heart of a sinner so He can change their heart and mind for the better.

PRAYER:

Father God, in the name of Jesus, I come before You today because Your Word in Revelation 3:20 (AMP) declares, "Behold I stand at the door (of the church) and continually knock. If anyone hears my voice and opens the door, I will come in and eat with him (restore him), and he with me." So, Lord, I surrender my life and open my heart for You to come and live in me and restore me back to You from this day forward in Jesus' name. Amen.

January 4th

JOHN 14:1 (AMP) "Do not let your heart be troubled (afraid, cowardly). Believe (confidently) in God and trust in Him, (have faith, hold on to it, rely on it, keep going and), believe also in me."

The word "believe" in the Merriam-Webster Dictionary is to consider to be true or honest.[9] In the Greek, the word believe is "pisteuo" meaning to think and be true or place confidence in.[10] In the Scripture above, Jesus told the disciples that He was getting ready to leave them. Jesus said to them that they would need to continue to fully trust in God and not to be troubled in their mind. So, this Word applies to us today. As we read it, get it into our hearts, and continue to stand on it, we can lean on God for support or help with all our life situations. Christ is sitting at the right hand of the Father interceding for you and me. He is our mediator between God and us. We don't have anything to worry about as long as our hands, hearts, and spirits are rooted and grounded in the Word of God. God is just a "hello" away. All we need to do is call out to Him, and imme-

9. "Believe" Merriam-Webster.com 2019. https://www.merriam-webster.com July 2020
10 "Pisteuo" Greek word   https://www.biblestudytools.com July 2020.

diately He is there with us to lead, guide, and help us through rough spots in our lives. God says in the Word that He will never leave or forsake us but will be with us until the end of the world. If you need Him today, just call the name of Jesus because there is power in that name; that will solve all things and calm all your fears.

PRAYER:

Father God, in the name of Jesus, I come before You today to ask that You will help my unbelief and doubt. Lord, in your Word in Mark 9:24 (AMP) says, "A father had taken his son to Jesus so that he could be healed and the father immediately cried out (with a desperate, piercing cry), saying, "I do believe; help (me overcome) my unbelief." Lord, help me to believe and take You at Your Word when You tell me that You will supply my every need, such as Your riches in glory by Christ Jesus. Lord, help me to believe that You love me and care about the same things that concern me. Lord, I thank You for coming to my rescue in Jesus' name. Amen.

January 5th

Joshua 1:8 (AMP) states, "This Book of the Law shall not depart from your mouth, but you shall read (and meditate on) it day and night, so that you may be careful to do (everything) in accordance with all that is written in it, for then you will make your way prosperous, and then you will be successful."

Law in the Merriam-Webster Dictionary is a binding custom or practice of a community.[11] The Greek word for law is "Nomos," which means divine laws, a force or influence impelling to action.[12] We are to read, study, and meditate day and night on the Word of God. So, we can know what the Word says, and we can pattern our life to line up with the Word. Whether it be male or female, no person can set themselves up above the law of God. We should always refer to the Word of God in any situation that comes up in our lives, so we can see what it says about a matter. When we know the Word for ourselves, we won't blindly follow any other doctrine. Hebrews 4:12 (NLT) says, "God's Word is alive and powerful. It is sharper than the

---

11. "Law" Merriam-Webster.com https://www.merriamwebster.com accessed July 2020
12. "Nomos" Greek word for law https://www.biblehub.com accessed July 2020

sharpest two-edged sword, cutting between soul and spirit, between joint and marrow. It exposes our innermost thoughts and desires." The Law of God must be followed to reach victory in our lives.

PRAYER:

Father God, in the name of Jesus, we come before you today to ask that You help me to remember everything that I have studied, read, and meditated on about Your Word. Whenever I need it to minister or console someone, the Word of God would come back up to my remembrance so that You can be glorified in Jesus' name. Lord, help me to hide the Word of God in my heart so that I will not sin against thee in Jesus' name. Holy Ghost, thank You for being a counselor when I needed to talk. Thank you for telling me who I am in You at this point in my life in Jesus' name. Thank You for always encouraging me to keep moving forward in You in Jesus' name. Amen.

January 6th

MATTHEW 6:10 SAYS, "YOUR kingdom come, thou will be done, on earth as it is in heaven."

The word "will" in the Merriam-Webster Dictionary is the power or the control over one's actions and emotions."[13] The Greek word for will is "thelemia" which means the act of will, [14]wishes, and desires. In the Scripture above, we refer to the 'will of God' because His will in heaven is what He wants to bring to the earth. But we are the ones that must decree and declare His will to come to earth. When we speak the Word of God over our lives, God responds because it is His Word. This Scripture teaches us to seek God's will for everything that concerns us. God's Word reigns everywhere, and when it is obeyed in the earth, God will send heaven down to earth. It is God's Will to advance His kingdom here on earth, and He will use His people to make the advancements. It is God's Will for His Word to reach all over this nation and the world.[15] He wants ev-

---
13. "Will" Merriam-Webster.com 2019 https://www.merriamwebster.com accessed July 2020
14. "Thelema" Greek word for Will https://www.biblehub.com accessed July 2020
15. Matthew 6:10 Matthew Henry's Concise Bible Commentary & Barnes Notes on the Bible. https://www.biblehub.com accessed July 2020

eryone to hear the Word in their own language to have a better understanding of Him. It is God's will for all His people to be blessed, prosperous, and to be able to help build up His Kingdom. It is His will to provide us with witty inventions and new streams of income. It is His Will to bless His people spiritually, mentally, physically and financially abundantly, so we can live whole and fulfilled lives in Him.

PRAYER:

Father God, in the name of Jesus, I come before You today to ask that Your Will be done on earth as it is in heaven in my life. Lord, help me always to know Your will before I venture out and do something that is not pleasing to You. Lord, help me read Your Word every day and hide it in my heart, so I will not sin against You. Lord, bring heaven to earth in my life so that I can do what You are calling me to do for Your Kingdom. Lord, I will love You. Lord, I will serve You for the rest of my life. Lord, I will always bring my fears and doubts before You to rest assured that You will work things out for me. Lord, I pray that Your will for my family will be shown to us to stay in the right alignment for Your Will in our lives. Lord, I thank You for the inheritance that You give to those that love and serve You in Jesus' name. Amen.

January 7th

Luke 6:21 says, "Blessed are ye that weep now; for ye shall laugh."

Laugh in the Merriam-Webster Dictionary is to show emotion (such as joy).[16] The Greek word for laugh is "gelos" which means laughter.[17] You may have been weeping, but the above Scripture says that you will laugh now, meaning that you will be happy, joyful, and no longer grieved. Psalm 30:5 (AMP) states, "Weeping may endure for night, but a shout of joy comes in the morning." God sees the pain in your heart, and you may be wondering why this is happening to you now because it is not God's best. Perhaps you have settled for something because it seemed to be taking too long to get to you. You must trust God and wait on the answer no matter how long it takes to come to fruition. It is not God's will for us to be mourning always. You should be walking around with joy on your faces because God deeply loves and cares about you. It is not God's will for us to be hurt physically, mentally, emotionally, or spiritually. He loves us, and He is a good Father to us. He wants the best of

---
16. Laugh" Merriam-Webster.com 2019 https://www.merrriam-webster.com accessed July 2020
17. "Gelos" Greek word laugh https://www.biblehub.com accessed July 2020

everything for His people. Just remember that sorrow will not last forever because everything has an expiration date. God is sending you joy, peace, love, and protection through His Word. We must read it to see what it says and how it applies to each of us. God wants to restore what we have lost. He will give us seven times back of what we lost or what the enemy took from us.[18] God wants to restore everything in Joel 2:25 (AMP), "And I will compensate you for the years That the swarming locust has eaten, The creeping locust, the stripping locust, and the gnawing locust—My great army which I sent among you."

God will bless us so much that all you will be able to do is laugh and scratch your head in awe. Joel 2:26 states, "You will have plenty to eat and be satisfied. And praise the name of the Lord your God. Who has dealt wondrously with you; And My people shall never be put to shame." So, get ready for a happy and joyous time in your life. The days of not having enough will no longer be your portion. You have graduated to the land of overflow, more than enough, so that you can be a blessing to other people you know and some you don't know. You will be a glory carrier for the kingdom.

PRAYER:

Father God, in the name of Jesus, we come before You today to ask that You restore to me everything that the devil has stolen from our family dating back to the generation of Adam and Eve. Lord, You said in Joel 2:25 (AMP) "And I will compensate you for the years That the swarming locust has eaten, the

---

18. "Weeping my do for a night but Joy comes in the morning article. https:/www.fromhispresence.com accessed July 2020

creeping locust, the stripping locust, and the gnawing locust that has stolen for me." Lord, I thank You for restoring it all back into my possession. Lord, help make me a good steward or manager of my finances to make good sound decisions on how to manage it in Jesus' name. Lord, thank You for wiping every tear away from my eyes and giving me joy and beauty for ashes in Jesus' name. Amen.

January 8th

Colossians 4:2 says, "Be persistent and devoted to prayer, being alert and focused in your prayer life with an attitude of thanksgiving."

In the Merriam-Webster Dictionary, persistence is existing for a long or longer than usual time or continuously.[19] The Greek word for persistent is "anaideia," which means shamelessness, without shame, or not backing down.[20] The above Scripture says to be persistent in prayer, which means never backing down from it and praying both in and out of season. Daniel prayed three times a day without ceasing, even though King Nebuchadnezzar decreed that nobody could pray to any other person except him. Daniel refused to pray to him and only chose to pray to God, our Abba Father, and the One who will continually answer our prayers. Before we can have any significant moves of God in our ministry, prayers must go up before Him to get the instructions on how to be effective. Jesus prayed all the time before He went to do any miracles for anyone. That is why the disciples asked Jesus to show them how to

---
19. "Persistent" Merriam-Webster.com 2019 https://www.merriam-webster.com accessed July 2020.
20. "Anaideia" Greek for persistent https://www.biblehub.com accessed July 2020

January 8th

pray. In Matthew 6:9-14, Jesus led them in the Lord's Prayer, and that prayer is still efficient for those that need to know how to pray effectively. The fervent prayers of the righteous availeth much and produces wonderful results because prayer is our lifeline to God. Make sure that you always keep the lines open between you and God through prayer.

PRAYER:

Father God, in the name of Jesus, we come before You today in prayer. Lord, You said in Your Word to be persistent, devoted to prayer, alert, and focused in my prayer life with an attitude of thanksgiving. Lord, give me a burden for intercessory prayer so that I can pray for whomever You drop into my spirit in Jesus' name. Lord, we are living times where we need to have an effective prayer life. Lord, help me continuously pray until it is manifested in the natural realm in Jesus' name. Lord, I know that great movements of Your Spirit must be birthed in prayer before they can manifest in the natural realm. Lord, help me to pray effectively and remind You of Your word so the solution will manifest in Jesus' name. Amen.

January 9th

1 Peter 4:8 (AMP) says, "Above all have fervent unfailing love for one another, because love covers a multitude of sins (it overlooks unkindness and unselfishly seeks the best for others)."

Fervent in the Merriam-Webster Dictionary means hot burning or glowing.[21] The Greek word for fervent is "zeo" which means to boil, be hot, boiling, or burn in spirit.[22] The Scripture above says that we are supposed to have a burning hot love for one another because love is the badge of the profession for a child of God. When doing anything in ministry, there has to be love between God's people. Love needs to be seen in the Body of Christ so the world may see and believe that God sent Jesus, who suffered, bled, died, and rose again with all power in the palm of His hand. When the world sees that kind of love in the Body of Christ, they will be drawn to Him by that love (agape). Proverbs 10:12 says, "Love covers a multitude of sins." We must not knowingly cover up a person's sins when they are out of the will of God for their lives. Give them the word that

---
21. "Fervent" Merriam-Webster.com 2019 https://www.merriam-webster.com accessed July 2020
22. "Zeo" Greek word for fervent https://www.biblehub.com accessed July 2020

January 9th

God has given you for them because He wants to get them back on the right track and back in His will.

PRAYER:

Father God, in the name of Jesus, I humbly come to you again. Lord, forgive me of all sins right now in Jesus' name. Forgive me of all sins, knowingly and unknowingly, in thought and deed, omission, and commission right now in Jesus' name. Lord, help me to have a fervent and burning love for the people that you put around me and the ones in my family, church, neighborhood, and anybody that I may encounter, in Jesus' name. Also, help me to have a burning to see many souls saved for Your kingdom. Lord, let every time I go to the grocery stores, Walmart, doctor's office, etc., be a divine opportunity to help build up Your kingdom in Jesus' name. Lord, help me to boldly tell them about You and the depth of Your love for them in Jesus' name. Lord, help me to love my enemies and pray for them to get to know You God, in Jesus' name. Lord, I thank You for teaching me how to love like You in Jesus' name. Amen.

January 10th

1 Thessalonians 5:11 (AMP) says, "Therefore encourage and comfort one another and build up one another, just as you are doing."

Encourage, in the Merriam-Webster Dictionary, means to inspire with courage, spirit, or hope.[23] The Greek word for encourage is "parakaleo," which means to call to or for, exhort, or encourage.[24] In the Scripture above, God wants us to encourage one another and comfort them when they are going through trials, so they will know they are not alone in this world. A kind word or gesture can make someone's day better. Your encouragement could give someone the strength they need to keep moving on in God. Many of us have testimonies that we need to share with someone who is going through. Tell them what God has done in your life. Your testimony will boost their confidence about what God can do for them. The people to whom you are witnessing in a dark place right now, but after you shed the light of the Word on the matter, it will encourage them

---

23. "Encourage" Merriam-Webster.com 2019 https://www.merriam-webster.com accessed July 2020
24. "Parakaleo" Greek word for encourage https://www.biblehub.com accessed July 2020

January 10th

to keep going on in God. When you give enough of the right encouragement, a person may leave their sinful lifestyle and give their life to Christ. We must step out and say something to them. Many of them are waiting on a Word from the Lord, and God wants to use His people to do it. God will bring everyone to seek Him out to a new place in Him and life in general. God wants to change everything in your life that is dead and will speak life into it. God said live. There should be no more walking around like the walking dead, wandering about aimlessly, and not having a purpose. True purpose can only be found in Jesus, so continue to run after Jesus because He is the only way on this earth to get to eternal life.

PRAYERS:

Father God, in the name of Jesus, I stand before You now asking that You empower me to be an encourager to everyone that I meet from this day forward in Jesus' name. Lord, help me to be a beacon of light to someone who has lost their way in this world. Lord, help me not to be ashamed of my testimonies because I know that it will help someone overcome a dark place to come to a peaceful place in their lives. Lord, help me to be a beacon of light in every dark place that I will encounter. Holy Spirit, lead and guide me to be a blessing in someone's life. As I am that blessing, Lord, send someone to our children's lives to encourage them to change their wayward ways in Jesus' name.

January 11th

Psalm 55:22 (AMP) "Cast your burdens on the Lord (release it) and He will sustain and uphold you; He will never allow the righteous to be shaken (slip or fail)."

Cast in Merriam-Webster Dictionary means moving or sending forth by throwing, getting rid of, or discard.[25] The Greek word for cast is "rhipto" which means to throw, to cast, to throw off, or toss.[26] God wants us to cast our burdens onto Him. We need to be laying them at His feet and leaving them there. Cast all your cares, fears, affairs, relationships, marriage, children, grandchildren, business, careers, or etc. All of these need to be cast at the feet of Jesus so that He can work it out on our behalf. God will work it out so well that it will be in our best interest, and that is what He desires for His people. So, leave your troubles and trials at the altar and leave it there. Stop getting in the way and let God work it out on your behalf. Trust me. God has everything under control. Even during the chaos, God is in the background putting people and situations

---
25. "Cast" Merriam-Webster.com 2019 https://www.merriam-webster.com accessed July 2020
26. "Rhipto" Greek word for Cast https://www.biblehub.com accessed July 2020

January 11th

in place so that it will bless your life. Our trials and struggles aren't meant to destroy us, but they are meant to build up your strength and muscles. We can walk in strength because God is our source of strength for the believer. Often, if things are going well in our lives, we tend to slack off our prayer lives. But when things rub us the wrong way, we are more apt to fall on our faces or knees before God. Staying in the presence of God is so essential for our lives and ministries. God wants all of His people to have an intimate relationship with Him, and prayer is the key to having that relationship with Him. God is our Abba Father, and we are His children.

PRAYER:

Father God, in the name of Jesus, I come before You today to lay all my burdens, trials, and tribulations at Your feet and to leave them there in Jesus' name. Lord, I cast all my fears today on You too. Lord, You know better than me and know my future from my beginning. You also know what I need in Jesus' name. Lord, strengthen me in Jesus' name. Lord, help me to be intentional about everything I do that concerns You in Jesus' name. Lord, I cast those troubles off, and I will stop picking them back up again in Jesus' name. Lord, I thank You for what You are getting ready to do in my life. Thank you for making a new creature out of me in Jesus' name. Amen.

January 12th

Acts 20:24 (AMP) says, "But I do not consider my life as something of value or dear to me, so that I may(with joy) finish my course and the ministry which I received from the Lord Jesus, to testify faithfully of the Good News of God's (precious undeserved grace(which makes me free of the guilt of sin and grants us eternal life)."

Good News in the Merriam-Webster Dictionary means something new that will be useful to someone.[27] The Greek word for Good News is "euaggelion, which means the Good News of Jesus?[28]

Are you telling the Good News of Jesus? Here are three things to ask yourself:

1. When was the last time that you told someone about the Good News of Jesus?

---

27. "Good News" Merriam-Webster.com 2019 https://www.merriam-webster.com accessed July 2020
28. "evaggelin" Greek word for Good News https://www.biblehub.com accessed July 2020

January 12th

2. Challenge: After reading this devotional, are you willing to tell someone how God has delivered you?

3. Do people know that you are a child of God by the way you carry yourself?

If not, then here is your opportunity to start telling the Good News to everyone at your job because God wants to draw people to Him. Let the people you meet every day know that you are a child of God. Also, inform them that God has taken care of you all these years, and He isn't going to stop now. Let them know that God can take care of them as well. Paul taught the Good News of the gospel to whomever he encountered. Paul taught that to gain salvation, a sinner must repent for their sin. They must believe that God sent Jesus to die for their sins, and that He rose on the third day with all power in the palm of His hands. Every sin that we could ever commit was placed on Jesus. We must no longer walk in sin because of Jesus's sacrifice. So, if we confess with our mouths and believe it in our hearts that God raised Jesus from the dead, we can all be saved through His sacrifice. The Holy Spirit comes to live in us when we are saved, and we are sealed with the promise of what Jesus has done for us.

Receiving Christ is as easy. All you must do is make up your mind, speak the words, and believe in your heart; then you are a new creature in Christ. But to grow from milk to meat, you must get into a 5-Fold ministry so you can be equipped for the work of God. You will have to read your word, pray, fast, worship, live a holy and righteous lifestyle to continue to grow in Christ. Allow God to do a work in you by removing all the old deeds out of your heart, mind, and soul and making a new creature out of you. Because in this Christian walk, we must die daily, take up our cross, and follow Christ daily so we can start to look more like Christ. The crowd of people we used to hang around before we were saved should also change because two cannot walk together without agreement. We should be changing the way we talk and walk and the places that we use to go because God is taking us through a process; so, He can use us the way He wants. We must submit to the process and not fight it. God wants to develop godly character in us. He wants us to walk in integrity because we will be standing for Him. We must continue to be yielded vessels open to the changes that God wants to do in our lives. We all are a work in progress under the hands of the potter.

PRAYER:

In the name of Jesus, Father, guide me to who You want me to witness and share my testimonies. Help me be a good steward of the Good News so that I can tell it to the people that You send to me in Jesus' name. Lord, help me be more sensitive to Your voice when you prompt me to move in Jesus' name. Lord, I am a willing vessel to be used by You for Your glory in Jesus' name. Lord, give me a passion for lost souls from this day forward in Jesus' name. Because I have many family members who need to know about You, use me to minister to them in Jesus' name. Lord, thank You for giving me a chance to serve You in Jesus' name. Amen.

January 13th

2 Thessalonians 3:3 (AMP) says, "But the Lord is faithful, and He will strengthen you (setting you on a firm foundation) and will protect and guard you from the evil one."

Foundation in the Merriam-Webster Dictionary is a basis (such as a tenet, principle, or axiom) upon which something stands or is supported.[29] The Greek word for a foundation is "themelio," which means to put down, groundwork, or substructure.[30] We must put our trust in God instead of man to work things out for us in our lives. We can't even do it in our own strength. We must totally depend on the strength that God gives us through His grace. God will set us on a firm foundation and will put His hedge of protection around us to keep us covered from the fiery darts of the enemy. The enemy wants to shake our faith and get us to take our eyes off God as Peter did. We must continue to move forward and not stop because our breakthrough is just on the horizon. Sometimes we must fast

---

29. "Foundation" Merriam-Webster.com 2019 https://www.merriam-webster.com accessed July 2020
30. "Themelios" Greek word for Foundation https://www.biblehub.com accessed July 2020

and pray to get through many challenging situations or obstacles that we face in our lives, marriages, careers, and families. God has everything that we need wrapped up in Him.

PRAYER:

Father God, in the name of Jesus, I come before You today to ask for more strength to make it through these trying times that I am going through right now in my life. Lord, thank You because Your Word declares that You would strengthen, protect, and guard me against the evil one. Lord, I ask that You strengthen my spirit, soul, and body to make it through this hard test that I am presently going through at this moment of my life. Lord, heal my negative emotions and send them back to the pit of hell from which they came. I realize that the enemy is trying to stop me from reaching my destiny in God by continuing to throw things at me to block my path. Lord, thank You for helping me move forward in You in Jesus' name. Amen.

January 14th

Psalm 27:14 (NLT) says, "Wait (rely) patiently for the Lord, be brave and courageous, Yes, wait (rely) patiently for the Lord."

Wait in Merriam-Webster Dictionary is to stay in place or in expectation of.[31] The Greek word for wait is "perimeno" to wait for, I wait for, or await.[32]

Sometimes we must encourage ourselves while we are encouraging others too. Have you ever needed prayer or encouragement, and someone would always call or text you, asking you for prayer, and you will say to yourself, "Lord, how can I encourage someone else when I need it myself?" The Scripture above reminds us to wait and rely on the Lord for whatever we need. I realize that sometimes it seems like it is taking years for a promise to come to pass. But even in our waiting, we still must continue to rely on the Lord. God knows what is best for us, and He will give it to us in His timing. So be of good cour-

---

31. "Wait" Merriam-Webster.com 2019 https://www.merriam-webster.com accessed July 2020
32. "Perimeno" Greek word for Wait http://www.biblehub.com accessed July 2020

age. God knows all about our prayer needs. He wants to come and take care of your problems for you, so you can walk in victory in your life.

PRAYER:

In the name of Jesus, Father God, I come to You today to ask that You help me be patient and learn how to wait on You and take care of the things that I have prayed about Lord, You said in Your word to not to get weary in well doing because we will reap if we faint not. So, Lord, strengthen me physically, mentally, financially, and emotionally so that I can continue to move forward in You. Lord, I am trying to continue to think positively about the situation, but it seems to be taking a long time coming to pass in my life. I know that You have the best intentions for me. You are working some things out in me. Lord, I thank You for finishing what You have started in me in Jesus' name. Amen.

January 15th

Luke 6:27-28 (NLT) states, "But to you who are willing to listen, I say, love your enemies! Do good to those who hate you. 28. Bless those who curse you, pray for those who mistreat you."

Bless in the Merriam-Webster Dictionary is to invoke divine care for.[33] The Greek word for bless is "makarios," which means blessed, happy, or to be envied.[34]

God wants us to love our enemies. Yes, this includes the person who has slandered your name all over the neighborhood you live in. Yes, God wants you to forgive them and love them like He loves them. We often think this is a challenging task for us, but God said to do it and we should make every effort to be obedient to what He is telling us. God said to pray for our enemies, so if you are praying for them, it will help you to forgive them too. You cannot continue to be angry with someone that you are praying for regularly. God will start to soften your heart

---
33. "Bless" Merriam-Webster.comn2019 https://www.merriam-webster.com accessed July 2020
34. "Makarios" Greek word for Bless https://www.biblehub.com accessed July 2020

toward them. This is an important step in keeping our hearts pure and our hands clean before God.

PRAYER:

In the name of Jesus, Father God, I come to You today to ask that You help me love my enemies and those that despitefully misuse me for Your namesake. Lord, I forgive them so that I can keep my heart pure and move on in my walk with You. O God, create in me a clean heart and renew a right spirit within me. Lord, help me release my heart's issues to You and leave it there, so I can walk in total freedom in Jesus' name. Amen.

January 16th

Isaiah 41:13 (NLT) says, "For I hold you by your right hand—I, the Lord your God. And I say to you, "Don't be afraid. I am here to help you."

Hold in the Merriam-Webster Dictionary is to have possession or ownership of or have at one's disposal.[35] The Greek word for hold is "katecho," which means to hold fast or hold back.[36]

God will hold each of us with His right hand, and He will be our God if we let Him. God wants to make things better for us. He is telling us not to fear anything because He is looking out for us. God has us covered under His blood and He has given us the keys to His Kingdom. We need to put on the whole armor of God, continue to pray, and let Him know what is going on with us. God is saying that He is here to help us with whatever we need, no matter what. If you need emotional healing, He is there to help you with it. "Lord, we lay all our burdens on You so You can help us with them."

---
35. "Hold" Merriam-Webster.com 2019 https://www.merriam-webster.com accessed July 2020
36. "Katecho" Greek word for hold https://www.biblehub.com accessed July 2020

PRAYER:

Father God, in the name of Jesus, I come before You today asking that You help me with everything that is going on in my life right now in Jesus' name. Lord, I need You so much and I need You to heal every area in my life that is broken, so I can walk in wholeness in Jesus' name. Lord, cover me under Your blood and keep me from all harm from the tricks and schemes of the enemy in Jesus' name. Lord, always help me keep the full armor of God on and to consult You for everything in my life in Jesus' name. Amen.

January 17th

Psalm 119:2 (NLT) says, "Joyful are those who obey his laws and search for him with all their hearts."

Joy in the Merriam-Webster Dictionary is the emotion evoked by well-being success, good fortune or by the prospect of possessing what one desires.[37] The Greek word for joy is "chara," which means joy, delight, gladness, or a source of joy.[38]

God knows our hearts and He knows what our intentions are even if we try to keep it from Him by saying one thing but doing another. This does not work with God because He is all-knowing. He knows everything about us. He knows what our intentions are always concerning Him. In the Scripture, God tells us to obey His laws (Word) and search for Him with all our hearts. God wants us to be true and sold out to Him and not just use Him as a sugar daddy when we need something. God is more than a one-time fling. He is continuous, and wants to be put first in our lives. Matthew 6:33 says, "Seek ye first the King-

---

37. "Joy" Merriam-Webster.com 2019 https://www.merriam-webster.com accessed July 2020
38. "Chura" Greek Word for Joy https://www.biblehub.com accessed July 2020

dom of God and His righteousness and all other things will be added unto you." So, this verse explains that when we put Him first and let Him take full control, God will add all the things that we will ever need to our lives. This is a promise that we can rely on because God's Word is true and powerful.

PRAYER:

Jehovah God, we come before You today to put all our trust in You and in Your word because we know that Your Word is powerful and sharper than any two-edged sword. Lord, Your Word declares that we have not because we ask not. Today I am asking You to help me to be real and live a life that is pleasing to You. I want to please You with my life and ministry in Jesus' name. Lord, thank You for opening my eyes and ears so that I hear and see the things that you need me to see at any given time in Jesus' name. Amen.

January 18th

James 1:19-20 (AMP) "Understand this, my beloved brothers and sisters. Let everyone be quick to hear (be a careful, thoughtful listener), slow to speak (a speaker of carefully chosen words and) slow to anger (patient, reflective, forgiving). 20. For the (resentful, deep-seated) anger of man does not produce the righteousness of God (that standard of behavior which He requires from us)."

Anger in the Merriam-Webster Dictionary is a strong feeling of displeasure and usually of antagonism.[39] The Greek word for anger is "orge," which means wrath, passion, or punishment.[40]

The enemy knows our weaknesses, so he continues to bring things our way to get us upset and acting out of character with our spouses, families, and on our jobs. We must ask God to help us with anger because we will not be able to do it independently. Most of the time with anger you will have to go through deliverance to get rid of it altogether. We must not take the

---

39. "Anger" Merriam-Webster.com 2019 https://www.merriam-webster.com accessed July 2020
40. "Orge" Merriam-Webster.com 2019 https://www.biblehub.com accessed July 2020

bait of Satan because we know that he aims to steal, kill, and destroy our lives and destinies in God. When we are upset with our family members, it is sometimes best to go into the other room to keep from doing something that we will regret later. For example, we usually get upset when someone does something against us like stealing. As a result, we want justice and revenge, but God said in His word that vengeance was His and not ours. Sometimes we may be led to pray that God gets those to whom our anger is directed, but that is not right. God wants us to pray for their salvation and that they will be blessed. It is extremely hard to forgive people for this offense, but we must do it because God commanded it. We need to pray and ask God to help us do this. It is always okay to ask God for more grace to forgive the people who have wronged you. "Lord, I forgive the people who have stolen from me with false claims in Jesus' name." Give it all to Jesus, and He will work it all out for you. Nothing goes unnoticed by God. He will use it all to propel you to your destiny in Him.

PRAYER:

Father God, in the name of Jesus, Your Word declares that we are to be slow to speak and slow to anger. Lord, every time I turn around, my enemies are trying to set a trap for me. Lord, thank You for our precious blood that has my family and me covered, so nothing by any means shall harm us. Satan, we serve you notice you cannot stop what God says is blessed in Jesus' name. Lord, put a guard over my mouth to not say anything that would harm or injure anyone's hearts. Lord, I repent for letting my feelings and emotions get the best of me in Jesus' name. I cast down every word curse that I have spoken over all my family members, and I will say what God says on the matter. I will no longer speak what I see but will speak the solution to the problem. Lord, put the coals of fire on my mouth and tongue so that I can think before I speak from this day forward in Jesus' name. Amen.

January 19th

EPHESIANS 4:2 (AMP) STATES, "With all humility (forsaking self-righteousness), and gentleness (maintaining self-control), with patience, bearing with one another in (unselfish) love.

Humility in the Merriam-Webster Dictionary is freedom from pride or arrogance.[41] The Greek word for humility is "tapeinophrosune," meaning lowliness of mind, humility, or modesty.[42]

A meek person has a gentle spirit and can get along with anyone that they meet. A humble person is teachable and does not mind serving God and their leaders as well. Many people walk in false humility, and this is not being humble at all. Nobody is unable to tell them anything because they think that they know it all. This kind of person will never take responsibility for their actions. They will blame others for what is going on in their lives, homes, or churches. We need to humble ourselves and

---

41. "Humility" Merriam-Webster.com 2019 https://www.merriam-webster.com accessed July 2020
42. "tapeinophrosune" Greek for Humility https://www.biblehub.com accessed July 2020

January 19th

get low. Then God will raise us up to where He wants to take us. People who have false humility are also self-righteous. They think that they have done everything for themselves independently and feel they do not need God. They will see what the other person is doing and point out their flaws and issues, but will not deal with their problems. No one is correct all the time. We all can learn something new from God. Humility is one of the fruits of the Spirit and to be able to please God, we will need humility. In His word, God said that He hates pride, so we cannot walk in arrogance and please Him. We cannot walk in humility and pride at the same time. It is impossible.

PRAYER:

Father God, in the name of Jesus, I come before You today to ask that You forgive me for walking in pride when I should have been walking in humility in Jesus' name. I know that humility is one of the nine fruits of the Spirit. I need to be walking in all of them to be effective in the Kingdom of God. Pride has no place in me, and God hates the spirit of Leviathan. Leviathan (pride) cannot take me to my next level in You, God. Lord, change my heart and create a new and right spirit in me to walk in humility. Everything that I have, You gave it to me, and it is because of You that I can go forward in the calling that You have on my life in Jesus' name. Lord, help me to keep my heart clean and pure in Jesus' name. Amen.

January 20th

Jude 1:20 (AMP) states, "But you, beloved, build yourselves up on (the foundation of) your most holy faith (continually progress, rise like an edifice higher and higher), pray in the Holy Spirit."

Tongues in the Merriam-Webster Dictionary are ecstatic or typically unintelligible utterances, especially in a moment of religious excitement.[43] The Greek word for tongues is "glossa, which is a tongue or language.[44]

We can build our spirits up every day if we continue to pray in tongues about whatever is going on in our lives and families. Tongues are praying directly to God. Our tongues will pray the heart of God for a situation that may be going on in our lives. In an article on kcm.org, Pastor Kenneth Copeland talks about five benefits of speaking in tongues that will help your life. Here are the five so you can get a good understanding of them.

FIVE BENEFITS OF SPEAKING IN TONGUES

---

43. "Tongues" Merriam-Webster.com 2019 https://www.merriam-webster.com accessed July 2020
44. "Glossa" Greek for Tongues https://www.biblehub.com accessed July 2020

January 20th

1. Praying in tongues allows you to speak directly to God. (1 Corinthians 14:2)
2. Praying in tongues keeps you in tune with the Holy Spirit. (Acts 2)
3. Praying in tongues strengthens your spirit. It will help you to live a Spirit-led life. (1 Corinthians 14:4)
4. Praying in tongues allows you to pray even when you don't know what to pray. (Romans 8:26)
5. Praying in tongues is a weapon against the work of the enemy. (Mark 16:15-18)[45]

PRAYER:

Father God, in the name of Jesus, I come to You today to ask that You would give me the gift of tongues to start praying in my heavenly language each day in Jesus' name. Lord, just like the day when the Holy Spirit fell in the upper room, let Your Spirit fall on me and pray through me. Holy Spirit, I welcome You into my life so that You will be there to lead and guide me into all truths and to help me get stronger in my prayer life. Lord, as I open my mouth, let the gift of tongues come upon me now, and I will speak with other tongues as Your Spirit gives me utterance. Lord, when I don't know what to pray for or how to pray, I can now pray in tongues and pray perfect prayers to You in heaven in Jesus' name. Amen.

---

45. Benefits of Praying in Tongues by KCM.org Accessed July 2020

January 21st

John 15:7 (AMP) says, "If you remain in Me and My words remain in you (that is, if we are vitally united and My message lives in your heart), ask whatever you wish and it will be done for you."

Remain in the Merriam-Webster Dictionary is to stay in the same place or with the same person or group.[46] The Greek word for remain is "meno," meaning to stay, abide, or remain.[47]

The Scripture above talks about abiding in God and letting Him abide in our hearts and live a holy and righteous lifestyle that we can ask for what we need, and it will be given to us. So, we need to abide in Jesus once we know Him as our Lord and Savior. The only way we get what we need spiritually, physically, mentally, financially, and get all of our needs met is by abiding in Jesus. There is no way that we can make anything happen on our own without God. We need God for everything. We need Him to wake us up every morning because we would have never woken each day without Him. We need God to breathe

---

46. "Remain" Merriam-Webster.com 2019 https://www.merriam-webster.com accessed July 2020
47. "Meno" Greek word for Remain https://www.biblehub.com accessed July 2020

January 21st

because He is the One that supplies the oxygen that we breathe. If there were no oxygen, we would have suffocated already. We need God to set the temperatures for Spring, Summer, Fall, and Winter. We need God to be able to move our bodies, feed, and dress ourselves. I don't know why anyone would think that they didn't need God when He made everything here on earth that we use daily. When we abide in the Word of God and allow it to change us and make all things new, we can walk the faith walk. The Bible states that without faith, it is impossible to please God. Everything that we do for God and what He does through us is obtained by faith. In His Word, God also said that we could have what we say when we are saying it in faith, and it is lining up with His will for our lives.

PRAYER:

Father God, in the name of Jesus, it is again that we come to the throne of mercy and grace. Lord, I say thank You for watching over me day by day. Lord, I do not take anything for granted because I know that You are the one that is making everything good happen in my life. Lord, I will forever abide in You as You will abide in me. I can do all things through Christ that strengthens me in Jesus' name. Lord, continue to make and mold me into the person that You want me to be in Jesus' name. Lord, I take my faith and believe that You can do anything but fail in my life. Thank You for shaping me, just like the potter shapes the clay into Your beautiful masterpiece in Jesus' name. Lord, let our wills align concerning my life from this day forward in Jesus' name. Amen.

January 22nd

HEBREWS 12:14 (AMP) SAYS, "Continually pursue peace with everyone, and the sanctification without no one will (ever) see the Lord."

Merriam-Webster Dictionary's definition for sanctification is to set apart as or declare holy; consecrate, free from sin; purify.[48] The Greek word for sanctification is "hagiasmos," which means the process of making or becoming holy, set apart, holiness, or consecration.[49]

Faith and patience enable believers to follow peace and holiness. Peace with men of all sects and parties will be favorable to our pursuit of holiness. Peace and holiness go together. There can be none without the other.[50] The Word of God states not to indulge in such passions, which leads to litigations, strife, wars, and confusion. We are supposed to be operating in the

---

48. "Sanctification" Merriam-Webster.com 2019 https://www.merriam-webster.com accessed August 2020
49. "Hagiasmos" Greek word for Sanctification https://www.biblehub.com accessed August 2020
50. Hebrews 12:14 Matthew Henry Concise Commentary https://www.biblehub.com accessed August 2020

January 22nd

spirit of kindness toward all people, especially toward those that have scandalized your name. In His Word, God said that we are supposed to do good to those who despitefully misuse us. Continue to love them and treat them the way God commanded by showing them His agape love, and you will do good. God also said that we need to be praying for our enemies regularly. Since we are born-again Christians, God's love should be seeping from our pores for our fellow man. Often, people will have disagreements, which is okay. When a disagreement occurs, the two individuals should be able to get together and talk the matter out according to Scripture. But if they can't come to a common ground, they can bring a neutral person to the meeting to resolve the conflict between them. Mature Christians should be able to work out their differences. Someone should be operating in the Spirit of Wisdom. God doesn't like confusion. If confusion is present, the enemy has crept in somewhere through an open door. All doors must be closed to confusion, so that the spirit can be cast out of the situation, and peace can take root in a person's life.

PRAYER:

Father God, in the name of Jesus, I come before You to ask that You will help me deal with these issues that I have going on in my life right now. Lord, I surrender my life to you all over again. I ask that You will teach me how to remove the spirit of offense out of my life so that I can walk in perfect peace and harmony with my fellow man. Help me be slow to speak and anger about changing things in my life for the better. Lord, help me to walk in Your peace and lay all of my cares, fear, and worries at Your feet so that I would be set free in my emotions in Jesus' name. Lord, I thank You for answering this prayer in Jesus' name. Amen.

January 23rd

Philippians 1:6 (AMP) says, "I am convinced and confident of this very thing, that He who has begun a good work in you will (continue to) perfect and complete it until the day of Christ Jesus (the time of His return)."

The definition of convinced in the Merriam-Webster Dictionary is to be completely certain about something.[51] The Greek word for convinced is "peitho," which means to persuade to have confidence, or urge.[52]

The perfect work that Jesus has done in His children is one of perfection so they will start looking, acting, and talking like Him. Jesus never doubted God or His word. We must do the same and believe in God at all costs. God has a future and an expected end waiting on the ones who have turned over their lives totally to Him. We must lay down our will for His and

---

51. "Convinced" Merriam-Webster.com 2019 https://www.merriam-webster.com accessed August 2020
52. "Peitho" Greek word for convinced https://www.biblehub.com Accessed August 2020

continue to move forward in Him. We must take up our cross daily and follow Christ, the "Hope of Glory." All our faith, hope, and trust should be in Jesus. What good is it to say that we are followers of Christ, but refuse to follow His lead? We need to stop leaning to our understanding and acknowledging that God knows more than we could ever know about our now and our future.

PRAYER:

Father God, in the name of Jesus, I come to You today to thank You for finishing the work that You have started in me, so that I can make it to my expected end in You Jesus. Lord, I know that You have the way prepared for me. Before I was even formed in my mother's womb, the plan for my life was already laid out. Lord, help me to be obedient to Your will and Word so that I can walk in the destiny that You have for my life in Jesus' name. Lord, I repent for going astray or listening to other voices when I should have been listening only to Your voice. Lord, I thank You for another chance to get back into right standing with You in Jesus' name. Amen.

January 24th

JAMES 1:24 (AMP) SAYS, "For once he has looked at himself and gone away, he immediately forgets what he looked like."

Forgets in the Merriam-Webster Dictionary means to lose the remembrance of; be unable to think of, or recall. [53] The Greek word for forgets is "epilanthanomai," which means to forget, or neglect.[54]

We should demonstrate God's Word in our everyday conduct and language. We should be circumspect in our behavior and gracious in our speech. In the verse above, James had a complaint against those who hear the truth of God's Word but do not act on it by changing their behavior—professing Christians who know the truth, but do not reflect a Christlikeness in their daily lives. He likens this to a man's experience of glancing into a mirror, but immediately forgetting the details of the reflected image he saw. To know the truth of who God is and

---

53. "Forgets" Merriam-Webster.com 2019 https://www.merriam-webster.com accessed August 2020
54. "epilanthanomi" https://www.biblehub.com accessed August 2020

what He has done in our lives without there being a significant change in our actions, attitudes, and words is counterintuitive. In other words, one that has taken a superficial glance into God's Word, but once he has looked at himself and gone away, has immediately forgotten his personhood. The Word of God identifies our flaws, faults, and failings. It provides the means to correct them and live godly in Christ Jesus. An inner change of heart by grace through faith in Him should be translated into an outward demonstration of a changed life that is being transformed into the image and likeness of Jesus Christ through the power of the indwelling Spirit.[55]

Prayer:

Father God, in the name of Jesus, I come before You today to help me surrender fully to You so that when I hear or read Your Word, I can apply it to my life instead of forgetting it. Lord, I will allow You to come and remove everything inside my heart that is not pleasing to Your Word in Jesus' name. Lord, I desire for my life to change and become new in Your Word and ways in Jesus' name. Lord, there is a yes in my spirit that wants everything that You want for my life. Lord, show me what needs to be removed in my life, so that I can be a doer of the Word instead of a hearer. Help me lay aside every weight and sin that so easily beset me so that I can continue in Your will and way for my life in Jesus' name. Lord, make all things new in me and in my life in Jesus' name. Amen.

---

55. Dailyverse.knowing-jesus.com , https://www.dailyverse.knowing-jesus.com accessed August 2020

January 25th

1 Corinthians 15:58 (AMP) states, "Therefore, my beloved brothers and sisters, be steadfast, immovable, always excelling in the work of the Lord (always doing your best and doing more than is needed), being continually aware that your labor (even to the point of exhaustion) in the Lord is not futile nor wasted (it is never without purpose).

Steadfast in the Merriam-Webster Dictionary is to be firmly fixed in place, or immovable.[56] The Greek word for steadfast is "hedraios" which means sitting, steadfast, or firm.[57] The Scripture above explains that we are to stay rooted and grounded in the Word of God and also doing the work that God has ordained for our lives. We are God's mouthpieces, His feet and hands on this earth. We will do what He tells us to do so His Kingdom can be advanced in this world. Our life is not our own. It belongs to God. Many people are assigned to us and waiting for us to get ourselves together. Say "Yes" to God and get busy working in the Kingdom. When our lives start lining up with the Bible, only then will God be able to use us for His service fully.

56. "Steadfast" Merriam-Webster.com 2019 https://www.merriam-webster.com accessed August 2020
57. "Epilanthanomai" Greek word for Steadfast https://www.biblehub.com accessed August 2020

Everything that we do in the Lord is not wasted, no matter how small or large it is. Nothing is wasted in God's sight.

PRAYER:

Father God, in the name of Jesus, we come to You today to thank You for reminding me that everything that I have ever gone through will not be wasted because You will use everything for my good. Lord, give me the strength to continue to move forward in the calling that You have on my life from this day forth. Lord, help me to find comfort in Your word and Your presence. Bless me with more energy so that I can keep going forth in Your Word in Jesus' name. Amen.

January 26th

Romans 8:18 (AMP) states, "For I consider (from the standpoint of faith) that the sufferings of the present life are not worthy to be compared with the glory that is about to be revealed to us and in us!

The definition of Glory in the Merriam-Webster Dictionary is worshipful praise, honor, and thanksgiving.[58] The Greek word for glory is "doxa," which means honor, renown, and especially divine quality, or the unspoken manifestation of God.[59] The world that we live in is a fallen one. It is a place of suffering, trials, heartaches, and problems. Since the COVID 19 pandemic, we have witnessed many people die. If the people that have died were in Christ, their souls went to live with Jesus. Jesus warned us that we would go through sufferings, sicknesses, and trials while living here on earth. There is no way to escape these trials. If we are rooted and grounded in Jesus, when going through the storms of life, we will walk on a certain level of peace because we have a loving God that is with us.

58 "Glory" Merriam-Webster.com 2019 https://www.merriam-webster.com accessed August 2020
59. "Doxa" Greek for Glory https://www.biblehub.com accessed August 2020

The 180-Days of Communing with God Daily Devotional

PRAYER:

Father God, in the name of Jesus, I come before You today asking for more grace to make it through this warfare that I have been going through lately. Deuteronomy 31:6 (NIV) says, "Be strong and courageous. Do not be afraid or terrified because of them, for the Lord, your God, goes with you; he will never leave you or forsake you." Lord send Your unmerited favor and empowerment so I can continue to move forward in You. I have been attacked in my body every time that I start getting closer to You. The enemy tries to use illnesses or even my family members as a distraction to get me off course. I refuse to stop moving forward in You, and I refuse to give up. So regardless of the attacks, I am going to keep moving to my next level in You. Thank You for Your grace because I know that I wouldn't be able to make it through anything without it. Your grace helps me do what I couldn't do in my ability, and that is a major milestone because I know that I can't do anything without You. But with You, I can do all things through Christ that strengthens me, which I depend on daily. Lord, I love You and thank You for keeping me hedged in the arc of safety in Jesus' name. Amen.

January 27th

ROMANS 13:8 SAYS, "OWE no man anything, but to love one another: for he that loveth another hath fulfilled the law."

Owe in the Merriam Webster Dictionary is to be under the obligation to pay or repay in return for something received.[60] The Greek word for owe is "opheilo" which means to owe, to repay, or to be indebted.[61]

It is the love of the world that caused the Father to give His only begotten Son so that we would have the right to the tree of life. Only through the love that God showed for us and through His grace can we love someone else the way He loves us. We are to love our neighbors as we love ourselves, but many times we don't really love ourselves because of the trauma and wounds we have had in our lives. The only way that we will ever find true love is through Jesus. What Jesus has done for us has set the stage for us to walk in a more profound love for our fellow man, especially those that are in the body of Christ. We all know that

---

60. "Owe" Merriam-Webster.com 2019 https://www.Merriam-webster.com accessed August 2020
61. "Ophelio" Greek word for Owe https://www.biblehub.com accessed August 2020

God is love and if we say we love God but hate our neighbors, then we are lying to ourselves. Our love for people has to be unconditional because we all have our flaws. God is working in every one of us that allows Him to change our old man into the new man. I learned a father's love when I realized that God is the Father that I have desired all my life. He was with me when I didn't know that He was, and after I felt His love, my life has changed for the better. "Lord, let Your love flow to every person who reads this book in Jesus' name. Amen."

PRAYER:

Father God, in the name of Jesus, You said in Your Word that we are to love our neighbors as ourselves. Lord, help me to love people the way You commanded despite their flaws and shortcomings because You loved me despite my flaws and imperfections, in Jesus' name. Lord, go deep inside of my heart and remove anything that blocks me from loving people the right way in Jesus' name. Lord, move in my life and make a new creature out of me so that I can be pleasing in Your sight in Jesus' name. Lord, create a clean heart and renew a right spirit in me from this day forward in Jesus' name. Amen.

January 28th

MARK 8:36 (AMP) STATES, "For what does it benefit a man to gain the whole world (with all its pleasures), and forfeit his soul?"

In the Merriam Webster Dictionary, the word benefit is any object that produces good or helpful results or effects or promotes well-being.[62] The Greek word for benefit is "opheleia" which means usefulness, profit, advantage, benefit, or gain.[63]

The Scripture above reminds us that if we forfeit our relationship with Christ, go out into the world, live a rowdy or partying lifestyle and be very successful without God, it will not profit us anything. You may have recognition from the world but will be in trouble with God. When a person leaves this world without knowing God, then in hell, they will lift up their eyes. But on the other hand, if we seek ye first the Kingdom of God and His righteousness, then all other things will be added unto us. So, any success without God is empty success and it

---
62. "Benefit" Merriam-Webster.com 2019 https://www.merriam-webster.com accessed August 2020
63. "Ophelia" Greek Word for Benefit https://www.biblehub.com accessed August 2020

will not be fulfilling to the person that is trying to obtain it. I would rather have Jesus as the head of everything that I will ever do in this life than not to have Him by trying to do it in my own strength. Trying to do it in your own strength will get exhausting. But with God putting His stamp of approval on it, it will blow up in a day. So, stay with Jesus and let Him lead and guide you to your destiny because He knows what is best for each of us.

PRAYER:

Father God, in the name of Jesus, I come to You today to let You know that I depend on You for everything in my life. Lord, there is no way that I can move forward in my destiny without You by my side. Lord, let me lay my will down in exchange for Your will so my life will line up with what You have for me in this season of my life. Lord, I thank You for bringing it back to my remembrance that You do have my best interest at heart. Lord, open up my ears so I will be able to hear you clearer, move when you tell me to, and be still when You instruct me. Lord, I thank You for loving me and pulling the best out of me, in Jesus' name. Amen.

January 29th

1 John 1:7 (AMP) states, "But if we (really) walk in the Light (that is, live each and every day in conformity with the precepts of God), as He Himself is in the Light, we have (true, unbroken) fellowship with one another(He with us, and we with Him), and the blood of Jesus His Son cleanses us from all sin(by erasing the stain of sin, keeping us cleansed from sin in all its forms and manifestations).

Conformity in the Merriam Webster Dictionary means in form, manner or character.[64] The Greek word for conformity is "suschematizo," which means to conform to another's pattern, or to fashion self-according.[65]

The Scripture reminds the Body of Christ to walk in the light because Jesus is the light. Our lives should reflect Jesus and if it doesn't, then we are not walking in the light but in sin. Sin and the light of God cannot co-exist. No matter how someone tries to force it, those two can have no parts of each other. God

---
64. "Conformity" Merriam-Webster.com 2019 https://www.merriam-webster.com accessed August 2020
65. "Suschematizo" Greek word for Conformity https://www.biblehub.com accessed August 2020

wants our lives to start conforming to Jesus and the manner He walked on this earth over 2,000 years ago. Our speech should line up with the way Jesus spoke. When Satan tempted Him in the wilderness, Jesus used the Word of God against him. Each time the devil proposed something to Him, Jesus said, "It is written." Satan was no match for the Word of God and couldn't penetrate the faith that Jesus walked in. We are supposed to be using the Word of God just like Jesus did. The Bible said to resist the devil and he will flee from you. The way that we resist the devil is by the Word of God. Speak it over any situation that comes against you and your family. The enemy doesn't have any authority, but with Jesus we have all the authority that we need to tread upon his lies.

PRAYER:

Father God, in the name of Jesus, I come to You today walking in the same faith that You walked in when You were on this earth. Lord, You said in Your word that faith comes by hearing and hearing by the Word of God. I will not let the Bible depart from my hearing in Jesus' name. Lord, help me to study Your word and to understand what I am reading so that I can apply it to my life in Jesus' name. Lord, help me to lay all my troubles and trials at your feet instead of worrying about things that I have no control over because You care for me. Holy Spirit have Your way in me. Lead and guide me in all truth to start to understand what I read and study in Jesus' name. Holy Spirit, I lay down my will for the will of the Father in Jesus' name. Lord, strengthen me where I am weak and build me up where I have been torn down in Jesus' name. Amen.

January 30th

1 John 5:12 (AMP) says, "He who has the Son (by accepting Him as Lord and Savior) has the life (that is eternal); he who does not have the Son of God (by personal faith) does not have life."

Accepting in the Merriam Webster Dictionary means to be able or willing to accept something or someone.[66] The Greek word for accepting is "dechomai" which means to take, receive, accept, welcome.[67]

The Scripture above is talking about being in Christ. If you have accepted Him as Your Lord and Savior, then you are walking in the light of the Word. If you are refusing to come to Christ, then this means that you are walking in darkness, and sin and eternal damnation will be your destination. We can't be straddling the fence. Either we belong to God, or we don't. If we belong to Christ, then our eternal home is heaven, where there will be no more sickness, COVID-19, or death. When we

---

66. "Accepting" Merriam-Webster.com 2019 https://www.merriam-webster.com accessed August 2020
67. "Dechomai" Greek for Accepting https://www.biblehub.com accessed August 2020

are in Christ, we have nothing to worry about because God has each of us covered under His blood. The person that doesn't have Christ is on their own in this world. God is steadily pursuing them by trying to get their attention so they will change their mind about Him. So, if you are undecided about God today, this is the best opportunity to give your life to Christ so you will have eternal life when you leave this earth.

PRAYER:

Father God, in the name of Jesus, I come to You today to ask that You would have mercy on me. Give me another chance to give my life to You. Lord, I have sinned and come short of Your glory of God. Forgive me. Lord, create in me a clean heart and renew a right spirit within me O' God. I have realized that I need a Savior. I do not have everything together. Lord, I need You more than ever before right now in Jesus' name. Lord, forgive me of every sin I have committed knowing and unknowing, through deed and omission and commission right now in Jesus' name. In Roman 10:9, You said that if I would confess with my mouth and believe in my heart that God raised Jesus from the dead that I would be saved. Lord, come into my heart and make a new creature out of me. Lord, I want better for my life than what's currently happening because I am doing things in my strength. Lord, help me to be all that I can be in You Jesus. Lord, remove all my doubts about You and Your unconditional love for me in Jesus' name. Amen.

January 31st

*1*Corinthians 6:19-20 (AMP) "Do you not know that your body is the temple of the Holy Spirit who is within you, whom you have (received as a gift) from God, and that you are not your own (property)? 20. You were bought with a price (you were actually purchased with the precious blood of Jesus and made His own). So then, honor and glorify God with your body."

Temple in the Merriam Webster Dictionary is a place devoted to a special purpose.[68] The Greek word for temple is "naos," which is part of the temple where God resides.[69]

The Scriptures above let us know that our bodies are the temple of the Holy Spirit, and we don't need to be doing anything that would grieve Him. We are not supposed to be in fornication, homosexuality, cursing, drinking, lying, or any other sins. We can't watch sinful things on TV or YouTube. We should not post provocative pictures on social media if we are men and women of God. We are supposed to be representing

---
68. "Temple" Merriam-Webster.com 2019 https://www.merriam-webster.com accessed August 2020
69. "Naos" Greek word for Temple https://www.bbiblehub.com accessed August 2020

Christ with our lives, so the world will see and want God too. Jesus brought us a price by the shedding of His blood. Through His sacrifice, we can live clean and productive lives here on earth. So, since my body is the temple of the Holy Spirit, then I must treat it with respect and glorify God only with it.

PRAYER:

Father God, in the name of Jesus, I come before You today to ask that You forgive me for defiling my body by doing things that are unpleasing to You. Lord, help me use self-control and not indulge in anything that would shorten my life here on earth. I realize that I have only one body, and I must take care of it so I can live a long time in Jesus' name. Lord, I repent for doing things out of Your will for my life. Help me to get back on track, Jesus. Lord, help me to keep my mind on the things of God instead of the things of this world. I surrender my will for Your will from this day forward in Jesus' name. Amen.

February 1st

COLOSSIANS 3:15 (AMP) SAYS, "Let the peace of Christ (the inner calm of one who walks daily with Him) be the controlling factor in your hearts (deciding and settling questions that arise). To this peace indeed you were called as members in one body (of believers). And be thankful (to God always)."

Peace in the Merriam Webster Dictionary is a state of tranquility, freedom from disquieting or oppressive thoughts or emotions.[70] The Greek word for peace is "eirene," which means peace of mind, quietness, or rest.[71]

The Scripture above says that we are supposed to be at peace in our hearts no matter what we are going through. Because we have Christ, and He is the Prince of Peace, we should be walking in His peace instead of stressing about things that we have no control over. It doesn't matter if COVID-19 is breaking out globally and social injustices are happening. We still can

---

70. "Peace" Merriam-Webster.com 2019 https://www.merriam-webster.com accessed august 2020
71. "Eirene" Greek word for Peace https://www.biblehub.com accessed August 2020

walk in peace because we know that God is on our side. He has our back. Just stay rooted and grounded in His love. We all should be a working organism in the body of Christ instead of warming a bench every Sunday. We should be working with our communities so we can help change people's lives. Everyone should be walking around every day with a thankful heart toward God because of the many blessings that He has rained down on our lives.

PRAYER:

Father God, in the name of Jesus, I come to you today lifting Your son and daughters in the faith in Jesus' name. Lord, help every one of Your children to walk in the peace of God. Lord, let everything that we do represent You in this earth in Jesus' name. So, help every one of Your people let their lights shine so that men and women of this world would turn away from their sin. Lord, help us be thankful for everything You have done in our lives in Jesus' name. Lord, give Your people peace amid the chaos occurring in the world. Lord, You said in Your word that we would have the peace that passeth all understanding and it would guard our hearts and minds through Christ Jesus. Lord, let peace rule and abide in our hearts daily in Jesus' name. Amen.

February 2nd

James 1:2-3 (AMP) says, "Consider it nothing but joy, my brothers and sisters, whenever you fall into various trials. 3. Be assured that the testing of your faith (through experience) produces endurance (leading to spiritual maturity, and inner peace)."

Joy in the Merriam Webster Dictionary is the emotion evoked by well-being, success, good fortune or by the prospect of possessing what one desires.[72] The Greek word for Joy is "chara," meaning joy, delight, or gladness.[73]

In the Scriptures above, James reminds us whenever we go through various trials and hardships to count it all. The trials were not sent to break you but to make you. When you are going through, you tend to pray, fast, read the Bible, and stay in God's presence more. You are growing spiritually during these times. God wants to grow every one of us up so we will start to look like Him, saying the things that Jesus would say, and

---

72. "Joy" Merriam-Webster.com 2019 https://www.merriam-webster.com accessed August 2020
73. "Chara" Greek word for Joy https://www.biblehub.com accessed August 2020

getting the results that Jesus did. Trials come to test our faith in God and His Word. God has promised you that He will do a certain thing for you or your family. When you don't have anything to stand on, seek the word of God in the matter. Before we can obtain something, we must go through a refiner's fire so all the impurities can be removed and we can be pure as gold. God must refine us so we can have hearts like Jesus. We are the clay on the wheel of the potter. He must make and mold us to turn out like the expensive pottery that we see in stores. This pottery doesn't have any flaws because the potter took His time to make you. So, rejoice when you go through trials and make it through to the other side. You are an overcomer in Christ Jesus.

PRAYER:

Father God, in the name of Jesus, I come before You today to ask that you strengthen me as I go through this trial. Lord, help me to see that these trials are for my good. Lord, You said that You would work everything out for my good. Nothing shall be wasted but used to refine me into that flawless piece of pottery that you want me to be. Lord, help me to go through the process with grace in Jesus' name. Lord, I know that You wouldn't allow these trials unless You want me to learn something from them in Jesus' name. Lord, increase my faith in You and Your Word in Jesus' name. Lord, I want to grow to be more like You every day in Jesus' name. Amen.

February 3rd

1 Peter 4:16 (AMP), "But if anyone suffers (ill treatment) as a Christian (because he is considered worthy to suffer) in this name."

Suffers in the Merriam Webster Dictionary is to submit to or forced to endure.[74] The Greek word for suffers is "pathema," which means that which befall one, suffering, passion, or affliction.[75]

The Scripture above says that we cannot be ashamed to be called a Christian, the doctrines taught by Jesus, the Savior whom we profess to love, fellowship with other believers, and perform the duties that God has put before us.[76] Romans 1:16 (AMP) states, "I am not ashamed of the gospel, for it is the power of God for salvation (from His wrath and punishment) to everyone who believes (in Christ as Savior), to the Jew first and also to the Greek." Jesus said in Luke 9:26 (AMP),

---

74. "Suffer" Merriam-Webster.com 2019 https://www.merriam-webster.com accessed August 2020
75. "Pathema" Greek word for Suffer https://www.biblehub.com accessed august 2020
76. 1 Peter 4:16 Barnes Notes on the Bible https://www.biblehub.com accessed August 2020

"For whoever is ashamed (here and now) of Me and My words, the Son of Man will be ashamed of him when He comes in His Glory and the glory of the (heavenly) Father and of the holy angels." So, if we want to hear Jesus say, "Well done, my good and faithful servant," then we need not be ashamed to do anything that He has called us to do on this earth.

Prayer:

Father God, in the name of Jesus, I come to You today to ask that You forgive me for the times that I was ashamed of You and when I disobeyed You. Lord, it doesn't matter what the people in this world say about me because I am totally sold out to You in Jesus' name. Lord, please don't turn Your back on me. Give me another chance to get it right, God. Lord, I would rather have man mad at me than to be in trouble with You about anything in Jesus' name. Lord, help me be the person You made me to be before I was formed in my mother's womb in Jesus' name. I bind shame and all the symptoms that come with it and lose confidence in my heart and mind right now in Jesus' name. Lord, I cannot do anything in my own strength, but I can do all things through Your strength, in Jesus' name. Amen.

February 4th

Philippians 4:8 (AMP) states, "Finally, believers, whatever is true, whatever is honorable and worthy of respect, whatever is right and confirmed by God's word, whatever is pure and wholesome, whatever is lovely and brings peace, whatever is admirable and of good repute; if there is any excellence, if there is anything worthy of praise, think continually on these things(center your mind on them, and implant them in your heart)."

Whatever in the Merriam Webster Dictionary is anything or everything that.[77] The Greek word for whatever is "hostis, hetis, hoti," which means whoever, anyone, or who.[78]

Confirmed in the Merriam Webster Dictionary is to assure the validity of, or remove doubt about.[79] The Greek word for confirmed is "bebaioo," which means confirm, secure, establish, pass, or guarantee.[80]

77. "Whatever" Merriam-Webster.com 2019 https://www.merriam-webster.com accessed august 2020
78. "hostis" Greek for Whatever https://www.biblehub.com accessed August 2020
79. "Confirmed" Merriam-Webster.com 2019 https://www.merriam-webster.com accessed August 2020
80. "Bebaioo" Greek for Confirmed https://www.biblehub.com accessed august 2020

The Scripture above will help us determine if it's okay to participate in certain things we see in the world. Is the thing that you want to do true and honorable? Does it line up or go against God's Word? We have to be very careful because the enemy will dress it up to look innocent, but in actuality, it goes against the Word of God. It doesn't matter who is doing it because we don't want to grieve the Holy Spirit who lives inside us. Is it pure and wholesome? Many TV shows are not. For instance, reality shows always have foul language and fighting in them. We should not be watching these because they contaminate our spirits. We shouldn't watch Jerry Springer because the content is so worldly. You can judge everything you see and hear on TV, YouTube, and social media by Philippians 4:8. After watching certain shows, are you weighed down? If so, then don't watch it. But if you have been watching them for a while and see nothing wrong with it, repentance is necessary because you have moved away from your close relationship with Christ. As believers, we should be hating what God hates and loving what He loves. There is no in-between. Either we are for Christ or against Him.

PRAYER:

Father God, in the name of Jesus, we come to You today to ask that You forgive me for watching shows that have been grieving the Holy Spirit. Lord, I desire to get back into my rightful place with You. Lord, forgive me for all the sin that I had committed when I overrode the Holy Spirit and fed my spirit contaminated material. Lord, create in me a clean heart and re-

February 4th

new a right spirit within me. Lord, cleanse me of all unrighteousness so that I can move forward in You, God. Lord, thank You for forgiving me in Jesus' name. Lord, from this day forward, I will turn off the TV, get back into Your presence, and in Your word so that I will not sin against You in Jesus' name. Lord, make me over again in Jesus' name. Amen.

February 5th

ROMANS 1:17 (AMP) STATES, "For in the gospel the righteousness of God is revealed, both springing from faith and leading to faith (disclosed in the way that awakens more faith). As it is written and forever remains written, "THE JUST AND UPRIGHT SHALL LIVE BY FAITH."

Faith in the Merriam Webster Dictionary is a belief and trust in loyalty to God.[81] The Greek word for faith is "pistis," which means faith, belief, trust, confidence, fidelity, or faithfulness.[82]

The just shall live by faith. Faith is like a muscle, and it has to be used for it to continue to grow. God has given us faith the size of a mustard seed. A mustard seed is a very tiny seed, but once it is planted, it will grow into a big tall tree with its roots way down deep in the soil. When strong winds blow or storms come along, the tree may bend but it won't break or be uprooted. This is how our faith needs to be in God. Despite what we

---
81. "Faith" Merriam-Webster.com 2019 https://www.merriam-webster.com accessed August 2020
82. "Pistis" Greek word for Faith https://www.biblehub.com accessed August 2020

February 5th

may be going through, God has us. We need to start seeing our situations in the spiritual realm instead of the natural realm. What seems difficult for us will be easy for God. Things that are impossible with us are possible with God! We need to pray in faith, believing that God will do it for us. Without faith, it is impossible to do anything in the Kingdom of God. It takes faith even to get saved. It is impossible to live a holy and righteous lifestyle without faith. Our unbelief is stopping us from advancing in the Will of God for our lives! We can't even please God without faith. Faith is the currency to get anything from God. If we have faith that a chair will hold us when we sit down, then our faith in God should be stronger just because of Him!! When we started as a babe in Christ, our faith should be the mustard seed size. But as we grow and mature in God, our faith should be growing. Our faith should be so strong that we should be able to jump-start ourselves off someone else's faith after we give our testimonies and encouragement to those who need it.

PRAYER:

Father, in the name of Jesus, I come before You today to ask that You help me with my faith. Lord, You said in Your Word that we would go from faith to faith in Jesus. Lord, You also said that faith comes by hearing and hearing the Word of God. Lord, help me to be able to study Your word and speak it aloud over my family and me when I need to strengthen my faith in You. Lord, help me to tell my testimony instead of keeping it to myself, so I can help to increase other people's faith. Lord, help me get away from the negative individuals and start gravitating to positive people. Lord, thank You for removing those in my life that doesn't mean me any good and replacing them with people who will speak life into me in Jesus' name. Lord, order my steps and guide me to people who will encourage and lift me in prayer in Jesus' name. Amen.

February 6th

2 Corinthians 10:5 (AMP) states, "We are destroying sophisticated arguments and every exalted and proud thing that sets itself up against the (true) knowledge of God, and we are taking every thought and purpose captive to the obedience of Christ, being ready to punish every act of disobedience, when your own obedience (as a church) is complete."

Destroying in the Merriam Webster Dictionary is to ruin the structure, organic existence, or condition of.[83] The Greek word for destroying is "portheo," which means to destroy, to waste, or ravage.[84]

In the Scripture above, we are casting down any thought that doesn't line up with the Word of God. The enemy will bring thoughts to our minds to make us feel guilty when God already forgave us. Satan has a bad habit of bringing up our past and trying to blackmail us into staying quiet, but he is a liar. Our

---
83. "Destroying" Merriam-Webster.com 2019 https://www.merriam-webster.com August 2020
84. "Portheo" Greek word for Destroying https://www.biblehub.com accessed August 2020

past and present are already covered under the blood if we have asked God to forgive us for all sins we have committed against His Word. We must steadily put the Word of God in our minds, so our thoughts can be transformed. After our mind changes, then our behaviors will follow suit. First, we must admit that we have a problem with sin in a certain area to get help from the Holy Spirit. If we continue denying it and trying to work it out in our own strength, we will never receive the deliverance we need. The enemy knows what we like and our weaknesses so he continues to tempt us with those things. If we find that we have sinned against God, then we need to repent, renew our minds and ask God to help us with the problems so we can finally overcome them. Deliverance is obtainable with Jesus' help.

PRAYER:

Father God, in the name of Jesus, I come before You today to ask that You forgive me for sinning against You Jesus' name. Lord, I admit that I need Your help to overcome this temptation to sin against You. Lord, strengthen me by Your Spirit so that I can become an Overcomer in Christ Jesus. Lord, help me to cast down anything that didn't come from You in Jesus' name. Your Word says that I am supposed to cast down every thought that is not like You that comes to try and snare me in Jesus' name. Lord, help me walk in the authority that You have given me so that I can move forward in my walk with You, God. Lord, thank You for forgiving and setting me free in Jesus' name. Amen.

February 7th

1 Corinthians 3:16 (AMP) states, "Do you not know and understand that you (the church) are the temple of God, and that the Spirit of God dwells (permanently) in you (collectively and individually)?"

Understand in the Merriam Webster Dictionary is to perceive the intended meaning of (words, a language, or a speaker).[85] The Greek word for understand is "nous," which means the mind, the understanding, the reasoning, or intellect.[86]

Permanently in the Merriam Webster Dictionary means a permanent manner: in a way that continues without changing or ending, or a way that is not brief or temporary.[87] The Greek word for permanently is "aparabatos," which means unchangeable, not passing away.[88]

The Scripture is talking about the church not being a building, but we are the church or individuals who make up the body of Christ. Our bodies are the temples of God, and we need to

---

85. "Understand" Merriam-Webster.com 2019 https://www.biblehub.com accessed August 2020
86. "Nous" Greek for Understand https://www.biblehub.com accessed August 2020
87. "Permanent" Merriam-Webster.com 2019 https://www.merriam-webster.com accessed August 2020
88. "Aparabatos" Greek for Permanent https://www.biblehub.com accessed August 2020

be pure and flee fornication and sin. We should not be doing anything that would grieve the Holy Spirit on the inside of us. The Holy Spirit is our teacher, and He will lead and guide us in all truth. We shouldn't be doing anything unholy with our bodies. We need to preserve our temples so our lives on this earth will be long. The Holy Ghost dwells in all true believers and we should not be sinning as if we are not saved. We should be pure, clean in heart and in profession. That means walking in integrity, not stealing, and scamming people out of their hard-earned money. Keeping our hearts pure means to have a forgiving heart and not being bitter or walking in hatred when someone has hurt or mistreated you. We are supposed to show the love of God to our enemies and pray for them to be saved because when we are praying for them, we have no time to be hating them. We can pray God's blessing over them and that God will touch their hearts for them to give their lives totally to Christ.

PRAYER:

In the name of Jesus, Father God, I come to You today to ask that You give me the strength and help me forgive those people who are hard to forgive because they have hurt or mistreated me. Lord, I want to do what Your Word declares, forgive 70 times 7, meaning continuously so that I will not get bitter about them. Lord, help me to keep my body as the temple of the Holy Spirit by not doing anything to grieve the Holy Spirit that lives on the inside of me. Lord, give me more grace to treat people the right way instead of behaving unseemly toward them. Lord, I command my emotions to line up with Your Word so that I

February 7th

can be pleasing in Your sight in Jesus' name. Lord, I will continue to intercede for them until their lives begin to line up with Your Word in Jesus' name. Amen.

February 8th

Ephesians 3:20 (AMP) says, "Now to Him who can (carry out His purpose and) do superabundantly more than that we dare ask or think (infinitely beyond our greatest prayers, hopes, or dreams), according to His power that is at work within us."

Superabundantly in the Merriam Webster Dictionary is an amount of supply more than sufficient to meet one's needs.[89] The Greek word for superabundantly is "perisseuma." It means an excessive quantity, redundancy, or extreme plenty.[90]

The Scripture above says to let us expect more from God and take Him out of the box because He can do so much more for us than we can comprehend with our natural minds. One thing we must get in our hearts that God is not broke, and He owns everything. He has resources that never run out. God can speak things into existence in our lives, but we must have the faith to believe that He can do it for us. Faith is the currency

---
[89]. "Superabundantly" Merriam-Webster.com 2019 https://www.merriam-webster.com accessed August 2020
[90]. "Perisseuma" Greek for Superabundantly https://www.biblehub.com accessed August 2020

February 8th

for the Kingdom of God. We must have it because without it, we cannot please God. We need to ask for more because we are often used to having just enough, but God wants to give us the overflow. He wants us to live an abundant life in every area of our lives, not to lack or want anything. God can move the mountains in our lives that seem to have us blocked in. God can make all your books become best sellers overnight. God will put your book in the right person's hands so it would go viral. God can send someone wealthy to your home and pay all your bills off, leaving you with a zero balance on all of them. God is so amazing and wonderful. He wants all His children blessed and prosperous. He wants us so blessed that we wouldn't mind sowing into His kingdom here on earth. Stay in expectation no matter what you see in the natural. Just know that God has already released it in the spiritual after He knows that He can trust you with your finances, ministry, people, etc.

PRAYERS:

Father God, in the name of Jesus, I come before You today to thank You for opening up the windows of heaven and pouring me out a blessing that I don't have room enough to receive in Jesus' name. Lord, thank You for watching over my family and me day by day and protecting us from things seen and unseen in Jesus' name. Lord, thank You for giving me new streams of income so that I can build up an inheritance for my children's children in Jesus' name. Lord, thank You for supplying my every need, such as Your riches in Glory by Christ Jesus. Lord, continue to bless me to be a blessing to everyone that I come into contact with in Jesus 'name. Lord, move mightily on my behalf in Jesus' name. Lord, I love You and all the glory and honor belongs to You in Jesus' name. Amen.

February 9th

Proverbs 4:23 (AMP) states, "Watch over your heart with all diligence, For from it flow the springs of life."

Diligence in the Merriam Webster Dictionary is steady, earnest, and energetic effort, or persevering application.[91] The Greek word for diligence is "spoude," meaning earnestness or enthusiasm.[92]

We are to watch over our hearts to keep bitterness and unforgiveness from settling in it. We all need to be practicing forgiveness instead of running to our friends and gossiping. We need to go to God first and pray about the situation and the people involved with the incident. We can pray and ask God for wisdom on how to handle the situation without letting it turn into something that wouldn't be pleasing to Him. Remember, we are not fighting against flesh and blood, but we are fighting things in the spiritual realm. Our battles can not be handling

---
91. "Diligence" Merriam-Webster.com 2019 https://www.merrian-webster.com accessed August 2020
92. "Spoude" Greek word for Diligence https://www.biblehub.com accessed August 2020

matters the way the world handles them. They must be handled according to the Word of God and not in our flesh. God is our vindicator. We do not have to retaliate against anyone. Just pray for them and let the Lord handle the situation. God can work it out better than we can any day of the week.

PRAYER:

Father God, in the name of Jesus, I come before You today to thank You for more grace to handle tough situations and not regress into my flesh in Jesus' name. Lord, help me remember that I must guard my heart and make sure I examine it every day to see if anything is in it that would hinder my walk with You, God. Lord, I have learned to forgive and keep it moving because it is not worth losing my intimate relationship with You. Lord, strengthen me so that I can walk closer to You and be pleasing in Your sight in Jesus' name. I will examine my heart to make sure it stays pure in Jesus' name. Nothing or no one is worth losing my salvation over in Jesus' name. Lord, help me be quiet and use self-control when the enemy tries to tempt me to get into my flesh in Jesus' name. Amen.

February 10th

PSALM 119:93 STATES, (AMP) "I will never forget your precepts, (how can I?) for it is by them You have quickened me (granted me life)."

Precepts in the Merriam Webster Dictionary is a command or principle intended especially as a general rule of action.[93] The Greek word for precept is "entalma," which means an injunction, religious precept, or ordinance.[94]

The Scripture above is talking about the Word of God. I will never forget or cease to read, study or speak it over myself and situations that come up in my life because it gives me life. The Word of God is life and gives life to anything that you speak it over. The Word will give us life and life more abundantly if we follow the precepts that are written in it.

DECLARATIONS

---

93. "Precepts" Merriam-Webster.com 2019 https://www.merriam-webster.com accessed August 2020
94. "Entalma" Greek for Percepts https://www.biblehub.com accessed August 2020

Lord, I will never forget Your Word.

Lord, Your Word keeps me going strong.

Lord, Your Word is sharper than any two-edged sword.

Lord, I will meditate on Your promises daily, in Jesus' name.

Lord, Your Word keeps me encouraged and gives me hope in an expected end and a future.

Lord, I will use Your Word to speak life over every dead situation in my life.

Lord, let Your Word lubricate and water every dry place in my life in Jesus' name. Amen.

February 11th

Hebrews 4:16 (AMPC) says, "Let us then fearlessly and confidently and boldly draw near to the throne of grace (the throne of God's unmerited favor to us sinners), that we may receive mercy (for our failures) and find grace to help in good time for every need (appropriate help and well-timed help, coming just when we need it)."

Boldly in the Merriam Webster Dictionary is fearless before danger and showing or requiring a fearless daring spirit.[95] The Greek word for boldly is "tolmao," meaning to have courage, to be bold, or to make up your mind.[96]

All who declare the name of Christ can come to the throne of mercy and grace with boldness and believe that God hears your prayers. We do not have to be scared to pray to God about any situation that has come up in our lives. God wants us to pray to Him about everything. God will give us His grace when

---
95. "Boldly" Merriam-Webster.com 2019 https://www.merriam-webster.com Accessed August 2020
96. "Tolmao" Greek word for Boldly https://www.biblehub.com accessed August 2020

we need more strength to accomplish things or for the required tasks. God will send the help exactly when you need it. His help is always on time. It is never late. Lord, we thank You for being there when we need You the most in Jesus' name. Amen.

DECLARATIONS

I will come boldly to the throne of mercy and grace to seek God's face.

From this day forward, I will only be praying bold prayers.

I decree and declare, and I will take back everything that the enemy has stolen for me.

Lord, I thank You for Your mercy and grace to help me in the time of need.

Lord, overwhelm me with Your Presence from this day forward in Jesus' name.

Lord, I stand on Your word each day of the week.

Lord, thank You for having my best interest at heart and loving me unconditionally.

Lord, I believe that You will supply my every need, such as Your riches in glory by Christ Jesus.

February 11th

Lord, thank You for moving every stubborn mountain out of my life in Jesus' name.

February 12th

John 15:10 (AMP) says, "If you keep my commandments (if you continue to obey My instructions), you will abide in My love and live on in it, just as I have obeyed My Father's commandments and live on in His love."

Commandments in the Merriam Webster Dictionary are something that is commanded.[97] The Greek word for commandments is "entole," meaning an injunction order, command, or law.[98]

When we keep the Word of God and apply it to our lives daily, we start to grow. Other people can see the changes that God made in our lives for the better. Obeying God is the key to everything. When you obey Him, it opens the door for more responsibility because He trusts You with more things and assignments. God loves each of us. He wants you to know just how much He loves you. He will love you until the end of time.

---

97. "Commandments" Merriam-Webster.com 2019 https://www.merriam-webster.com Accessed August 2020
98. "Entole" Greek for Commandments https://www.biblehub.com accessed August 2020

God's love doesn't stop for us even if we mess up. He still loves us and continues to draw us back into right standing with Him.

DECLARATIONS

Lord, I will continue to live a holy lifestyle to be pleasing unto You God.

Lord, I want to continue to abide in Your love forever.

Lord, I forever want to stay in Your will for my life.

Lord, I long for your presence every day of the week.

Lord, I need You to come into my life and make a new creature out of me.

Lord, forgive me for any sins that I have committed that will keep me away from Your presence.

Lord, touch my heart and do a great work in me in Jesus' name.

February 13th

John 1:7 (AMP) states, "This man came to witness, that he might testify of the Light, that all men might believe in it (adhere to it, trust it, and rely upon it) through him."

A witness in the Merriam Webster Dictionary is one that gives evidence, one who testifies in a cause or before a judicial tribunal.[99] The Greek word for witness is "martureo," which means to be a witness, to bear witness, to affirm that one has been seen or heard. It also means to give (not to keep back) a testimony.[100]

When we are walking in the Word, we are walking in the light. God's Word is life and light. A person that walks in the light should be hating what God hates and loving what He loves. God hates sin and anything evil, but He loves that which is good and glorifies Him in your life. God is light and in Him, there is no darkness. Light and darkness can never be mixed. Either

---
99. "Witness" Merriam-Webster.com 2019 https://www.merriam-webster.com Accessed August 2020.
100. "Martureo" Greek word for Witness. https://www.bibletools.org Accessed August 2020.

February 13th

you are for the darkness (the enemy) or light (Jesus). There can be no in between. No man can be in communion with God unless he walks in the light.

DECLARATIONS

Lord, thank You for Your blood that cleanses us from every sin.

Lord, thank You for Your hedge of protection that surrounds me like a shield.

I bind the spirit of death seeking my life and my bloodline in Jesus' name.

Lord, I love the light of Your Word in Jesus' name.

Lord, I will not fulfill the lust of the flesh, but I will walk in the light of Your Word.

Lord, let Your light shine in every dark area of my life from this day forward in Jesus' name.

Lord, I am a light-bearer in Jesus' name.

February 14th

2 Corinthians 1:3-4 (AMP) states, "Blessed be the God and Father of our Lord Jesus Christ, the Father of sympathy (pity and mercy) and the God (Who is the Source) of every comfort (consolation and encouragement). 4.Who comforts (consoles and encourages) us in every trouble (calamity and affliction), so that we may also be able to comfort (consolation and encouragement) with which we ourselves are comforted (consoled and encouraged) by God."

Consoles in the Merriam Webster Dictionary is to alleviate the grief, sense of loss, or trouble of comfort.[101] The Greek word for consoles is "paramutheomai," which means comfort, encouragement, admonish, and invite.[102]

Jesus is our comforter. He will console us anytime that we need comforting. We just need to cast our cares on Him because He cares for you. John 14:1 (NLT) "Don't let your hearts

---

101. "Consoles" Merriam-Webster.com 2019 https://www.merriam-webster.com August 2020.
102. "Paramutheomai" Greek word for Consoles. https://www.biblehub.com Accessed August 2020

be troubled. Trust in God, and trust also in me." God doesn't want us to be troubled about anything, but trust in Him for everything. When God strengthens us, then it will come at a time that we should be able to encourage someone else. Because the time and season that we are in many people need to be encouraged and pushed into their next level in their walk with God.

DECLARATIONS

Lord, thank You for comforting me in my tribulations.

Lord, strengthen me so that I can help strengthen someone else.

Lord, help me to always say something that is positive and uplifting to someone who is need.

Lord, help me to encourage those that are less fortunate than me.

Lord, let the light of Your Word come out of my mouth so someone will receive it and be blessed.

Lord, order my steps and lead me to the right people who need encouraging.

February 15th

Nahum 1:7 (AMP) states, "The Lord is good, a Strength and Stronghold in the day of trouble. He knows (recognizes, has knowledge of, and understands) those who take refuge and trust in Him."

Strength in the Merriam Webster Dictionary is the quality or state of being strong, capacity for exertion or endurance, power of resisting attack.[103] The Greek word for strength is "ischus" which means strength (absolutely), power, might, force, or ability.[104]

God knows those who trust in Him. We are to take refuge in Him, and He will care for us. God loves us so much and wants to give us good things. God is our strength in the time of trouble. The Holy Spirit will guide us in all truth through His Word. We need to trust God with our lives, marriages, relationships, businesses, children, grandchildren, etc. God is our stronghold

---

103. "Strength" Merriam-Webster. Com 2019 https://www.merriam-webster.com August 2020.
104. "Ischus" Greek Word for Strength https://www.biblehub.com Accessed August 2020.

February 15th

in the day of trouble. The righteous run to Him and will find safety from the storm.

PRAYER:

Father God, in the name of Jesus, I come before You today to say thank You for always being there for me whenever I needed You. Lord, thank You for being my stronghold and strength during the times that I felt so weary in Jesus' name. Lord, I trust You with my life, families' lives, and those that are in my circle in Jesus' name. Lord, I permit You to do whatever You want to do in my life in Jesus' name. Lord, come into my heart and make a new creature out of me. Lord, I know that I can find safety from the storms of life in Your presence in Jesus' name. Lord, that You for Your love and understanding in Jesus' name. Amen.

February 16th

*S*AMUEL 16:7 (AMP) STATES, "But the Lord said to Samuel, look not on his appearance or at the height of his stature, for I have rejected him. For the Lord sees not as a man sees; for a man looks on the outward appearance, but the Lord looks on the heart."

Look in the Merriam Webster Dictionary is to exercise the power of vision, examine.[105] The Greek word for look is "apoblepo," which means to look away from all else at an object.[106]

The Lord told Samuel, you are looking at him in the natural, but I am viewing his heart in the spirit. That is the same way that God looks at every one of us today. God cares about what you have in your heart more than anything. God is looking for the ones who are pure in heart and have good character. But if you are not there yet, God will mold you, like the potter molds clay, to get you to that point. God will not turn His back on us, but will perfect us by taking us through the refiner's fire until

---
105. "Look" Merriam-Webster.com 2019 https://www.merriam-webster.com August 2020.
106. "Apoblepo" Greek word for Look https://www.merriam-webster.com August 2020

February 16th

all the impurities are out of our lives. God will clean us up if we allow Him too. He wants to perfect His spirit in us. He wants to make us new in Him because we are to take up our cross daily and follow Him. Allow God to do what He wants to do in you. If you allow the process then can you go on to Your God given destiny. It is better to have Jesus behind you 100% than try to do things on your own. When you try to do anything without God, it will not last because only what you do for Christ will last now and forever more.

PRAYER:

Father God, in the name of Jesus, I come before You today to ask that You create a clean heart and renew a right spirit in me, O God. Lord, give me a little more grace so that I can walk worthy of my calling in Jesus' name. Lord, strengthen me to go through Your process to be made into the image of Christ. Lord, heal every broken place in my heart and go deep down into the areas of my heart where I have suppressed things that were painful to me. Lord, I release myself to You so that I can go through the refiner's fire and be purified from all that is holding me back from my best life in You God. Lord, thank You for making a new creature out of me and keeping me safely in Your arms in Jesus' name. Amen.

February 17th

*P*ROVERBS 22:6 (AMP) STATES, "Train up a child in the way he should go (and in keeping with his individual gift or bent), and when he is old, he will not depart from it."

Train in the Merriam Webster Dictionary is to teach to make fit, qualified or proficient, or discipline.[107] The Greek word for train is "gumnazo," which means to train, to teach, or to show.[108]

God holds each one of us accountable for raising our children and teaching them about what is right and wrong. He expects even the grandparents to help raise children and to teach them about Him every chance that we get. If we start training them up young about Godly things, they will have a chance to get to know God at a very young age before they get to experience all the world has to offer them. The world and the enemy wants to kill, steal and destroy our children. God has given the adult, whether parent or grandparent, raising the children a

---
107. "Train" Merriam-Webster.com 2019 https://www.merriam-webster.com September 2020.
108. "Gumnazo" Greek word for Train https://www.biblehub.com September 2020

February 17th

mandate that if you don't teach them, the enemy and the world will. They will teach them that it is okay to live alternate lifestyles and that God agrees with it. We that are seasoned in the Word know that is a lie from the pit of hell. God does not approve of sin in any form. God hates sin, but He doesn't hate the person that is caught in sin. God wants to save people that are bound in sin. He doesn't want anyone to die and go to hell, but it is a choice that we all must make: Jesus or the enemy. If you keep denying Jesus, then your answer has already been made for you. Life without Jesus is lonely. God's strength is better because if God is for you who can be against you? God has the believers' back and He will make sure that we are taken care of and not lacking anything.

PRAYER:

Father, in the name of Jesus, we come before You today to ask You to cover our children under Your precious blood. Lord, help me to teach my children and grandchildren what they need to know to make it in this world today. Lord, touch my child so that they would want to fall deeply in love with you and live a life that is pleasing unto You. Lord, help me not to do anything in front of them that would cause them to stumble and walk away from You God. Lord, as I continue reading Your Word, instruct me to effectively teach my child or grandchild what they need to know concerning You in Jesus' name. Lord, move mightily over the younger generation from 1 to 60 years old right now in Jesus' name. Lord, let them know just how much you love, care for them, and that they can always have someone to lean on during their time of need. Lord, touch every parent, grandparent, or whoever is raising children right now. Help them teach the children the lessons they will need to be better to walk in Your love God. Lord, help us as grandparents, and parents to teach our children to flee evil and run to You. God, in You, we can find safety in the middle of the storms that are raging in their lives in Jesus' name. Amen.

February 18th

Colossians 3:16 (AMP) states, "Let the word (spoken by) Christ (the Messiah) have its home (in your hearts and minds) and dwell in you in (all its) richness, as you teach and admonish and train one another in all insight and intelligence and wisdom (in spiritual things, and as you sing) psalms and hymns and spiritual songs, making melody to God with (His) grace in your hearts."

Admonish in the Merriam Webster Dictionary is to give friendly earnest advice or encouragement.[109] The Greek word for admonish is "noutheteo," which means to exhort, to counsel, or to warn.[110]

The Gospel or Good News is the Word of Christ. The Word is supposed to have power over us. Our soul prospers when we are full of Scriptures and the grace of God. When we are singing hymns, we must be affected by what we are singing at some point through the ministry of the Holy Spirit. God is not wor-

---

109. "Admonish" Merriam-Webster.com 2019 https://www.merriam-webster.com Sep.tember 2020.
110. "Noutheteo" Greek word for Admonish https://www.biblehub.com September 2020

ried about whether you can sing or not. He takes pleasure in hearing us during our worship. The Holy Spirit that dwells on the inside of us will let you know what song to sing at any given time. It is so important to be sensitive to the Holy Spirit. He can change the song list that you may have practiced because someone in the house needs to hear a different song. When we are obedient to what the Holy Spirit commands, the Shekinah Glory will come in and wreck the service by taking it another way. The Holy Spirit may need to touch people's hearts because it could be a life and death situation. The Holy Spirit knows who is in the service and their need for deliverance at that time. We should always submit to the Holy Spirit because He knows exactly what needs to be done in all of us to reach our breakthroughs. If we would lay our agendas down and let God's agenda take over, we would see more signs, wonders and miracles in our homes, churches, and families. Never rush the Holy Spirit when He is moving. He wants to make someone new and give us a fresh refilling of Himself so we can be empowered to keep moving on in our walk with Christ.

DECLARATIONS

I decree and declare the Word of God over my life every day. The Word is a light and a lamp to my feet.

Lord, send Your Holy Spirit, now, to refresh me with Your Presence.

Lord, I need You to come into my heart and make a new creature out of me.

February 18th

Lord, let Your Holy Spirit burn up anything that is in me that is not of You.

Oh, create in me a clean heart and renew a right spirit in me.

Lord, I will sing praises to Your name and will forever walk in Your Word.

The prayers of the righteous availeth much and produce wonderful results in my life.

February 19th

James 5:16 (AMP) states, "Confess to one another therefore your faults (your slips, your false steps, your offenses, your sins) and pray (also) for one another, that you may be healed and restored (to a spiritual tone of mind and heart). The earnest (heartfelt, continued) prayer of a righteous man makes tremendous power available (dynamic in its working)."

Faults in the Merriam Webster Dictionary is a moral weakness, less serious than a vice.[111] The Greek word for faults is "memphomai," which means to blame, find fault, or censure.[112]

The Scripture above tells you to confess your sins to each other. We must discern who to tell our sins too, so our business won't be all over the neighborhood. Basically, it is saying tell your shortcomings and sins to people who can help pray you through, to become an overcomer. Everyone can not necessarily get a prayer through, so confide in the ones that will take your situation before God. We all need prayer partners and

---

111. "Faults" Merriam-Webster.com 2019 https://www.merriam-webster.com August 2020
112. "Memphomai" Greek word for Faults https://www.biblehub.com September 2020

February 19th

someone to intercede for us who loves and tells us the truth. The person who prays for you has an intimate relationship with God and can tell you what He says concerning the issue you are going through. Remember, iron sharpens iron. We are supposed to be helpers to one another. Whoever we tell, prayer partner or mentor, it needs to stay between the two of you. It is not for anyone else's ears. We can pray for our unsaved loved ones by continuing to pray to God. He will do the work to change them into new creatures in Christ.

DECLARATIONS

Lord, I confess my sins and faults to you.

Lord, help me find a prayer partner or mentor who can help me pray through life issues.

Lord, we come against the works of the flesh that tries to tempt me into sin.

Lord, open up a way of escape, so I do not sin against you.

Lord, help me to grow more in Your Word so that I can resist the wiles of the enemy.

Lord, cover my faults and weakness under the blood of Jesus from this day forward in Jesus' name.

Lord, help me pray with the power, authority, and passion You have given me to help strengthen Your children.

February 20th

Ephesians 6:10 (AMP) states, "In conclusion, be strong in the Lord (be empowered through your union with Him); draw your strength from Him (that strength which His boundless might provide)."

Conclusion in the Merriam Webster Dictionary is a reasoned judgment, result, or outcome. [113] The Greek word for conclusion is "sumbibazo," which means unite or knit together, to join together, to consider, or to teach.[114]

The Scripture above talks about being strong in the Lord, drawing your strength from Him by staying in His Word, and living a life that is pleasing in His sight. God will give us the strength that we need when we cry out to Him. When we lay before Him, be real about what we are going through, and give Him the issue or problem. He can strengthen us. God will strengthen us for the tasks ahead of us so we can continue to move forward in Him and His will and purpose for our lives.

---

113. "Conclusion" Merriam-Webster.com 2019 https://www.merriam-webster.com September 2020
114. "Sumbibazo" Greek word for Conclusion https://www.biblehub.com September 2020.

February 20th

PRAYER:

Father God, in the name of Jesus, I come before You today to ask that You continue to strengthen me through the troubles and trials that I am going through at this time. Lord, I look to You for strength. Bless me to move closer and forward in You right now, in Jesus' name. Lord, help me to continue to grow and make You a priority in my life right now, in Jesus' name. Lord, make, mold, and use me for Your glory in Jesus' name. Lord, thank You for caring, loving, strengthening, and sustaining me in Jesus' name. Amen.

February 21st

Jeremiah 17:7-8 (AMPC) states, "(Most) blessed is the man who believes in, trusts in, and relies on the Lord, and whose hope and confidence the Lord is. 8. For he shall be like a tree planted by the waters that spreads out its roots by the river; and it shall not see and fear when heat comes; but its leaf shall be green. It shall not be anxious and full of care in the year of drought, nor shall it cease yielding fruit."

Hope in the Merriam Webster Dictionary is to cherish a desire with anticipation. It also means to want something to happen or be true. [115] The Greek word for hope is "elpis," meaning expectation, hope, trust, or confidence.[116]

A person is blessed when he believes in the Lord and trusts totally in Him. Whatever we are praying for in our lives or children's lives, God is the only person who can change things or make new things happen. So, when we trust Him, we can take

---
115. "Hope" Merriam-Webster.com 2019 https://www.merriam-webster.com September 2020.
116. "Elpis" Greek word for Hope https://www.biblehub.com Accessed September 2020.

our hands off the situation and let Him work it out without our help. Often, we say that we trust Him, but we really don't because our actions say otherwise. If God told us to be still and stand on His word, then that is what He means. Stop dabbling in it and wait on Him. Every time I have tried to do it on my own, I have always messed things up. I had to repent to God for overstepping my boundaries by trying to do His job. God certainly doesn't need any help from us, although at times we think He does . He truly doesn't need our help. He has everything in our lives fully under control before our birth and after we leave this earth. Give up control of your life and give it to Him. Amen.

Declarations

You are blessed if you continue to trust in God.

God is sending you water in every dry place in your lives.

My leaves will turn green and I will produce a bountiful harvest in my life.

I will produce fruit all season long and it will be a blessing to other people.

The Glory of God will follow my life, ministry, and everything that I put my hand to do for the glory of God.

Trust in God and lean not to your own understanding for whatever you are believing Him for in your life.

February 22nd

1 Chronicles 29:12 (AMPC) states, "Both riches and honor come from You, and You reign overall. In Your hands are power and might, in Your hands it is to make great and to give strength to all."

Might in the Merriam Webster Dictionary is the power, energy, or intensity of which one is capable.[117] The Greek word for might is "ischus," which means might, strength, power, force, or ability.[118]

David gives thanks to the Lord for the unsearchable riches that He holds and has given to us. In turn, give it back to Him. God deserves all the glory and adoration from us. We are to praise and serve God for who He is in our lives and what He has done for us. He sent His Son Jesus to die for all of our sins and redeem us back to Him. "Lord, in Your hands are power and might. You are the Almighty God and there is no other god who can do what You do. Lord, we glorify Your name because

---

117. "Might" Merriam-Webster.com 2019 https://www.merriam-webster.com September 2020
118. "Ischus" Greek word for Might https://www.biblehub.com Accessed September 2020

February 22nd

You are worthy to be praised every day of the week. Lord, it is all about You, God, and not about us."

DECLARATIONS

Lord, You are great and give strength to all that ask of You.

Lord, glory and honor belongs to You God.

Lord in Your hands are power and might.

Lord, Your love is from everlasting to everlasting.

Lord, we declare that You are Jehovah Rapha.

Lord, You are Jehovah Jireh.

Lord, You are our Redeemer. I thank You for redeeming us back to God.

February 23rd

Zephaniah 3:17 (AMPC) states, "The Lord your God is in the midst of you, a Mighty One, a Savior (Who saves)! He will rejoice over you with joy; He will rest (in silent satisfaction) and in His love He will be silent and make no mention (of past sins, or even recall them); He will exult over you with singing."

Exult in the Merriam Webster Dictionary is to be extremely joyful, rejoice, or to leap for joy. [119] The Greek word for exult is "agalliao," meaning rejoice greatly or full of joy.[120]

The Scripture above talks about the abundant peace, comfort, and prosperity of the church in the happy times yet to come. He will save. He will be Jesus. He will answer to His name. For He shall save His people from their sins. The Lord will save the weakest believer and cause true Christians to be greatly honored where they have been treated with contempt. God is going to sing and rejoice over you. This Scripture was

---

119. "Exult" Merriam-Webster.com 2019 https://www.merriam-webster.com September 2020
120. "Agalliao" Greek word for Exult https://www.biblehub.com Accessed September 2020.

February 23rd

written for Israel, but it applies to us today because we are His people. Also, the same thing that He promised for them is our promise. God is happy with the person who fully trusts in Him and is obedient to His Word and living a life that is pleasing unto Him. God loves us and yes, He is rejoicing over the things that we are doing for Him so that He can get the glory from our lives. God is not mad at you according to this Scripture. He is happy and rejoicing over His obedient children.[121]

PRAYER:

Father God, in the name of Jesus, we come before You today to thank You for loving me. Lord, thank You for being in the middle of Your people and guiding us in the way You want us to go. Lord, thank You for saving me and filling me with Your Holy Spirit and fire. Zephaniah 3:17 says, "He will rejoice over you with joy." Thank You for rejoicing over the changes that You are making in my life. According to Your Word, you are rejoicing and singing over us because You are pleased with my life. Lord, I surrender to You so You can continue to remove anything that is in my life or me that doesn't need to be there. Perfect me. Make a new creature out of me so I can continue to live a pleasing life before You in Jesus' name. Amen.

---

121. Zephaniah 3:17 Mattew Henry's Concise Commentary. https://www.bibblehub.com Accessed September 2020.

February 24th

Psalm 18:1-2 (AMPC) states, "I LOVE You fervently and devotedly, O Lord, my Strength. 2. The Lord is my Rock, my Fortress, and My Deliverer, My God, my keen and firm Strength in Whom I will trust and take refuge, my Shield, and the Horn of my salvation, my High Tower."

Fervently in the Merriam Webster Dictionary is exhibiting or marked by great intensity of feeling or zealous.[122] The Greek word for fervently is "zeo, " meaning burn (in spirit) or fervent.[123]

Those that truly love God can triumph in His strength. The Lord is my rock and my refuge. I can confidently call upon Him when I am praying or crying out to Him. God is my deliverer. He will deliver me from things that are not healthy and wounds from the past that have been troubling or plaguing me. "Lord, You are my God, my Abba Father, my Daddy God, and someone I can call my own. I will trust You and take refuge in Your arms in the secret place. I will trust You with my life and destiny for my family, marriage, and career. Lord, I will trust You

---

122. "Fervently" Merriam-Webster.com 2019 https://www.merriam-webster.com September 2020

123. "Zeo" Greek word for Fervently https://www.biblehub.com Accessed September 2020

February 24th

for everything that I need today and, in the days, months, and years to come. God, You are all that I will ever need to help me be the person You called. Lord, empower and anoint me with Your glory so that I can move in the gifts and talents that You have placed on my life. Lord, I thank You for Your strength and empowerment to keep moving forward in You in Jesus' name."

DECLARATIONS

Lord, empower me to move in all the gifts that You have given me.

Lord, I stir up the gifts that are lying dormant in me.

Abba Father, You are my One and only true Father.

I will trust the Lord with my whole life, family, marriage, business, and children in Jesus' name.

Lord, You are gracious and worthy to be praised.

Lord, I honor and adore You for now and forever more in Jesus' name.

Lord, I take refuge in Your shadow in Jesus' name.

February 25th

*P*SALM 37:39 (AMPC) STATES, "But the salvation of the (consistently) righteous is of the Lord; He is their refuge and secure Stronghold in the time of trouble."

Salvation in the Merriam Webster Dictionary is deliverance from the power and the effects of sin.[124] The Greek word for salvation is "soteria," which means deliverance, salvation, prosperity, or preservation.[125]

The salvation of the righteous will be the Lord's doing. He will help you to do what He has called you to do before you were formed in your mother's womb. He will help you bear your every burden and be with you in the times of troubles. God is with us. God is for us. We must stay rooted, grounded in Him and His love. Continue to lay before Him and stay at His feet. God will continue to strengthen you for all the tasks that

---

124. "Salvation" Merriam-Webster.com 2019 https://www.merriam-webster.com Accessed September 2020
125. 'Soteria" Greek word for Salvation https://www.biblehub.com Accessed September 2020

February 25th

He has given you to do in your lifetime. With God on our side, we are more than conquerors through Christ who loves us.

DECLARATIONS

Lord, my salvation is found in only You.

Lord, thank You for saving and giving me a new lease on life.

God, You are for me and care about me. You Love me with an everlasting love.

Lord, I have put down my roots in You so that I will not be moved.

Lord, I will cry out to You until You move on my behalf.

Lord, I thank You for Your never-ending strength.

February 26th

Psalm 138:3 (AMPC) states, "In the day when I called, You answered me; and You strengthened me with strength (might and inflexibility to temptation) in my inner self."

Inflexibility in the Merriam Webster Dictionary is rigidly firm in will or purpose, and unyielding.[126] The Greek word for inflexibility is "akamptos," meaning rigid, stiff, or unbending.[127]

On the day that I cried, I called upon God. He answered and delivered me from all ungodliness into salvation. I can resist the temptation from my enemy Satan. God will give us strength in our souls to bear the burdens that plague us from time to time. We need to lean on and trust the Lord to make a way out of no way.

PRAYER:

---

126. "Inflexibility" Merriam-Webster.com 2019 https://www.merriam-webster.com Accessed September 2020
127. "Akamptos" Greek word for Inflexibility https://www.wordhippo.com Accessed September 2020

February 26th

Father God, in the name of Jesus, I come before You today to say thank You for being there for me when I needed You the most in my life. I will not be bending to the wiles of the enemy, but I will be unyielding to anything that is not like God. God purify and purge me so that I can be cleaned in my mind, soul, and body in Jesus' name. Lord, mold me in the creature that You desire me to be in Jesus' name. Lord, I thank You for helping me to be able the fight off and get rid of wrong thinking in Jesus' name. Amen.

February 27th

Isaiah 40:28 (AMPC) states, "Have you not known? Have you not heard? The everlasting God, the Lord, the Creator of the ends of the earth, does not faint or grow weary, there is no searching of His understanding."

Everlasting in Merriam Webster is lasting or enduring through all time, eternal.[128] The Greek word for everlasting is "aionios," meaning eternal, unending; partaking of the character of that which lasts for an age.[129]

The Scripture above says that you don't know who God is and do not trust Him to work things out for you. God is the creator of the universe. He does not grow weary or faint with anything. Your understanding is definitely not like God's because we can't even comprehend His ways, no matter how hard we try. Not even the most intelligent person in the world can

---

128. "Everlasting" Merriam-Webster.com 2019 https://www.merriam-webster.com September 2020
129. "Aionios" Greek word for Everlasting https://www.biblehub.com Accessed September 2020

February 27th

comprehend on the same level as God. God will not stop being God!!

PRAYER:

Father God, in the name of Jesus, I come before You today to ask that You forgive me for not believing and trusting in You completely when You tell me something. Lord, forgive me for leaning to my own understanding instead of acknowledging You first in Jesus' name. Lord, help me get stronger in my faith by staying in Your Word and presence in Jesus' name. Lord, I know that when I get weary, You don't stop or get weary. You continue to work out things in my best interests in Jesus' name. Lord, I will acknowledge You in all that I do from this day forward in Jesus' name. Lord, thank You for being God in my life. Matthew 6:33 (AMPC) says, "But seek (aim at and strive after) first of all His kingdom and His righteousness (His way of doing and being right), and then all these things taken together will be given you besides." Lord, thank You for reminding me of Your Word in Jesus' name. Amen.

February 28th

Proverbs 18:21 (AMPC) says, "Death and life are in the power of the tongue, and they who indulge in it shall eat the fruit of it (for death or life)."

Indulge in the Merriam Webster Dictionary is to yield to the desire of. [130] The Greek word for indulge is "poreuomai," which means to go their way.[131]

The Scripture above is talking about using our tongue to bless. What we speak and say on a regular basis matters because either you are speaking life or death over yourself. The way to speak life over yourself is to speak the Word of God over ourselves and to speak positive things. A lot of times we think that what we say doesn't matter but it really does because many people have spoken curses over themselves. When we say things like, "This is how I am," it is a trick of the enemy. We can become new creatures in Christ when we accept Him

---

130. "Indulge" Merriam-Webster.com 2019 https://www.merriam-webster.com Accessed September 2020
131. "Poreuomai" Greek word for Indulge https://www.biblehub.com Accessed September 2020

February 28th

as our Lord and Savior. When you continue to say "you are broke," then that is what you will be. God has given us the His Word to speak over ourselves and our families so changes can be made in our lives. The Word of God says, "Let the weak say they are strong." God is obligated to answer His Word, so speak His word out loud every day.

DECLARATIONS

Lord, I will decree and declare Your Word every day.

I am rich in every area of my life because God's Word says I am.

I will stop speaking negative things over myself, my family, my marriage, etc.

I will speak life and life more abundantly into every situation.

God's Word says, "I am more than a conqueror through Christ who loves me."

Lord, I bring Your Word back up to You to call in a harvest in Jesus' name.

February 29th

2 Corinthians 4:8 (AMPC) "We are hedged in (pressed) on every side (troubled and oppressed in every way), but not cramped or crushed, we suffer embarrassments and are perplexed and unable to find a way out, but not driven to despair."

Hedged in the Merriam Webster Dictionary is a means of protection or defense.[132] The Greek word for hedged is "phragmos," meaning a fencing, fencing in.[133]

Friends and families may forsake believers. Enemies may persecute them, but God will never leave or forsake them. There may be fears from within and fighting without, yet we are not destroyed.[134] God has us hedged in and has a shield of protection surrounding us like a shield. The enemy must get permission from God before He can do anything to us. Testing comes to make us strong and not destroy us. God has each of

---
132. "Hedged" Merriam-Webster.com 2019 https://www.merriam-webster.com Accessed September 2020
133. "Phragmos" Greek word for Hedged https://www.biblehub.com Accessed September 2020
134. 2 Corinthians 4:8, Matthew Henry's Concise Commentary https://www.biblehub.com Accessed September 2020

February 29th

us covered under the blood of Jesus. We may suffer embarrassments, but we will not quit or be in despair because we have the Lord on our side. We are never alone. We always win because God is with and for us. Just keep the faith and trust God and hold on to Him.

PRAYERS:

Father God, in the name of Jesus, I come to You today to ask that You will keep me covered under the blood of Jesus. Lord, I thank You for having me hemmed in on every side so I will not lean too far to the left or the right but stay on the narrow path. Lord, You said in Your Word that when we are persecuted we will not be forsaken because You are with us. Lord, I lay down my life to You so You can take full control over it, in Jesus' name. Lord, help me continue to grow more in You, day-by-day as I lay my will down for Yours, in Jesus' name. Lord, You said in Your Word that no weapon that is formed against me shall prosper and every tongue that rises up against me in judgement, I shall utterly condemn for this is the heritage of the saints in Christ Jesus. Lord, thank You for Your love in Jesus' name. Amen.

March 1st

*P*SALM 94:19 (AMPC) STATES, "In the multitude of my (anxious) thoughts with me, Your comforts cheer and delight my soul!"

Anxious in the Merriam Webster Dictionary is characterized by extreme uneasiness of mind or brooding fear about some contingency, worried.[135] The Greek word for anxious is "merimnao," meaning to care for, to be anxious, or distracted.[136]

The world's comforts give little delight to the soul. When hurried with anxious thoughts, God's comforts bring that peace and pleasure, which the world cannot give or cannot take away. God is our refuge in the time of troubles. We can flee to God and be safe within His shadow. Our security can be found in the Most High God because the world doesn't have nor does it offer any security to anyone, not even its own.[137] True joy can only be found in Jesus. Many people have searched all over the

---

135. "Anxious" Merriam-Webster.com 2019 https://www.merrian-webster.com Accessed September 2020

136. "Merimnao" Greek word for Anxious https://www.biblehub.com Accessed September 2020

137. Psalm 94:19, Matthew Henry's Concise Commentary https://www.biblehub.com Accessed September 2020

world looking for joy in relationships, marriages, businesses, etc., but to find it is simpler than they will ever know. All they must do is to cry out to Jesus with repentance in their hearts and confess with their mouths that God raised Him from the dead and they would be saved. True love, peace, joy, patience, and long-suffering can only come from the Son of God and His name is Jesus.

DECLARATIONS

Lord, I repent of every sin that I have ever committed knowingly and unknowingly, in thought, deed, omission and commission in Jesus' name.

Jesus, I confess with my mouth and believe in my heart that God raised You from the dead that I would be saved.

Lord, thank You for saving me and making a new creature out of me.

Lord, I know that true joy, peace, love, longsuffering, and patience can only be found in You.

Lord, thank You for changing my way of life today, in Jesus' name.

Lord, thank You for giving my life new meaning, in Jesus' name. Amen.

March 2nd

*1*Chronicles 16:34 (AMPC) says, "O give thanks to the Lord, for He is good, for His mercy and loving-kindness endure forever!"

Loving-kindness in the Merriam Webster Dictionary is tender and benevolent affection.[138] The Greek word for loving-kindness is "storigiki kalosyni," meaning kindness, goodness, or benevolence.[139]

We need to be thanking God for He is good. His mercy and kindness is everlasting. Everything about God is good and perfect. We should be thanking God for everything, such as waking us up in the morning, being in good health, having eyes to see, and a tongue to talk. So many people didn't wake up this morning even with their alarm clocks going off. God's grace has kept us alive. We cannot do anything on our own. We need God to even breathe. He supplies us with oxygen and He keeps our mind right if we keep it stayed on Him. When we praise, deliv-

---
138. "Loving-Kindness" Merriam-Webster.com 2019 https://www.merriam-webster.com Accessed September 2020
139. "Storgiki Kalosyni" Greek word for Loving-Kindness https://www.wordhippo.com Accessed September 2020

erance and miracles are released. Open your mouth and sing a song of praises to our God, who keeps us from all hurt, harm and danger. Singing praises to God can get heavy burdens off our hearts and give us peace that only God can give.

DECLARATIONS

Lord, I thank You for Your grace and mercy in my life.

Lord, I cannot do anything unless You and with and for me.

Lord, I sing praises to Your name Oh Lord.

Lord, Your name is worthy to be praised and honored.

Lord, we give You the glory, honor, and praise just because of who You are.

Lord, I cast down every heavy burden that has me stressed out and worried.

Lord, I thank You for life, health, strength, and the roof that is over my head in Jesus' name.

March 3rd

James 1:12 (AMPC) states, "Blessed (happy, to be envied) is the man who is patient under trial and stands up under temptation, for when he has stood the test and been approved, he will receive (the victor's) crown of life which God has promised to those who love Him."

Temptation in the Merriam Webster Dictionary is the act of tempting or the state of being tempted especially to evil, enticement.[140] The Greek word for temptation is "peirazo," meaning to make proof of, to attempt, or test.[141]

It is trials and tribulations a Christian's life that refines our trust in God and increases our dependence upon Him. The personal difficulties and dangers that we face in our everyday life, and our reaction to the distresses and despair of others is often the determining factor in whether we hold fast to what we believe of Christ's sufficient strength.Otherwise, we allow seeds

---

140."Temptation" Merriam Webster.com 2019 https://www.merriam-webster.com Accessed September 2020
141. "Peirzo" Greek word for Temptation https://www.biblehub.com Accessed September 2020

March 3rd

of doubt to darken our hearts to the goodness of God. In which case, we become tossed to and fro in a sea of uncertainty. We have a vicious enemy that is seeking to shipwreck our faith in the goodness of God and his strategy is to plant seeds of doubt in the mind of the believers, so that their life is not fruitful, nor honoring to the Lord Who bought them.[142] But the trials can be used for our gain instead of our distrust in God. Our faith could grow stronger in God. What the devil meant for bad, God will turn it around for our good.

PRAYER:

Father God, in the name of Jesus, I come to You today to ask if You would help me go through these trials that I am going through, in Jesus' name. Father, help me to always depend on You for whatever I need, in Jesus' name. Lord, I will endure until the end of my life, in Jesus' name. Lord, help me pass the test so I don't repeat the same mistakes. Lord, I thank You for always being there for me when I needed You the most. Lord, I take on the crown of life and place it on my head. Lord, You said that You would give me life and life more abundantly in Jesus' name. Lord, let my life be found pleasing in Your sight in the heavens, in Jesus' name. Amen.

---

142. James 1:12 https://www.dailyverse.knowing-jesus.com Accessed September 2020

March 4th

Psalm 103:5 (AMPC) states, "Who satisfies your mouth (your necessity and desire at your personal age and situation) with good so that your youth, renewed, is like the eagle's (strong, overcoming, soaring)!"

Renewed in the Merriam Webster Dictionary is to make like new, restore to freshness, vigor, or perfection.[143] The Greek word for renewed is "anakainoo," meaning to make new again.[144]

God is going to renew our strength and joy even in our old age. You are never too old for God to use you for His glory. As the eagle renewed its youth by casting all its old feathers, getting new ones, God is going to do this His seasoned saints that have been on the battlefield a long time. God will give us His favor, loving-kindness, and grace so we can continue to go forward in Him. If God used Abraham and Sarah at an old age, He can use us too. No matter how late in life your calling may

---

143. "Renewed" Merriam-Webster.com 2019 https://www.merriam-webster.com Accessed September 2020
144. "Anakainoo" Greek word for Renewed https://www.biblehub.com Accessed September 2020

March 4th

come, you must accept it and move forward in God. Many people that are assigned to us need to hear what you have to say to them.

DECLARATIONS

Lord, You said that they that wait on You shall renew their strength.

Lord, I will run and not be weary. I shall walk and not faint.

Lord, I will wait in Your presence until You renew my strength.

Lord, I will continue to fly high as I stay in Your will for my life.

Lord, I will make it through this testing with a greater level of anointing on my life.

Lord, I will stop trusting in myself to do everything and I will fully put my trust in You.

March 5th

Psalm 103:6-7 (AMPC) states, "The Lord executes righteousness and justice (not for me only, but) for all who are oppressed. 7. He made known His ways (of righteousness and justice) to Moses, His acts to the children of Israel."

Executes in the Merriam Webster Dictionary is to carry out fully, put completely into effect.[145] The Greek word for executes is "poieo," means to do, or to make.[146]

Truly God is good and special to us all. God has revealed Himself and His grace to us. We need to understand His precepts, the ways He requires us to walk in, and His promises and purposes. He has always been full of compassion. God has given us a great deal of His mercy and not giving us what we deserve. He pities His children that are weak in knowledge, froward and sick, and teaches, bears, and comforts them. Thank God for His grace. He empowers us to move forward in Him.

---

145. 'Executes" Merriam-Webster.com 2019 https://www.biblehub.com Accessed September 2020
146. "Poieo" Greek for Executes https://www.Gospelhall.org Accessed October 2020

March 5th

Not in our own ability but in His with His unmerited favor. God enables us to do what we couldn't do on our own.[147]

PRAYER:

Father God, in the name of Jesus, we come to You today to thank You for Your grace and mercy. Lord, we thank You that You have not given us what we deserve, in Jesus' name. Thank You, Lord, for having mercy on us when we sin and fall short of Your glory. Lord, we activate Your grace with our faith right now, in Jesus' name. God Your Word says that without faith, it is impossible to please You. So, increase our faith to help our unbelief. Lord, help us to stay in Your word so we can grow into the knowledge of You, in Jesus' name. Lord, continue to have Your way in our lives right now in Jesus' name. Make a new creature out of me, in Jesus' name. Amen.

---

147. Psalm 103:6-7, Matthew Henry's Concise Commentary https://www.biblehub.com Accessed September 2020

March 6th

Psalm 73:25-26 (AMPC) states, "Whom have I in heaven but You? and I have no delight or desire on earth besides you. 26. My flesh and my heart may fail, but God is the Rock and firm Strength of my heart and my portion forever."

Rock in the Merriam Webster Dictionary is foundation, support, or something like a rock in firmness.[148] The Greek word for rock is "petra," which is like a rock, by reason of firmness and strength of soul.[149]

Matthew 16:18 (AMP) says, "And I tell you, you are Peter (Greek Petros a large piece of rock), and on this rock (Greek Petra a huge rock like Gibraltar) I will build My church, and the gates of Hades (the powers of the infernal region) shall not overpower it (or be strong to its detriment or hold out against it)."

---

148. "Rock" Merriam-Webster.com 2019 https://www.merriam-webster.com Accessed September 2020
149. "Petra" Greek word for Rock https://www.Thayer'sGreekLexicon Accessed September 2020

March 6th

"You are the only One that I can rely on for help in the time of trouble. You are the One that can guide, save, and lead me. Even on this earth, there is no substitute for You. Lord, You are not replaceable in my life. I need You for everything in my life and You are the only One that can move things on my behalf. Lord, I long for You with every fiber of my being, and I love You more than words could ever say. My soul thirsts for You, Lord because You are the living God in heaven and earth."

The sooner we recognize that God is our all-sufficient source, the better off we will be. We must put our total trust in God alone, continue to get close to Him, and stay in His presence continually so we can walk in the peace that God has for us. We can find strength in God in our hearts. If you need an extra touch today, call on Jesus. He is the One that will give you peace, and release His joy in your life when there is none. Jesus is just a whisper away. Say His name while you are in your prayer closet, car, or wherever you are, and He will come to rescue to see about you.

DECLARATIONS

Lord, You are my rock and my very present help in the storm.

Thank You, Lord, for being my sanctuary place that I can run to for safety.

Lord, in Romans 9:33, You said, " If I believe in You, I will not be disappointed."

Lord, I will not stumble because of being disobedient to Your Word.

Lord, You said in 1 Corinthians 3:11, "For no one can lay a foundation other than that which is laid, which is Christ Jesus."

1 Peter 2:5 states, "You yourselves like living stones are being built up as a spiritual house, to be a holy priesthood, to offer spiritual sacrifices acceptable to God through Jesus Christ."

Lord, You said in Psalm 61:2, "That You would lead me to the rock that is higher than I."

March 7th

Jeremiah 29:11 (AMPC) states, "For I know the thoughts and plans that I have for you, says the Lord, thoughts and plans for welfare and peace and not for evil, to give you hope in your final outcome."

Plans in the Merriam Webster Dictionary is a method for achieving an end, goal, or aim.[150] The Greek word for plans is "boule," which means counsel, deliberate wisdom, decree, purpose.[151]

The Scripture above means the Lord is telling Israel that He is resolved in His own thoughts on what to do for them. He said that He doesn't intend on blotting out the name of Israel from the earth but to give them an end to their troubles. There should be an end to their captivity in His time after they have fulfilled seventy years in bondage. God is saying the same thing to us today. He already knows the thoughts and plans that He has for us. He knew the plans and purpose for our lives be-

---

150. "Plans" Merriam-Webster.com 2019 https://www.merriam-webster.com Accessed September 2020

151. "Boule" Greek for Plans https://www.biblehub.com September 2020

fore we were formed in our mother's womb. God already knew who we are in Him, because He is in our future already. We are in the present, moving toward our future or purpose. God will show us who we are in Him or He will have prophets and other prophetic people to tell us so we can start to prepare ourselves for the calling on our lives. God will give us hope and a future. He will perfect and take us through the refiner's fire so we can become who He is calling us to be in Him.

PRAYERS:

Father God, in the name of Jesus, I come to You today to ask that You reveal to me who I am in You and my calling in life, in Jesus' name. Lord, send seasoned labors to help get me to my next level in You Jesus. Lord, remove anything that is not of You, in Jesus' name. Lord, help me to be more like You, Jesus as I journey to my destiny and purpose. Lord, remove anyone in my life that is not for me or really cares for me. Replace them with people that will help propel me forward in You, Jesus. Lord, no matter how painful it is, help me to pray and forgive them so I can move forward in You Jesus. Oh, create in me a clean heart and renew a right spirit in me, Jesus, so there will not be anything hindering my walk with You. You are the only reason that I can have hope and a future. Lord, I give You all the glory, honor, and praise, in Jesus' name. Amen.

March 8th

Isaiah 25:1 (AMP) says, "O Lord, You are my God; I will exalt You, I will praise Your name, for You have done wonderful things, even purposes planned of old (and fulfilled) in faithfulness and truth."

Exalt in the Merriam Webster Dictionary is to elevate by praise or in estimation, glorify.[152] The Greek word for exalt is "hupsoo," which means to lift or raise up, to exalt, uplift, raise on high, or set on high.[153]

God has always had a remnant of believers who trust His Word, believe His promises, and give glory to His name in spite of others living in ungodliness. Isaiah was warning of the coming judgment or the Great Day of the Lord. The coming tribulation period is when God will pour out His wrath on a sinful world that has rejected Christ. Never forget -no matter the trials and tribulations we face in this Church age, let us be part of today's little flock, who lifts up our voices in joyful praise and worship, singing: "Oh Lord, You are my God, I will exalt You.

152. "Exalt" Merriam-Webster.com 2019 https://www.merriam-webster.com Accessed September 2020
153. "Hupsoo" Greek word for Exalt https://www.biblehub.com September 2020

I will praise Your name, for You have done wonderful things, even purposes planned of old (and fulfilled) in faithfulness and truth."[154]

DECLARATIONS

Lord, I will forever trust in Your Word for all eternity, in Jesus' Amen.

Lord, according to the Word of God, every promise that belongs to Abraham belongs to me.

Lord, I worship and praise Your name because You are worthy to be praised.

Lord, I exalt You because You are my Lord.

Lord, I will praise Your name because You have done wonderful things.

Lord, all the purposes planned of old are fulfilled in faithfulness and truth.

---

154. Isaiah 25:1, https://www.knowingjesus.com Accessed September 2020

March 9th

DEUTERONOMY 7:9 (AMPC) STATES, "Know, recognize, and understand therefore that the Lord your God, He is God, the faithful God, who keeps covenant and steadfast love and mercy with those who love Him and keep His commandments, to a thousand generations."

Covenant in the Merriam Webster Dictionary is to promise by a covenant, pledge, contract, or to enter into a covenant.[155] The Greek word for covenant is "diatheke," which means a covenant between two parties, a will, testament. [156]

God is faithful, true to His word, and constant in performing all His promises. We must continue to stay rooted, grounded in God, and seek His kingdom and all other things will be added unto us. When we put God's business first, He will take care of our business. Even during the COVID-19 pandemic, God has never left us. He has been there all the time, healing our bod-

---

155. "Covenant" Merriam-Webster.com 2019 https://www.merriam-webster.com Accessed September 2020
156. "Diatheke" Greek word for Covenant https://www.biblehub.com Accessed September 2020

ies. The illness wasn't a death sentence because Jehovah Rapha, our Great Physician, is with us when we cry out to Him. God has been with us before we were formed in our mother's womb. He will be with us until the end of the world. Many people have realized in the pandemic that they really need God in their lives. His healing virtue has touched many bodies, so they know without a shadow of doubt that God is real. Jesus is alive and well.

Prayer:

Father God, in the name of Jesus, I come to You today to just say thank You for protecting us from COVID-19. Thank You for healing our hearts, minds, and bodies from this illness in Jesus' name. Thank You for the hedge of protection that You had surrounded me, my family, and everybody that is connected to me in Jesus' name. Lord, You are Jehovah Rapha, the God that healeth thee. I thank You for answering the prayers of the righteous in Jesus' name. Lord, thank You for never leaving me even when I didn't always do what was right in Your sight in Jesus' name. Thank You for the multiple chances that You have given me. Lord, continue to touch and show everyone in this world that You are still God. You hold the world in the palm of Your hands, in Jesus' name. Lord, we thank You for Your faithfulness and all the promises given by being the Sons and daughters of God, in Jesus' name. Amen.

March 10th

Psalm 32:8 (AMPC) states, "I (the Lord) will instruct you and teach you in the ways you should go; I will counsel you with My eye upon you."

Instruct in the Merriam Webster Dictionary is to give knowledge to, teach, or train.[157] The Greek word for instruct is "katecheo," which means to teach by word of mouth.[158]

God will teach us in His Word the way that we should go. If we follow His commands, we will do good. If we follow the way of the unrighteous, we will live in a world of sorrow. Living your life without God is a lonely place because He is not your source and strength. We, as children of God, don't have to do anything in our own strength. All we need to do is to put our total trust in God. He will work things out for our good. God has our best interests at heart. Anything that comes your way to hurt or destroy you, God will send His angels to block it. We will go through trials and tribulations. They are not meant to

---

157. "Instruct" Merriam-Webster.com 2019 https://www.merriam-webster.com Accessed September 2020
158. "Katecheo" Greek word for Instruct https://www.biblehub.com Accessed Spetember 2020

destroy us but to strengthen, help, and move us forward. Opposition keeps us on our knees praying, fasting, worshiping and reading the Bible so we can walk in peace, joy, or freedom during our darkest moments. We must study the Word of God and let it enter our hearts, so we can be transformed from the inside out.

DECLARATIONS

Lord, thank You for teaching me with divine instructions concerning Your Word.

Lord, You said in Your Word that if we need wisdom, we are to ask You.

Lord, give me more godly wisdom.

Lord, I will follow the way of the righteous and stay on the narrow path.

Lord, let Your divine will be done in my life as it is in heaven.

I will hide the Word of God in my heart, so I will not sin against thee.

March 11th

1 Timothy 2:5-6 (AMP) "For there (is only) one God, and (only) one Mediator between God and men, the Man Christ Jesus. 6. Who gave Himself as a ransom for all (people, a fact that was) attested to at the right and proper time."

Mediator in the Merriam Webster Dictionary is especially one that mediates between parties at variance (being different).[159] The Greek word for mediator is "mesites," means a go between, mediator, or arbiter.[160]

We know that Jesus is our one and only mediator between God and man. Jesus is sitting at the right hand of the Father interceding for each of us. Jesus gave His life as a ransom so we could be redeemed back to God. Because of Christ, we were made righteous to be the righteousness of God in Christ Jesus. Through Jesus's sacrifice, we have been reconciled back to God because He did a perfect work on the cross of Calvary. He did

---
159. "Mediator" Merriam-Webster.com 2019 https://www.merriam-webster.com Accessed September 2020
160. "Mesistes" Greek word for Mediator https://www.biblehub.com Accessed September 2020

it for the Jews and Gentiles, you and me. We now have an advocate with the Father and it is Jesus. We have to go through Jesus to get to God. When we give our lives to Jesus and allow His Spirit to come and live inside of us. The Holy Spirit will lead and guide us in the way that we should go on this Earth. We should be living holy and righteous lifestyles in the glory of God before we go to Heaven.

PRAYER:

Father God, in the name of Jesus, we thank You for the perfect sacrifice of Your life so that we could be made the righteousness of God in Christ Jesus. Without Jesus, we never would have been reconciled back to God. Lord, thank You for giving people from all nationalities and cultures a chance to get to know You as their Lord and Savior. Lord, thank You for Your Holy Spirit that will lead and guide me in all truth in Jesus' name. Lord, help me to read and study Your Word so that I can get it in my heart in Jesus' name. Lord, send Your glory to surround and move powerfully in my life, in Jesus' name. Amen.

March 12th

2 Corinthians 5:21 (AMP) says, "For our sake He made Christ (virtually) to be sin Who knew no sin, so that in and through Him we might become (endued with, viewed as being in, and examples of) the righteousness of God (what we ought to be, approved and acceptable and in right relationship with Him, by His goodness."

Endued in the Merriam Webster Dictionary is provided, endow, to provide something freely or naturally.[161] The Greek word for endued is "epistemon," meaning knowing, skilled, skillful, or experienced.[162]

Jesus endowed us with redemption when He gave His life as a ransom. Jesus knew no sin but all our sins: past, present, future were placed on Jesus at Calvary. When we become joint-heirs with Christ, we are made the righteousness of God. We must accept the finished works of Jesus, make Him our Lord and Savior, and live a life that is pleasing and lining up with the

---
161. "Endued" Merriam-Webster.com 2019 https://www.merriam-webster.com Accessed September 2020
162. "Epistemon" Greek for Endued https://www.biblehub.com Accessed September 2020

Word of God. Because we have justification that was given by Jesus, it is as if we have never sinned once we become children of God. When we take on Christ, we take on His divine nature to help us live a life free from habitual sin. But if we stumble and fall into sin, we can go to God and ask for forgiveness. Then we can get back into right standing with Him by making Jesus the head of our lives.

DECLARATIONS

I am the righteousness of Christ.

Jesus is my redeemer.

I am redeemed through the Blood of the Lamb.

I will activate the grace of God through faith.

Grace is more than unmerited favor; it is the ability to know that I can't do on my own.

Lord, thank You for sacrificing Your life for me so that I might live.

March 13th

Psalm 62:7 (AMPC) states, "With God rests my salvation and my glory; He is my Rock of unyielding strength and impenetrable hardness, and my refuge is in God."

Unyielding in the Merriam Webster Dictionary is characterized by a lack of softness or flexibility.[163] The Greek word for unyielding is "aklines," which means unbending, firm, or unbent.[164]

We have found it good to wait upon the Lord, and it should charge us to have some dependence on Him. Since God will save our souls, we can leave everything else to His disposal. David's faith advances to unshakeable steadfastness, so his joy in God improves into a holy triumph. Meditation on God's Word is a way to strengthen your faith and hope in the Lord. The more Word that you have in your heart, the better you are. When the enemy comes at you like a flood, you can use God's

---

163. "Unyielding" Merriam-Webster.com 2019 https://www.merriam-webster.com Accessed September 2020

164. "Aklines" Greek word for Unyielding https://www.biblehub.com Accessed September 2020

Word to lift up a standard against him. Prayer also strengthens your hope in God since prayer is not a monologue, but it is a dialogue. Dialogue means that we will talk to God and listen, and He will speak back to us. We can take refuge in God and He will protect us in the time of trouble. God is our very present help in the time of trouble.

PRAYER:

Father God, in the name of Jesus, thank You for hearing my cry and saving me from death and destruction. Lord, help me read and study Your Word so I can hide it in my heart, in Jesus' name. Lord, I will use Your Word when the enemy tries to come against me. Lord, You are my refuge when the world gets cold and lonely. You will put Your loving arms around me and help me face the storms. Lord, every time I pray Your Word back to You, it obligates You to answer my prayers in Jesus' name. I will forever hide Your Word in my heart so I will not sin against You, in Jesus' name. Lord, thank You for teaching me what to do, so I can glorify You in Jesus' name. Amen.

March 14th

Psalm 16:11 (AMPC) states, "You will show me the path of life; in Your presence is fullness of joy, at Your right hand there are pleasures forevermore."

Path in the Merriam Webster Dictionary is a track specially constructed for a particular use.[165] The Greek word for path is "tribos," which means a beaten track, a path, road, or highway.[166]

God will show us the path of life. Even after we leave this earth and go to heaven, there will be eternal life with God forever. David said to God that in His presence is fullness of joy, meaning that heaven is a blessed place where there is no more sickness, dying, suffering, or sorrow. In heaven, there will be praising and worshipping God forever more. The right hand of God is a place of power, where Jesus is sitting. When we go to heaven, it will be a glorious time, but God wants us to have the fullness of joy here on earth too. The only way that we can have

---

165. "Path" Merriam-Webster.com 2019 https://www.merriam-webster.com Accessed September 2020
166. "Tribos" Merriam-Webster.com 2019 https://www.merriam-webster.com Accessed September 2020

the fullness of joy is totally depending on Jesus to take care of our needs and be our source, so we don't have to struggle any longer in any areas of our life. Our full dependence is on Jesus and not us.

DECLARATIONS

Lord, I want to go deeper in Your presence so You can show me wondrous and mighty things.

Lord, I exchange every one of my burdens, and troubles with Your peace, in Jesus' name.

Lord, I cast all my cares at Your feet because You care for me, in Jesus' name.

Lord, I will seek You while you may be found, in Jesus' name.

Lord, I will worship You and in spirit and in truth and will stay in Your presence until I get everything I need.

Lord, I cry holy, holy to Your name because You are worthy to be praised.

March 15th

Psalm 145:9 (AMPC) says, "The Lord is good to all, and His tender mercies are over all His works (the entirety of things created)."

Lord in the Merriam Webster Dictionary is God, Jesus being perfect in power, wisdom, and goodness who is worshipped in Christianity.[167] The Greek word for Lord is "kyrios," meaning Lord.[168]

It can truly be said about our Lord Jesus, that His Words and works are ones of goodness and grace. He is full of compassion; hence, He came into the world to save sinners. When on earth, He showed His compassion both to the bodies and souls of men, healing the one, and making wise the other. He is of great mercy, a merciful High Priest, through whom God is merciful to sinners.[169]

---

167. "Lord" Merriam-Webster.com 2019 https://www.merriam-webster.com Accessed September 2020
168. "Kyrios" Greek word for Lord https://www.biblehub.com Accessed September 2020
169. .Psalm 145:9, Mattew Henry's Concise Commentary https://www.biblehub.com Accessed September 2020

The 180-Days of Communing with God Daily Devotional

PRAYER:

Father God, in the name of Jesus, thank You for being good to me and giving me your tender mercies when I fail to live according to Your commandments. Lord, Your grace is more than unmerited favor, but it is the ability to do what I couldn't do in my own strength, in Jesus' name. Lord, I want You to know that I am forever grateful for all the miracles and blessings that You have done in my life. Lord, I am grateful that You know my beginning and my end. You have great plans for my life. Lord, thank You for having compassion on me when I was sick in my body and didn't know what I would do. When I prayed and had other people to intercede for me, my body was totally healed. Lord, I thank You for having compassion for me when I was unstable in my mind. Thank You for regulating and giving me a sound mind, in Jesus' name. Lord, I will be forever grateful for saving me from a life of sin. Thank You for creating a new heart and renewing a right spirit within me in Jesus' name. Lord, thank You for Your unconditional love finding me in Jesus' name. Amen.

March 16th

Psalm 145:18-19 (AMPC) "The Lord is near to all who call upon Him, to all who call upon Him sincerely and in truth. 19. He will fulfil the desires of those who reverently and worshipfully fear Him; He also will hear their cry and will save them."

Near in the Merriam Webster Dictionary is in a close or intimate manner, closely.[170] The Greek word for near is "eggus," which means near in place or time, nearby, or close.[171]

God draws near to those that draw near to Him. He makes His presence felt, and we must call upon Him in truth, sincerely with an earnest desire. God is ready to hear and answer the prayers of His people. He is present everywhere, but in a special way He is nigh to them, as He is not to others. He is in their hearts dwelling there by faith, and they abide in Him. He is nigh to those that call upon Him for help in the times of need. They may have what they ask, and find what they seek if they call upon Him in truth and sincerity. Having taught men to love

---

170. "Near" Merriam-Webster.com 2019 https://www.merriam-webster.com Accessed September 2020
171. "Eggus" Greek for Near https://www.biblehub.com Accessed September 2020

His name and holy ways, He will save them from the destruction of the wicked. May we then love His name and walk in His ways, while we desire that all flesh should bless His holy name forever and ever. [172]

DECLARATIONS

The Lord is near to those that call upon Him.

I call upon Jesus in the truth of His word.

God will fulfill the desires of the hearts that fear and reverence Him.

I am about to experience God on another level in this season of my life.

Lord, I love Your name and I will walk in Your ways in Jesus' name.

The Lord is good to_____(name).

Thank You Lord for blessing my life and bringing me closer to You, in Jesus' name.

---

172. Psalm 145:18-19 Matthew Henry's Concise Commentary https://www.biblehub.com Accessed September 2020

March 17th

Mark 12:30 (AMP) states, "And you shall love the Lord your God out of and with your whole heart and out of and with all of your soul (your life) and out of and with all of your mind (with your faculty of thought and your moral understanding) and out of and with all your strength. This is the first and principal commandment."

Soul in Merriam Webster is a person's total self.[173] The Greek word for soul is "psyche," which means the vital breath, breath of life, the human soul, the soul as the seat of affections and will.[174]

We are to love God with all of our spirits. This is a place where the Holy Spirit dwells. Our soul consists of our emotions, wills, and feelings. Our bodies should be presented as living sacrifices wholly acceptable to God which is our reasonable service. So, in essence we should be putting God first above everyone and everything in our lives. God should be our prior-

---
173. "Soul" Merriam-Webster.com 2019 https://www.merriam-webster.com Accessed September 2020
174. "Psche" Greek for Soul https://www.biblehub.com Accessed September 2020

ity because in Matthew 6:33, it states that if we seek first the Kingdom of God and His righteousness then all other things will be added unto us. When we make the will and ways of God our main concern, He will in turn go to bat for us when we need Him too. God wants to know if we are going to be obedient to what He is telling us to do.

PRAYER:

Father God, in the name of Jesus, I come to You today to thank You for loving and me. Lord, I love You so much and I will be obedient to do what You are telling me to do, in Jesus' name. Lord, I love you with all my spirit, soul and body in Jesus' name. Lord, Your love is unfailing, and You are always there when I need You the most, in Jesus' name. Lord, thank You for renewing my mind as I continue to study Your Word, in Jesus' name. Lord, I will make my body a living sacrifice and not use it to stray into sin, in Jesus' name. Lord, help me to trust You in every area of my life so I can release to You all the cares of this world. I know that You have everything that concerns me fully under control, in Jesus' name. You are working it out for my good in Jesus' name. Amen.

March 18th

Psalm 103:2 (AMPC) states, "Bless (affectionately, gratefully praise) the Lord, O my soul, and forget not (one of) all His benefits."

Bless in the Merriam Webster Dictionary is to speak well of, praise, glorify, or approve.[175] The Greek word for bless is "markarios," which means blessed, happy, or position for receiving God's provisions.[176]

All of God's actions are beneficial. Worship God in spirit and truth, call on His name and show Him reverence in all the things that He has done in our lives so far. Deliverance is found in our praise. We need to welcome the Holy Spirit in our space, so He can do great works in us. Jesus wants us to have personal encounters with Him as He shows us great and marvelous things in the spirit. We can be happy to come into His presence to be strengthened as we go through this journey called life. Lord, we thank You for the benefits that You have poured out continuously. One of the greatest benefits we have is Jesus as

---

175. "Bless" Merriam-Webster.com 2019 https://www.merriam-webster.com Accessed September 2020
176. "Makarios" Greek for Bless https://www.biblehub.com Accessed September 2020

our Lord and Savior. When we go through in our lives and the cares of this world, we are never alone because God is by our side.

DECLARATIONS

Lord, thank You for the benefits that I find in Your Word and in knowing You.

Lord, I am never alone. You will be with me until the end of the world.

I will find strength in the presence of the Lord.

Lord, You are the God of multiplication. Thank You for multiplying me in every area of my life.

Lord, I know that my labor is not in vain.

Lord, thank You for brand new mercies every day.

March 19th

Habakkuk 3:19 (AMPC) states, "The Lord God is my Strength, my personal bravery, and my invincible army, He make my feet like hinds' feet and will make me to walk (not to stand still in terror, but to walk) and make(spiritual) progress upon high places (of trouble, suffering, or responsibility)! For the Chief Musician; with my stringed instruments.

Invincible in the Merriam Webster Dictionary is incapable of being conquered, overcome or subdued.[177] The Greek word for invincible is "anikitos," meaning unbeatable, unbowed, or unconquerable.[178]

We will be supplied with the graces and comforts of God's Spirit. We shall be strong in spiritual warfare and work. With the enlargement of heart, we may run the way of His commandments and outrun our troubles. We shall be successful in spiritual undertakings. Prophet Habakkuk began the above prayer

---
177. "Invincible" Merriam-Webster.com 2019 https://www.merriam-webster.com Accessed September 2020
178. "Anikitos" Greek word for Invincible https://www.biblehub.com Accessed September 2020

with fear and trembling, then ended it with joy and triumph. Our faith in Christ prepares us for every event. The name of Jesus is a balm for every wound, a cordial for every care. It is as ointment poured forth, shedding fragrance through the whole soul. In the hope of a heavenly crown, let us sit loose to earthly possessions and comforts, and cheerfully bear up under crosses. Yet a little while, and He that shall come will come, and will not tarry; and where He is, we shall be also. [179]

PRAYER:

Father God, in the name of Jesus, I come to You today to thank You for being my strength when I am weak. Habakkuk 3:19 says, (AMP), "You are my strength, and my confidence is found in You Jesus and my invincible army is surrounding me. Lord, You make my feet like hind's feet of a deer so that I could go up higher and walk-in higher places and make spiritual progress in those high places, in Jesus' name." Lord, thank You for giving me the confidence to move further in You, in Jesus' name. I will not let fear stop me from moving forward, in You in Jesus' name. I will do it if I must do it afraid, but I know that I don't have to do it alone because You are with me, in Jesus' name. Amen.

---

179. Habakkuk 3:19, Matthew Henry's Concise Commentary https://www.biblehub.com Accessed September 2020

March 20th

Matthew 6:34 (AMPC) says, "So do not worry or be anxious about tomorrow, for tomorrow will have worries and anxieties of its own. Sufficient for each day is its own trouble."

Sufficient in the Merriam Webster Dictionary is enough to meet the needs of a situation or a proposed end.[180] The Greek word for sufficient is "hikanos," which means considerable, worthy, suitable, of number quantity, or time.[181]

We are to pray about everything and not worry about the things that will happen on the following day but take care of things one day at a time. We are to give our troubles to God because He cares for you. Don't worry about the future. God has our future in His hands, and He has plans for each of us. We will reach our God-given destiny with Him as the rudder of our boats. Make the most of your present time and pray for

---

180. "Sufficient" Merriam-Webster.com 2019 https://www.merriam-webster.com Accessed September 2020
181. . "Hikanos" Greek word for Sufficient https://www.biblehub.com Accessed September 2020

what you need. God will build and hold you up when you need Him too.

Happy are those that take the Lord as their God and make full proof of it by trusting wholly to His wise counsel. Trusting in God will take away the worldliness of our hearts.[182]

DECLARATIONS

I will not let anything steal my peace.

God will give me supernatural grace to get through anything in my life.

I will walk from the place of victory in every area of my life.

I will step up my level of prayer, fasting, and consecration.

I will take one day at a time and will not worry about what the future holds for me.

Lord, I am happy that You are my God.

Lord, I will trust You with every fiber in me to take care of my best interests.

---

182. Matthew 6:34 Matthew Henry's Concise Commentary https://www.biblehub.com Accessed September 2020

March 21st

Psalm 119:11 (AMPC) states, "Your word I laid up in my heart, that I might not sin against You."

Sin in the Merriam Webster Dictionary is an offense against religious or moral law, transgression of the law of God.[183] The Greek word for sin is "hamartia," which means missing the mark, guilt, fault, or failure.[184]

God's Word is a treasure worth laying up in the safest place to store it in our hearts. We need to plea to God to teach us His statutes, that being partakers of His holiness, we may also partake of His blessedness. Those hearts that are fed with the Bread of Life should with their own lips feed many. In God's Word, there are unsearchable riches of Christ.[185] "I will not only be a hearer of the Word, but also a doer. I will meditate on God's Word and conceal it in my heart, so it will be renewed.

---

183. "Sin" Merriam-Webster.com 2019 https://www.merriam-webster.com Accessed September 2020
184. "Hamartia" Greek word for Sin https://www.biblehub.com
185. Psalm 119:11 Matthew Henry's Concise Commentary https://www.biblehub.com Accessed September 2020

As a result, I can see how I carry myself and the things that I speak out of my mouth. The places that I use to go, I don't desire to go to those types of places anymore. I have renewed my mind and now my behaviors will change for the better."

PRAYER:

Father God, in the name of Jesus, I come before You today to ask that You would help me read Your Word and obtain it in my heart in Jesus' name. Lord, help me to remember what I have read and meditated on so the Holy Spirit can bring it to my remembrance when I need it. Lord, I hide Your Word in my heart so I will not sin against You. I will use the Word of God on the enemy when he tries to tempt me to do evil. Lord, create a clean heart and renew a right spirit within me, in Jesus' name. Lord, You said in Your Word, "that we are supposed to guard our hearts because out of it flows the issues of life." Lord, help me keep a heart of flesh and not have a heart of stone, in Jesus' name. Go deep down in my heart and uproot anything that is not like You, in Jesus' name. Amen.

March 22nd

Psalm 107:13-14 (AMP) states, "Then they cried to the Lord in their trouble, and He saved them out of their distresses. 14. He brought them out of darkness and the shadow of death and broke apart the bonds that held them."

Bonds in the Merriam Webster Dictionary is something that binds or restrains, fetter.[186] The Greek word for bonds is "halusis," which means a chain or fetter.[187]

When God's children cry out to Him, He will come to our rescue, deliver us out of our troubles, or give us more grace to go through those trials in peace. The awakened sinner realizes that he needs a Savior and cries out to Jesus to save him from death, hell, and destruction. When he becomes godly repentant and he is humbled and broken, only then can he receive the forgiveness that God wants to give to him. The only help that a sinner can find is in the mercy and grace of God. God will par-

---
186. "Bond" Merriam-Webster.com 2019 https://www.merriam-webster.com Accessed September 2020
187. "Halusis" Greek word for Bonds https://www.biblehub.com Accessed September 2020

don their sin and deliver them from the power of sin and Satan by sanctifying them and filling them with the Holy Spirit.[188] But they will continuously renew their mind in the Word of God daily so they can continue to grow to maturity in Christ.

DECLARATIONS

Lord, I cried to You in my distresses and You delivered me out of them all.

Lord, thank You for saving me and giving me the victory in Jesus' name.

Lord, I stand on the Word of God as I bring Your Word back to Your remembrance.

Lord, You are protecting me in the middle of my distresses.

Lord, unshackle every chain that had me bound from my past up until this present time.

Jesus, You are the chain breaker.

Lord, break every chain off my bloodline back to Adam and Eve in Jesus' name.

---

188. Psalm 107:13-14 Matthew Henry's Concise Commentary https://www.biblehub.com Accessed September 2020

March 23rd

Romans 12:21 (AMPC) says, "Do not let yourself be overcome by evil, but overcome (master) evil with good."

Master in the Merriam Webster Dictionary is one that conquers or masters, victor, or superior.[189] The Greek word for master is "despotes," which means implies, someone exercising unrestricted power and absolute domination, confessing no limitations or restraints.[190]

The Scripture above is saying to not repay evil with evil. Do not try to pay people back when they do you wrong. We are supposed to show them love even though we know that they are talking about us. Always show the love of God to someone regardless of the circumstances. God is our vindicator. He said that vengeance was His and He means it. We are not to be rejoicing when our enemies are judged by God. We are to pray for them because they have a soul that needs to be saved. We don't

---

189. "Master" Merriam-Webster.com 2019 https://www.merriam-webster.com Accessed September 2020
190. "Despotes" Greek for Master https://www.biblehub.com Accessed September 2020

need to fight our battles because Jesus is there to fight them for us. Hold your peace and let the Lord fight your battles. Trust me. God has everything under control regarding your life.

PRAYER:

Father God, in the name of Jesus, my enemies are spreading lies about me all over the city that I live in. Lord, You commanded me to pray for my enemies and not try to defend myself from accusations. Lord, I surrender and allow You to vindicate me concerning the situation. Lord, I know that without a shadow of a doubt that You have my best interest at heart. You will only do what is best for me. Lord, help me to hold my peace and allow You to fight all my battles right now, in Jesus' name. There is no need to fight or respond to anyone at this point, in Jesus' name. Lord, You said in Your Word that You would keep me in perfect peace when my mind continues to stay on You in Jesus' name. Amen.

March 24th

James 3:13 (AMPC) says, "Who is there among you who is wise and intelligent? They let him by his noble living show forth his (good) works with the (unobtrusive) humility (which is the proper attribute) of true wisdom."

Unobtrusive in the Merriam Webster Dictionary is not obtrusive, not blatant, arresting, or aggressive.[191] The Greek word for unobtrusive is "tapeinos," which means lowly, humble, or reverent.[192]

The Scripture above shows the difference between men pretending to be wise and those who are truly wise. He who thinks or talks well, is not wise if he does not live or act well. True wisdom may be known by the meekness of the spirit in true temperance. Those who live in malice, envy, and contention live in confusion, and are liable to be provoked and hurried to any evil work. Such wisdom does not come from up above but

---

191. "Unobtrusive" Merriam-Webster.com 2019 https://www.merriam-webster.com Accessed September 2020
192. "Tapeinos" Greek word for Unobtrusive https://www.wordhippo.com Accessed September 2020

springs up from earthy principles, acts on earthly motives, and is intent on serving earthly purposes.[193]

DECLARATIONS

I will always walk in the fruit of the Spirit from this day forward in Jesus' name.

I am a fruit producer.

I will be slow to speak when a difficult situation comes before me.

A soft answer turns away wrath, but grievous words stir up strife.

I will walk in the peace that passeth all understanding, in Jesus' name.

If I lack any wisdom in any area of my life, I will ask God to give it to me so I can do what is always right.

I will not walk-in malice, envy, or have any contentions that would cause me to get out of right alignment with You, Jesus.

---

193. James 3:13 Matthew Henry's Concise Commentary https://www.biblehub.com Accessed September 2020

March 25th

Jeremiah 17:9 (AMP) states, "The heart is deceitful above all things, and it is exceedingly perverse and corrupt and severely, mortally sick! Who can know it (perceive, understand, be acquainted with his own heart and mind)?"

Perverse in the Merriam Webster Dictionary is turned away from what is right or good, corrupt.[194] The Greek word for perverse is "diasrepho," which means to distort, misinterpret, or corrupt.[195]

I have heard people tell others to "follow your heart." This Scripture above says not to follow our hearts because they are wicked and deceitful. Anything in our hearts without God's Holy Spirit leading us is wicked and can't be trusted. Those who trust their own righteousness and strength think that they can do it without Christ. They make flesh their foundation, and their souls cannot prosper in grace and comfort. Those who

---
194. "Perverse" Merriam-Webster.com 2019 https://www.merriam-webster.com Accessed September 2020
195. "Diastrepho" Greek word for Perverse. https://www.biblehub.com Accessed September 2020

make God their hope shall flourish like a tree that is always green, whose leaf does not wither. They shall be fixed in peace and satisfaction of mind; they shall not be anxious for anything in a year of drought. Those who make God their hope have enough in Him to make up the want of all creature comforts. They shall not cease from yielding fruit in holiness and good works. The heart, consciousness of a man in his corrupt and fallen state, is deceitful above all things. It calls evil good, and good evil, and cries peace to those whom it does not belong."[196]

PRAYER:

Father God, in the name of Jesus, I come to You today to ask that You remove the heart of stone and give me a heart of flesh in Jesus' name. Lord, I know that with You and reading Your Word, I can discern between good and evil, in Jesus' name. Lord, take the Spiritual cataracts off my eyes so that I can see clearly from this day forward. Lord, I ask You to come into my heart and make a new creature out of me, so I am underneath the umbrella of Your grace and mercy. Lord, send Your Holy Ghost fire to come into my spirit so my spiritual eyes can be opened, and I will be able to see the tricks and the roadblocks of the enemy against my life and destiny, in Jesus' name. Amen.

---

196. Jeremiah 17:9 Matthew Henry's Concise Commentary https://www.biblehub.com Accessed September 2020

March 26th

Colossians 1:28 (AMP) states, "Him we preach and proclaim, warning and admonishing everyone and instructing everyone in all wisdom (comprehensive insight into the ways and purposes of God), that we may present every person mature (full-grown, fully initiated, complete, and perfect) in Christ (the Anointed One)."

Admonishing in the Merriam Webster Dictionary is to say something as advice or a warning.[197] The Greek word for admonishing is "noutheteo," meaning admonish, warn, counsel, or exhort.[198]

As Christ is preached among us, let us seriously inquire, whether He dwells and reigns in us; for this alone can warrant our assured hope of His glory. We must be faithful to death, through all trials, that we may receive the crown of life, and obtain the end of our faith, the salvation of our souls."[199] God

---
197. "Admonishing" Merriam-Webster.com 2019 https://www.merriam-webster.com Accessed September 2020
198. "Noutheteo" Greek word for Admonished https://www.biblehub.com Accessed September 2020
199. Colossians 1:28 Matthew Henry's Concise Commentary https://www.biblehub.com Accessed September 2020

is perfecting us to full maturity by purging us of things that don't need to be there. He wants to develop our character so we can walk in integrity in every area of our lives. God wants to get negative emotions out of us, so we can stand, not falter or waver when the cares of life come at us. We must know that we can depend on God for everything that we need in our walk down here on this earth. God has an amazing future for us and we can hope for an expected end. God wants to use us as His mouthpieces and His legs, so we can go where He is sending us and speak what He tells us, resulting in building up His Kingdom.

DECLARATIONS

Lord, You said in the Word, "That if anyone needs wisdom, they are to ask of You."

Lord, give me Your supernatural wisdom to handle every situation that comes up in my life.

Lord, teach me Your purposes and ways.

Lord, I am depending on You to get me to my future and expected end.

I am complete and not lacking anything in Christ.

I will preach, teach, and proclaim Jesus to a lost and dying world.

March 27th

1 John 5:14 (AMP) states, "And this is the confidence (the assurance, the privilege of boldness) which we have in Him; (we are sure) that if we ask anything (make any request) according to His will (in agreement with His own plan), He listens to and hears us."

Assurance in the Merriam Webster Dictionary is the confidence of min or manner, easy freedom from self-doubt or uncertainty.[200] The Greek word for assurance is "hupostasis," meaning an underlying confidence, guaranteeing, reality, or substance.[201]

Let us thankfully receive and abound in the Word of God. Know that our labor is not in vain in the Lord. Christ invites us to come to Him in all circumstances, with your supplications and requests notwithstanding the sin that besets us. Our prayers must always be offered in submission to the will of God. Some things that we pray for are speedily answered. Oth-

---
200. "Assurance" Merriam-Webster.com 2019 https://www.merriam-webster.com Accessed September 2020
201. "Hupostasis" Greek word for Assurance https://www.biblehub.com Accessed September 2020

er prayers are granted if God thinks it is best for us. We should not just be praying for ourselves but other people because the effectual prayers of the righteous availeth much and produces wonderful results.[202]

PRAYER:

Father God, in the name of Jesus, I come to You today to thank You for working things out in my favor. I may have prayed for it to happen a different way, but You did what was best for me in Jesus' name. Lord, thank You for leading and guiding me in all truth. Philippians 4:6 (AMPC) says, "Do not fret or have any anxiety about anything, but in every circumstance and in everything, by prayer and petition (definite requests), with thanksgiving, continue to make your wants known to God." I will bring everything to You, no matter how small or big, in prayer before I will make a move or decision on anything. You have my best interest at heart, in Jesus' name. Lord, help me to trust You fully as You are working and moving on my behalf, in Jesus' name. Amen.

---

202. 1 John 5:14 Matthew Henry's Concise Commentary https://www.biblehub.com Accessed September 2020

March 28th

PSALM 56:3 (AMPC) SAYS, "What time I am afraid, I will have confidence in and put my trust and reliance in You."

Reliance in the Merriam Webster Dictionary is something or someone relied on.[203]. The Greek word for reliance is "exartisi," which means dependence, trust, confidence.[204]

We can flee to and trust the mercy of God when surrounded by difficulties and dangers. David is crying out to God because he was afraid. Many times, we are afraid of the unknown and the known. We are scared when God tells us to step out in faith on a new business venture. We are hesitant to step out when He tells us. We must remember the way has already been made, so stepping out will get the ball rolling. Stepping out will get things and events in motion. Fear is false evidence appearing real. The enemy wants us to walk in fear so we won't step out and be who God has called us to be. We cannot let fear stop us

---

203. 'Reliance" Merriam-Webster.com 2019 https://www.merriam-webster.com Accessed September 2020
204. "Exartisi" Greek word for Reliance https://www.biblehub.com Accessed September 2020

because perfect love cast out fear. God loves us so much that He has us hedged in His shield of protection. God will save us from impending dangers and traps set by the enemy. "Lord, I will trust You and do what You tell me to do." God has the power to deliver us always. If He doesn't deliver you from a trial, He wants to strengthen you to go through it. One day you will be able to help someone else that is going through the same thing. You will testify how you overcame and encourage them to keep moving forward in God. If God did it for me, there is no doubt in my mind that He will do it for you.

DECLARATIONS

Lord, I thank You for protecting me through the storms of life.

Regardless of the outcome God, I will trust You.

God is going to come through for you and me.

God will rescue me from the storms of life.

God will give strength to the ones that are weary in Him.

I am not alone in this world. Jesus is with me every day of my life.

March 29th

Isaiah 48:17 (AMP) states, "Thus says the Lord, your Redeemer, the Holy One of Israel; I am the Lord your God, Who teaches you to profit, Who leads you in the way that you should go."

Redeemer in the Merriam Webster Dictionary is a person who redeems, or Jesus.[205] The Greek word for redeemer is "lutrotes," meaning a redeemer, deliverer, or liberator.[206]

The Holy Spirit qualifies us for service, so we speak boldly when He sends us. Christ is also a sent One. God sent him to redeem man back to Himself. We had lost the image of God because Adam and Eve disobeyed the Lord and chose to eat the forbidden fruit. The enemy made them doubt what God had told them. The enemy told them that if they ate the fruit, they would be wise like God, knowing all that God knows. So, Eve took the bait of Satan, ate the fruit, then she gave it to Adam and he ate it too. They were expelled from the garden and God

---

205. "Redeemer" Merriam-Webster.com 2019 https://www.merriam-webster.com Accessed September 2020
206. "Lutrotes" Greek for Redeemer https://www.biblehub.com Accessed September 2020

put an angel with a flaming sword to guard the entrance. They couldn't go back into the garden ever again. So, now when a child is born, they are automatically born in sin and shapen in iniquity because of Adam and Eve's disobedience. So, Jesus agreed to come to earth and be born of a virgin so He could sacrifice His life so we could be redeemed back to God. Jesus put us back in right standing with God; through His shed blood, we are redeemed. When we give our lives over to Jesus and get filled with the Holy Spirit, all of our sins have been washed away by His blood. We can now walk uprightly in this Christian walk, but we have to start studying the word of God and get it in your heart. Also, pray to God and develop an intimate relationship with Him. Jesus needs to be first in our lives before anybody and that includes family members. Start worshipping God. Start fasting so you can walk in the same power that Jesus walked in when He walked the earth. It all requires some effort on your part. Jesus is a gentleman and will not force Himself on anyone. You have to come to Him willingly. If you need healing, deliverance, saving, redeeming, or forgiving, then Jesus is the man for the job.

PRAYER:

Father God, in the name of Jesus, I come to You today to thank You for sacrificing Yourself for me so that I could be made free by Your blood. Thank You for saving me when I was in my mess. You delivered me from a dark place and time in my life. Lord, thank You for forgiving my past, present, and future sin. Now since the veil has been torn, I can come to You myself and ask for forgiveness. Because of Your sacrifice and my

March 29th

surrendering to You, I can now live an abundant life on earth and have eternal life when I get to Heaven. Lord, thank You for throwing my sin in the sea of forgetfulness, never remembering it any more. Lord, thank You for Your Word that is now planted in my heart so I will not sin against You. Lord, help me keep short accounts by walking in forgiveness with others to continue to move forward in the destiny that You have mapped out for my life, in Jesus' name.

March 30th

Psalm 16:8 (AMPC) says, "I have set the Lord continually before me, because He is at my right hand, I shall not be moved."

Continually in the Merriam Webster Dictionary is in a continual manner, without stopping or interruption.[207] The Greek word for continually is "proskartereo," which means to attend constantly, persist, steadfast in, or wait upon.[208]

I have set the Lord before me in my private meditations as well in public professions. Always, I regard myself as in the presence of God. I have endeavored always to feel His eye was upon me. God is at my right hand and it was regarded as a place of honor, dignity, defense, and protection. To have Jesus at our right hand is to have Him near to protect and defend us. Psalm 121:5 (AMPC) states, "The Lord is my keeper; the Lord is your shade on your right hand (the side not carrying a shield." Jesus is sitting at the right hand of the Father interceding for us. Jesus

---
207. "Continually" Merriam-Webster.com 2019 https://www.merriam-webster.com Accessed September 2020
208. "Proskartereo" Greek word for Continually https://www.biblehub.com Accessed September 2020

wants us to succeed in our walk with Him. He will move things and people around in our lives if it seems like it will hinder us from reaching our destiny in Him. Jesus is here to help you. All you have to do is call out to Him. He will come and see about you. Life is more pleasant with Jesus as the head of your life because He is there to continually help you through the storms of life. You don't have to feel alone in this world when you have Jesus in your corner.

DECLARATIONS

I shall not be moved. I will be like the tree that is planted by the water.

I will not stop because of the storms or the warfare that I am going through.

Lord, send Your supernatural strength to build me back up where I have been torn down.

I can do all things through Christ who strengthens me.

I am going to fight my way to breakthrough and I will not give up!!

I will rest in the arms of Jesus and stay hidden in the secret place of the Almighty.

March 31st

Psalm 42:8 (AMPC) says, "Yet the Lord will command His loving-kindness in the daytime, and in the night His song shall be with me, a prayer to the God of my life."

Prayer in the Merriam Webster Dictionary is an address (such as a petition) to God.[209] The Greek word for prayer is "proseuchomai," meaning praying without ceasing.[210]

I shall have constant cause for praising my God both day and night for His loving kindness during the storms I face in life. Continue to worship God with a song in your heart because one word from Him will calm every storm and turn your midnight into day. When you trust in the name of the Lord, you will have nothing to fear. God has not forgotten us. He sees and knows everything that you are going through in your life.[211]

---

209. "Prayer" Merriam-Webster.com 2019 https://www.merriam-webster.com Accessed September 2020
210. "Proseuchomai" Greek word for Prayer https://www.biblehub.com Accessed September 2020
211. Psalm 42:8 Matthew Henry's Concise Commentary https://www.biblehub.com Accessed September 2020

March 31st

PRAYER:

Father God, in the name of Jesus, I come to You today giving You the praise for all that You have done for my family and I. Lord, You have brought us through many storms, trials, and tribulations. When the doctor had given me a bad report, I leaned to Your Word and decreed Your word back to You. Lord, when I was in the darkest night, You sent Your sustaining light to brighten up my dark days. Lord that is why I can worship You and sing a song of praise to You. When my back was against the wall, You provided a way of escape. When I lost my job during the pandemic, You continued to provide for my family and I. We haven't lost anything. You gave me a witty idea to start my own business even in the midst of what is going on globally. Thank You, Lord, for blessing me to step out of the poverty mindset into the kingdom mindset, in Jesus' name. Amen.

April 1st

*P*SALM 139:23 (AMP) STATES, "Search me (thoroughly), O God, and know my heart! Try me and know my thoughts!

Thoroughly in the Merriam Webster Dictionary is to complete or thorough manner.[212] The Greek word for thoroughly is "ekkathario," which means to cleanse thoroughly, or completely out.[213]

The Lord knows us thoroughly and every gift and talent that we have, He knows about it. God knows everything that is in our hearts and our thoughts. We need to keep our hearts pure. Take care of offenses and not let our hearts get hard from them. We need to practice walking in forgiveness because it is the right thing to do according to the Word of God. We cannot trust or follow our hearts. We need to pray like David, "Create in me a clean heart and renew a right spirit in me." When we pray this, we tell God to search our hearts and not just our out-

---

212. "Thoroughly Merriam-Webster.com 2019 https://www.merriam-webster.com Accessed September 2020
213. "Ekkathairo" Greek word for Thoroughly https://www.biblehub.com Accessed September 2020

ward appearance. What do I think about all the time? What are my purposes in this life? What occupies my imagination? What do I have in my short and long-term memory? What controls my will? Lord, help me keep my thoughts pure and my mind focused on You. Lord, I surrender my will for Your will in Jesus' name.

DECLARATIONS

Lord, I will think only good things so my thoughts can line up with Your Word.

God, I thank You for the many promises that You have in store for me.

Lord, I will strive every day to do the right thing so I can stay in right standing with You.

Search me O God and if You find anything in me that is not like You, take it out of me.

God if there is something that I need to take care of, reveal it to me, and I will work on it with Your help.

Lord, remove my heart of stone and give me a heart of flesh perfected in You.

April 2nd

*P*ROVERBS 29:11 (AMPC) SAYS, "A (self-confident) fool utters all his anger, but a wise man holds it back and stills it."

Self-Confident in the Merriam Webster Dictionary is confident in oneself and in one's powers and abilities.[214] The Greek word for self-confident is "pepoithesis," meaning confidence, trust, or reliance.[215]

A fool utters all his mind all at once unnecessarily, unseasonably, without reservation or caution. You call yourself telling it like it is and making a menace of yourself. But a wise man keeps it to himself because God will allow him to talk about it later after their tempers have calmed down. A person is foolish if he tells everything that he knows, and can keep no counsel (secrets).[216]

---

214. "Self-Confident" Merriam-Webster.com 2019 https://www.merriam-webster.com Accessed September 2020
215. "Pepoithesis" Greek word for Self-Confident https://www.biblehub.com Accessed September 2020
216. Proverbs 29:11 Matthew Henry's Concise Commentary https://www.biblehub.com Accessed September 2020

April 2nd

PRAYER:

Father God, in the name of Jesus, I come before You today to ask You to help me to study to be quiet. Lord, I need deliverance from anger and outbursts when things do not go my way. I realize that I am the one with the problem with anger and not everyone else. Lord, help me get all of this anger and rage out of me, so my relationships will be healthy and prosperous. Lord, help me consider other people's feelings before I blurt something out that can hurt someone. Lord, help me to keep other people's information to myself if they have confided in me. Lord put a bridle on my tongue, in Jesus' name. Lord, I repent for everything that I have done and said against anyone in my life before I gave my life to You Jesus. Lord, I give my life to You today. Take away the old man and transform me into the new man with a change of heart and mind, in Jesus' name. Lord, You said in Romans 10:9, "If I would confess with my mouth and believe it in my heart, that You raised Jesus from the dead that I would be saved." Lord, thank You for saving me and making a new creature out of me in Jesus' name. Lord, help me to walk in forgiveness and not hold grudges so that I can grow more in You in Jesus' name. Amen.

April 3rd

Psalm 119:165 (AMPC) says, "Great peace have they who love Your law; nothing shall offend them or make them stumble."

Stumble in the Merriam Webster Dictionary is to fall into sin or waywardness, error.[217] The Greek word for stumble is "ptaio," to cause to stumble, fall, sin, err.[218]

There is always disquietude (uneasiness, anxiety) where there is sin. A sense of perfect peace and rest belongs to those who love and keep God's Word. There will be no stumbling blocks and nothing will cause them to stumble, much less fall from grace.[219]

When we know the tricks, plans, and ploys of the enemy, we don't have to keep falling for the "okie-doke." The enemy will use anything to get us off track, but we must continue to use

---

217. "Stumble" Merriam-Webster.com 2019 https://www.merriam-webster.com Accessed September 2020
218. "Ptaio" Greek word for Stumble https://www.biblehub.com Accessed September 2020
219. Psalm 119:165 Pulpit Commentary https://www.biblehub.com Accessed September 2020

our discernment and wisdom so we will make the right decisions in every area of our lives. Instead of making the same mistakes over and over, we are to shun sin and any evil presence out of our lives. If we happen to get off track, we can go to God, ask for forgiveness and He will forgive us. We then can get back up, brush ourselves off, and keep running this race called life. Don't let the tricks of the enemy keep you down or cause you to be stagnant when God is pushing you forward in Him. Give the devil notice that you will serve God, regardless of what he throws at you. You will not give up, but will continue to hold on and move forward in the calling of God on your life.

DECLARATIONS

I will walk in the peace that passeth all understanding that will guard my heart and mind in Christ Jesus.

Lord, send Your supernatural healing to heal anything in me that is not of You.

No weapon that is formed against me shall prosper and every tongue that rises up against me in judgment, I will utterly condemn for this is the heritage of the saints and my righteousness is of You, Jesus.

I take back my peace from the enemy and prophesy that peace will chase me down.

Lord, remove anyone that is around me that doesn't mean my family and I any good.

Lord, replace them with covenant people who love and will speak life into me.

April 4th

Psalm 121:1-2 (AMPC) says, "I will lift up my eyes to the hills (around Jerusalem, to sacred Mount Zion and Mount Moriah) From whence shall my help come? 2. My help comes from the Lord, Who made heaven and earth."

Help in the Merriam Webster Dictionary is to give assistance or support to, to be of use to, or benefit.[220] The Greek word for help is "sunsntilambanomai," meaning to take hold with at the side, hence to take share in, generally to help, or properly to give assistance.[221]

The godly are safe. We must not rely on men by any means. We shall not depend on the President, the government, our jobs, or any other source, but we should be putting our total trust in God to take care of and protect us. God can do anything but fail, so all my trust is in Him to make a way for my family and I. We have to be obedient to what God is telling us to do

---

220. "Help" Merriam-Webster.com 2019 https://www.merriam-webster.com Accessed September 2020
221. "Sunantilambanomai" Greek word for Help https://www.biblehub.com September 2020'

in this hour. If He is telling us to start a business or a ministry while we are in the middle of the COVID-19 pandemic, then we need to be obedient. God wants to see if we trust Him with our lives. Everything that He tells you to do doesn't always have to make sense. Stop thinking with your natural mind and see in the spiritual realm. Remember that God is in our future and He sees us as a finished product. He knows when we should get started and launch to reach the outcome that He has for us at a specific time in our lives. So, if He has told you to do something, then you need to get started. There is no room for any more excuses.

PRAYER:

Father God, in the name of Jesus, forgive me for not moving forward when You told me too. Lord, give me another chance to do what You have called me to do in this season of my life. Lord, show me the blueprint for my life and ministry so I can align with what You are calling me to do, in Jesus' name. I cast down the spirit of fear that is keeping me from walking forward in You, God. I come out of agreement with the voice of the enemy that is speaking in my ear in Jesus' name. Lord, let Your voice be louder and the enemies voice get weaker as I continue to do it while I am afraid, in Jesus' name. Lord, I will open my mouth and let You fill it with Your Word, in Jesus' name. I will continue to study the Word and meditate on it so that I can get it in my heart in Jesus' name. Lord, if there is anything that I am lacking, download it in my spirit, in Jesus' name. Amen.

April 5th

ESTHER 4:14 (AMPC) SAYS, "For if you keep silent at this time, relief and deliverance shall arise for the Jews from elsewhere, but you and your father's house will perish. And who knows but that you have come to the kingdom for such a time as this and for this very occasion."

Deliverance in the Merriam Webster Dictionary is the act of delivering someone or something, or the state of being delivered, rescued.[222] The Greek word for deliverance is "soteria." When God rescues, He delivers believers out of destruction and into His safety.[223]

Mordecai had word sent to Esther that Haman lied and told King Ahasuerus that the Jews were detestable people. Their laws were different. They did not keep the King's laws, and it was not to the king's benefit to tolerate them. So, Haman convinced King Ahasuerus to write a decree to kill off the Jews. When Mordecai learned of the decree, he rent (tore) his clothes

---

222. "Deliverance" Merriam-Webster.com 2019 https://www.merriam-webster.com Accessed September 2020
223. "Soteria" Greek word for Deliverance https://www.biblehub.com Accessed September 2020

in mourning and sent a message to Esther for her to talk to the king to save the Jews. Mordecai told her that she had been placed in the kingdom as the queen for such a time as this to save her people. God had given her favor with the King because He chose her to be his wife and queen. The same thing applies to the Body of Christ. This is the time that God is calling His people to stand up and be counted because of what is occurring with the COVID-19 pandemic and social injustices. People are hurting and crying out to God. God is sending the unknown into the field to gather the harvest. People are looking for something different and an outlet to escape from the pain and suffering that is happening in the world. In this season, God is using everyone that is in the Body of Christ, from the young to the old to bring in the harvest of souls into the Kingdom. God is preparing us for the harvest or the Great Awakening to come. Those that are not in their rightful places need to step up and be who God is calling them to be.

DECLARATIONS

It is time for me to step into my rightful place in God and get from behind the winepress.

God has called me for such a time as this.

I am built for this.

I will not keep silent but speak what God is telling me to say in this hour.

April 5th

I will be one of the voices crying in the wilderness, "Repent. Repent for the Kingdom of Heaven is at hand."

I will not be scared or ashamed to tell my testimonies so people can get free from bondage.

April 6th

Psalm 52:8 (AMPC) states, "But I am like a green olive tree in the house of God; I trust in and confidently rely on the loving-kindness and the mercy of God forever and ever."

Green in the Merriam Webster Dictionary is covered by green growth or foliage, prosperous, or rejuvenated.[224] The Greek word for green is "prasinos," meaning greenery, tender, or fresh.[225]

Those who live by faith and love dwell in the house of God shall be like green olive trees there. We can have confidence in God and His grace. God's name alone shall be our refuge and strong tower. I have been protected by God and flourishing in His house. I am safe in His care and His sight. The green tree is the emblem of prosperity, meaning you are growing more mature in Christ as long as you stay rooted and grounded in Him. The church is the place where God resides. A tree planted

---

224. "Green" Merriam-Webster.com 2019 https://www.merriam-webster.com Accessed September 2020
225. "Prasinos" Greek word for Green https://www.biblehub.com Accessed September 2020

around the sanctuary would remain safe and be regarded as sacred because it was directly under the divine covering of God. [226]

Powerful! If you are rooted and grounded in God and in His divine covering, stay there. Do not let anyone or anything pull you out of His divine covering. Continue to be the green olive tree that is talked about in this passage. The olive tree has to be squeezed to produce olive oil. Don't give up in the pressing but keep going on in God. There is always a price that we have to pay for the oil. God wants you to be able to walk and operate in His glory. After the pressing, the glory will be manifested. Hallelujah!

PRAYER:

Father God, in the name of Jesus, I come before You today, thanking You for giving me the strength to go through the pressing, in Jesus' name. Lord, I know the pressing is the reason that I have been going through so many things lately. It is because there is a price for the oil that is on my life. Lord, I am like the green olive tree that is flourishing in Your house. Your presence is greatly needed in the ministry that You have given me. The enemy wants to stop and block me. I refused to be hindered and I must toil on through until I reach my breakthrough. Lord, when the storms get so heavy and weighty, I know I have to continue to pray and cry out to You to help me go through to the other side in Jesus' name. Lord, I thank You for making me who I am in You, in Jesus' name. Lord, continue to move

---

226. Psalm 52:8 Barnes Notes on the Bible https://www.biblehub.com Accessed September 2020

mightily in my life, in Jesus' name. Deliverance, healing, and breakthrough is coming right now in Jesus' name. Oh, I thank You, Lord! Glory to Your name, Jesus. Amen.

April 7th

Colossians 3:12 (AMPC) states "Clothe yourselves therefore, as God's own chosen ones (His own picked representatives), (who are) purified and holy and well-beloved (by God Himself, by putting on behavior marked by) tenderhearted pity and mercy, kind feeling, a lowly opinion of yourselves, gentle ways(and) patience (which is tireless and long-suffering, and has the power to endure whatever comes with good temper)."

Representatives in the Merriam Webster Dictionary is standing or acting for another especially through delegated authority.[227] The Greek word for representative is "presbeuo," meaning to act as an ambassador, to be the elder, or someone who is trusted to speak as God's emissary.[228]

We must not cause harm to any, but do good to all. God's elect, holy and beloved, ought to be lowly and be compassionate towards all. Where there is corruption in our hearts, quarrels

---
227. "Representatives" Merriam-Webster.com 2019 https://www.merriam-webster.com Accessed September 2020
228. "Presbeuo" Greek word for Representatives https://www.biblehub.com Accessed September 2020

sometimes arise. It's our duty to forgive one another, imitating the forgiveness through which we are saved. Let the peace of God rule in your hearts; it is His working in all who are His. Thanksgiving to God helps to make us agreeable to all men. The gospel is the Word of Christ. Many have the Word, but it dwells in them poorly; it has no power over them. The soul prospers when we are full of Scriptures and the grace of Christ.[229]

DECLARATIONS

I clothe myself as one of God's chosen ones, and I will represent Him on earth.

I will put on the behavior that is marked by God by putting on tenderhearted, mercy, and kindness toward others.

I will continue to walk in humility and not pride.

Lord, give me more patience so that I can stay strong in my walk with You.

Lord, help me to be able to endure with long-suffering whatever comes my way.

Lord, help me to always keep a good attitude without mumbling and complaining while I am waiting.

---

229. Colossians 3:12 Matthew Henry's Concise Commentary https://www.biblehub.com Accessed September 2020

April 8th

Psalm 116:1-2 (AMP) states, "I LOVE the Lord, because He has heard (and now hears) my voice and my supplications. 2. Because He has inclined His ear to me, therefore will I call upon Him as long as I live."

Inclined in the Merriam Webster Dictionary is willing, having a leaning or slope.[230] The Greek word for inclined is "proklisis," meaning tipped one way, towards, or the direction.[231]

We can call upon the Lord and He will hear and deliver us. When a sinner calls upon the Lord and repents of their sin, the Lord will incline His ear toward them. When a person has come to the end of themselves and realizes that they need God, He will listen to their cries when they ask for forgiveness of their sins. God always listens to the prayers of the righteous because we belong to Him. The prayers and the words of the righteous availeth much and produce wonderful results. When we remind God of His Word, our prayers and decrees will come to

---
230. "Inclined" Merriam-Webster.com 2019 https://www.merriam-webster.com Accessed September 2020.
231. "Prosklisis" Greek word for Inclined https://www.biblehub.com Accessed September 2020

pass in our lives. We need to pray, decree, and declare in faith. God will do what He has promised in the Scriptures.

PRAYER:

Father God, in the name of Jesus, I come to You today to ask You to forgive me of my sins. Live in me and make me a new creature in Christ. Lord, I have come to the end of myself and realize that I need You in my life before I can do anything. Romans 10:9 states, " If I would confess with my mouth and believe it in my heart that God raised Jesus from the dead that I would be saved." Lord, save me and remove everything in me that is not of You. Lord, I realize that my life is meaningless if I don't have You in it, in Jesus' name. Lord, forgive me for wasting many years, and believing the devil's lies concerning the lifestyle that I was leading in Jesus' name. Lord, I thank You for giving me another chance to get in right standing with You, in Jesus' name. Lord, send Your Holy Ghost fire to saturate my spirit, soul, and body so that I can be led into all truth in Jesus' name. Lord, I thank You for making a new creature out of me in Jesus' name. Amen.

April 9th

Jeremiah 31:25 (AMPC) says, "For I will (Fully) satisfy the weary soul and I will replenish every languishing and sorrowful person."

Languishing in the Merriam Webster Dictionary is to live in a state of depression or decreasing vitality, feeble, or weak.[232] The Greek word for languishing is "astheneo," meaning to be weak, feeble, or to be without strength.[233]

In the love and favor of God, the weary soul shall find rest, and the sorrowful shall find joy.

"The unrighteous cannot find neither food, for their famishing souls; weary in seeking righteousness to cover them, nor life nor rest till they come to Christ and all the saints are weary of the body of sin and death, with mourning over it, and groaning under it, weary of Satan temptations and buffetings; weary of the world, and the men of it, and with afflictive dispensa-

---

232. "Languishing" Merriam-Webster.com 2019 https://www.merriam-webster.com Accessed September 2020
233. "Astheneo" Greek word for Languishing https://www.biblehub.com Accessed September 2020

tions of Providence in it, as weary travelers passing through a waste land."

These the Lord satiates (satisfies), refreshes, and even inebriated (drunk) with His love, which is very reviving and refreshing. The Lord replenishes and refills those that are sorrowful and fills them to satisfaction with Christ and all good things by Him with peace, pardon, righteousness, salvation; with the Spirit, and His gifts and His graces.[234] A person that doesn't know God is weary. They are alone and cannot find any peace, but the weary Saints, God will refill, replenish, and give them His peace.

DECLARATIONS

Lord, You have satisfied my weary soul and replenished me with Your peace.

Lord, refresh me with Your presence.

Lord, I give my life to You completely so that my weary soul can be refreshed and satisfied.

Lord, here I am, a sinner. I need You to live in me so I can get rest for my weary soul.

I will stop running from You God and give my life over to You to be refreshed in Your peace and love.

---

234. Jeremiah 31:25 Gill's Exposition of Entire Bible https://www.biblehub.com Accessed September 2020

April 9th

Lord, I receive Your love, righteousness, peace, grace, and mercy in Jesus' name.

April 10th

1 Corinthian 13:1 (AMP) "If I can speak in the tongues of men and (even) of angels, but have not love (that reasoning, intentional, spiritual devotion such as inspired by God's love for and in us), I am only a noisy gong or a clanging cymbal."

Intentional in the Merriam Webster Dictionary is done by intention or design, intended.[235] The Greek word for intentional is "ek protheseo," meaning intentional or deliberate.[236]

The Scripture above is talking about God's love and without it, the gifts are of no significance to us, and no esteem in the sight of God. A clear head and a deep understanding are of no value without a benevolent and charitable heart. Doing good to others will not do anything for us if it is not done from the love of God, and goodwill to all men.[237] We have to walk in love with all people. How can we say we love God whom we

---

235. "Intentional" Merriam-Webster.com 2019 https://www.merriam-webster.com Accessed September 2020
236. "Ek Protheseos" Greek for Intentional https://www.wordhippo.com Accessed September 2020
237. 1 Corinthians 13:1 Matthew Henry's Concise Commentary https://www.biblehub.com Accessed September 2020

have never seen, when we don't love our sisters and brothers who we see every day? God loves everyone because He gave His only begotten Son so that we would have a right to the tree of life through His shed blood. Love is an action word and it means loving and caring for people when they don't care for you. When you reach this level in your walk with Christ, it shows maturity in Him. God will hold us accountable for how we treat others. Some people do not know true love. Help them to understand the love of God by committing to love them.

PRAYER:

Father God, in the name of Jesus, I come to You today to ask You to teach me how to love people like You do. Lord, help me look beyond their faults and shortcomings in Jesus' name. Lord, thank You for coming into my life and teaching me how to love people past their imperfections. Lord, thank You for showing me how to love myself, in Jesus' name. Lord, please help me to know my worth becauseYou are the author and finisher of my faith. I know that You are not holding me accountable for how other people treat me, but for how I treat them in Jesus' name. According to Your Word, if I speak with tongues but do not have real love, I am just like tinkling brass and sounding cymbals only making noise but not being effective in Your Kingdom. Lord, thank You for teaching me to love with Your agape love, that never-ending love that lasts for a lifetime in Jesus' name. Amen.

April 11th

Hebrews 12:2 (AMPC) states, "Looking away (from all that will distract) to Jesus, Who is the Leader and the Source of our faith (giving the first incentive for our belief) and is also its Finisher (bringing it to maturity and perfection). He, for the joy (of obtaining the prize) that was set before Him, endured the cross, despising and ignoring the shame and is now seated at the right hand of the throne of God."

Finisher in Merriam Webster is complete, to bring to an end, terminate.[238] The Greek word for finisher is "teleiotes," meaning a completer, finisher, or the one binging a life of faith to a complete conclusion.[239]

Jesus is the author and the finisher of our faith; He made the perfect sacrifice by laying down His life so we could be redeemed back to God. We need to look away from everything that will distract us and keep our focus and mind on Jesus. He

---
238. "Finisher" Merriam-Webster.com 2019 https://www.merriam-webster.com Accessed September 2020
239. "Teleiotes" Greek for Finisher https://www.biblehub.com Accessed September 2020

April 11th

died on the cross and declared that it was finished. There will never be another sacrifice like Jesus made at Mount Calvary. This perfect sacrifice was for us, so we don't have to live estranged from God. Through Jesus, we can now have an intimate relationship with God, our Father, and live a pleasing life unto Him. All we have to do is accept the finished works of Jesus, give our lives to Him and live according to His word. Isn't it amazing that all we have to do is accept Jesus and we will be in right standing with God? We should put our faith and trust in Jesus to see us through the trials, tribulations, and storms that we may encounter in our life. Jesus is our ever-present help in the time of storms. He will hold you up on your leaning side when troubles come.

DECLARATIONS

Lord, thank You for strengthening me to go through these storms in my life.

I will keep my focus on Jesus and not look to the right or the left, but I will continue to move forward in Him.

Lord, thank You for taking my sin and iniquities on Your body so that I could be redeemed back to God.

Jesus, I thank You for taking the 39 stripes on Your body for my healing .

Lord, I join my faith with Your faith, so I can believe for the impossible in my life.

Lord, thank You for Your redeeming blood that makes me justified (just as I never sinned) in Christ Jesus.

April 12th

JEREMIAH 23:29 (AMPC) SAYS, "Is not My word like fire (that consumes all that cannot endure the test)? Says the Lord, and like a hammer that breaks in pieces the rock (of most stubborn resistance)?"

Fire in the Merriam Webster Dictionary is the phenomenon of combustion manifested in light, flame, heat, and combustion.[240] The Greek word for fire is "pur," meaning fire, heat of the sun, lightning, eternal fire, or trials.[241]

Hammer in the Merriam Webster Dictionary is to strike blows especially repeatedly with or as if with a hammer, pound.[242] The Hebrew word for hammer is "halmuth" meaning a hammer or mallet.[243]

---

240. Fire Merriam-Webster.com 2019 https://www.merriam-webster.com Accessed September 2020
241. "Pur" Greek word for Fire https://www.biblehub.com Accessed September 2020
242. "Hammer" Merriam-Webster.com 2019 https://www.merriam-webster.com Accessed September 2020
243. "Halmuth" Hebrew word for Hammer https://www.biblehub.com Accessed September 2020

God's Word is the great purifier which destroys all that is false. A true prophetic word burns in the heart of a man, and will not be restrained, and when uttered it consumes the evil, and purifies the good. It will burn up the chaff of the utterances of the false prophets. As the hammer breaks the rocks, it shatters the pride and stubbornness of man, and is mighty in pulling down strongholds and the heart of him who hears it as it should be heard: broken and contrite.[244]

PRAYER:

Father God, in the name of Jesus, I come before You today to lift up myself and my family in prayer in Jesus' name. Lord, I realize that every time I pray and speak Scriptures back to You I am tearing something up in the spiritual realm, in Jesus' name. Lord, I pray that every stubborn situation that I see today will come down by the blood of the Lamb. I will not see it anymore in my life or my family's life in Jesus' name. I break the bounds of Satan and every demonic spirit that has attached itself to me and my bloodline. Be canceled and cast out, in Jesus name. Lord I know that Your Word is like a hammer breaking things and situations that are hard in the spiritual realm, in Jesus' name. Hebrews 4:12 (NLT) says, "For the word of God is alive and powerful. It is sharper than the sharpest two-edged sword cutting between soul and spirit, between joint and marrow. It exposes our innermost thoughts and desires."

---

244. Jeremiah 23:29 Ellicott's Commentary for English Readers https://www.biblehub.com Accessed September 2020

April 13th

Psalm 119:103 (AMP) says, "How sweet are Your words to my taste, sweeter than honey to my mouth!"

Sweeter in the Merriam Webster Dictionary is something that is sweet to the taste.[245] The Greek word for sweeter is "mathoq," meaning sweet or sweetness.[246]

To taste God's Word is sweet, yea sweeter than any of the gratifications of sense, even those that are most delicious. David here speaks as if he wanted words to express the satisfaction, he took in the discoveries of the divine will and grace; he judged no pleasure to be comparable to it. The Word of God is sweet to taste as we read, study, and meditate on it. How sweet and gracious is the Lord? The Word of God is nourishing and sweet as the virtue of honey.[247]

---
245. "Sweeter" Merriam-Webster.com 2019 https://www.merriam-webster.com Accessed September 2020
246. "Mathoq" Greek word for Sweeter https://www.biblehub.com Accessed September 2020
247. Psalm 119:103 Benson Commentary https://www.biblehub.com Accessed September 2020

DECLARATIONS

The promises of God are sweet in my life.

The Honey of the Word is sweet to my palate (mouth).

I decree and declare I will have a better job, house, and ideas.

Your Words, God, are sweeter than the honey in the honeycomb.

Lord, I will hold onto the prophetic promises that You have over my life and they will surely come to pass.

Lord, there are many promises in You like Joy, Hope, Strength, Love, and Peace. I receive them in my life.

April 14th

Psalm 126:5 (AMPC) says, "They who sow in tears shall reap in joy and singing."

Reap in the Merriam Webster Dictionary is to gather by reaping, or harvest.[248] The Greek word for reap is "therizo" meaning to reap, harvest, or gather.[249]

Suffering saints are often in tears; they share the calamities of human life, and commonly have a greater share than others. Weeping must not hinder sowing; we must get good from times of affliction. And they that sow in the tears of godly sorrow, to the Spirit, shall of the Spirit reap life everlasting and that will be a joyful harvest indeed. When we mourn for our sins, or suffer for Christ's sake, we are sowing in tears, to reap in joy. And remember that God is not mocked, for whatever a man soweth that shall he reap." (Galatians 6:7-9)[250]

---

248. "Reap" Merriam-Webster.com 2019 https://www.meriam-webster.com Accessed September 2020
249. "Therizo" Greek word for Reap https://www.biblehub.com Accessed September 2020
250. Psalm 126:5 Matthew Henry's Concise Commentary https://www.biblehub.com Accessed September 2020

The 180-Days of Communing with God Daily Devotional

PRAYER:

Father God, in the name of Jesus, I come before You today to ask that You strengthen me for the tasks set before me. There are a lot of things that are going on in my life that have me weeping and moaning for Your help. Lord, forgive me of my sins. I am godly sorry for the things that I have allowed to come into my life and wreak havoc. Lord, I surrender my will over to Your will so that I can have peace in the midst of what is going on in my life. Lord, Your words declare that those that sow in tears shall reap in Joy. I know that weeping may endure for a night but joy comes in the morning. I can see that my morning is near and my breakthrough is just around the corner. I know that regardless of the circumstances, I cannot give up but I must continue to move forward even in the midst of the pain I feel. Lord, I know that You love me and care about everything that is troubling and concerns me. Lord, I know that You will work everything out that concerns me for my good in Jesus' name. Lord, I love You and I thank You for watching over me and keeping me from the hurt, harm, and danger of the enemy, in Jesus' name. Lord, thank You for a double portion of everything that the devil has stolen from me. According to Your word, I will get it all back and then some, so double is coming to me and my house, in Jesus' name. Amen.

April 15th

MARK 11:25 (AMP) SAYS, "And whenever you stand praying, if you have anything against anyone, forgive him and let it drop (leave it, let it go), in order that your Father Who is in heaven may also forgive you your (own) failings and shortcomings and let them drop."

Forgive in the Merriam Webster Dictionary is to cease to feel resentment against (an offender), or pardon.[251] The Greek word for forgive is "aphesis," meaning a sending away, a letting go, a release, pardon, or complete forgiveness.[252]

The Scripture above talks about forgiving someone that has mistreated you. God wants us to forgive them and release all the hurt so we can move forth in Him without hindrance. Sometimes forgiving is hard but it can be done with God's help and grace. Grace is more than unmerited faith, but it is the ability to do what we couldn't do on our own. Nobody can do any-

---
251. "Forgive" Merriam-Webster.com 2019 https://www.merriam-webster.com Accessed September 2020
252. "Aphesis" Greek word for Forgive https://www.biblehub.com Accessed September 2020

thing on their own. We need God for everything that concerns us in this world. When you pray, forgive so your prayers can be heard and answered by God. Walking in unforgiveness blocks and hinders your prayers. Let people go and release them, because they are fickle. People will love you today and dislike you tomorrow and that is fine. If everybody liked you, that would be a problem, because then you will be a people pleaser instead of a God pleaser. It is not the end of the world when people don't like you. It is not you that they don't like but the God that is in you. Amen.

DECLARATIONS

I will walk in forgiveness and forgive everyone who has mistreated me.

Lord, thank You for forgiving me when I am wrong or have sinned.

I will love like Jesus said to love and walk in the love of God toward all people.

I will forgive, forget, and continue to move on.

Lord, I will forgive others and keep my heart pure from offenses.

Lord, I thank You for Your empowerment to be able to forgive and love as You commanded.

April 16th

Proverbs 2:6 (AMPC) says, "For the Lord gives skillful and godly Wisdom, from His mouth comes knowledge and understanding."

Skillful in the Merriam Webster Dictionary is possessed of or displaying skill, or expert.[253] The Greek word for skillful is "panourgos," meaning ready to do anything, crafty, skillful, or clever.[254]

Those who earnestly seek heavenly wisdom will never complain that they have lost their labor, and the freeness of the gift does not do away the necessity of our diligence. God's Word states that those that need wisdom are to ask Him and He will give it generously. So, by just asking we will obtain it because wisdom is an important thing to have on our Christian journey. With wisdom comes knowledge and understanding. We need both of these. Godly wisdom doesn't originate with us. Solomon asked for wisdom so he would know how to lead people.

---

253. "Skillful" Merriam-Webster.com 2019 https://www.merriam-webster.com Accessed September 2020
254. "Panourgos" Greek for Skillful https://www.biblehub.com Accessed September 2020

God gave it to him. As a result, he gained knowledge and understanding when it comes to any subject.

PRAYER:

Father God, in the name of Jesus, You said in Your Word that if I need wisdom to ask You for it. So Lord, give me wisdom, knowledge, understanding, and grace that I will need to succeed in Jesus' name. Lord, help me to study and meditate on Your Word so I can grow more in You. Lord, help me not to lean to my own understanding in anything, but to consult You about all things so I can be in Your timing. Lord, help me to see things like You see them and respond like You want in Jesus' name. Amen.

April 17th

James 4:3 (AMPC) states, "(Or) you do ask (God for them) and yet fail to receive, because you ask with wrong purpose and evil, selfish motives. Your intention is (when you get what you desire) to spend it in sensual pleasures."

Selfish in the Merriam Webster Dictionary is arising from concern with one's own welfare or advantage in disregard of others.[255] The Greek word for selfish is "eritheia," meaning the seeking of followers, ambition, rivalry, self-seeking, or carnal ambition.[256]

The Scripture above is saying that when we are praying to God to do something in our lives, we have to ask for the right reasons and motives. We shouldn't show off or try to be famous. God looks at the heart and knows the reason you are making the request. Many times, people are praying to win the lottery only to boast and act uppity. Once God finds our hearts

---
255. "Selfish" Merriam-Webster.com 2019 https://www.merriam-webster.com Accessed September 2020
256. "Eritheia" Greek word for Selfish https://www.biblehub.com Accessed September 2020

pure and can trust us with finances, He doesn't mind blessing us with it. God will bless someone financially who is already a giver because He knows that the money will not have them. The person will use the money to give their tithes and offering, pay their bills off and then help build up the Kingdom of God. God will continually give seed to a sower because they do not mind giving because they understand the seed principle.

Prayer:

Father God, in the name of Jesus, help me to have the right motives when I pray for something so it can be used in the right manner, in Jesus' name. Lord, You said that You will give seed to the sower and bread to the eater. Lord, help me not to eat up my seed but sow it in fertile ground in Jesus' name. Lord, I thank You for watering every seed that I have sown so it can produce a bountiful harvest, in Jesus' name. Lord, let every seed sown in my life produce a harvest that I will not have room enough to contain in my storehouse, in Jesus' name. Lord, I call forth every seed that has my name and spouse's name on it. I call it forth from the north, south, east and west to hit our lives like never before, in Jesus' name. I am calling for an increase in every area of our lives, in Jesus' name. Amen.

April 18th

Matthew 7:13-14 (AMP) says, "Enter into the narrow gate, for wide is the gate and spacious and broad is the way that leads away to destruction and many are those who are entering through it. 14. But the gate is narrow (contracted by pressure) and the way is straitened and compressed that leads away to life, and few are those who find it."

Narrow in the Merriam Webster Dictionary is limited in size and scope.[257] The Greek word for narrow is "stenos," meaning narrow, strait, or path.[258]

Jesus said to enter the Kingdom on the narrow gate where few may find it. The road to salvation is narrow because many people don't want to live right and stay in right standing with God. The narrow path is the one that will lead you to eternal life. Jesus is on the narrow path and not the broad path. If we are followers of Jesus, then we need to stay on the righteous-

---
257. "Narrow" Merriam-Webster.com 2019 https://www.merriam-webster.com Accessed September 2020
258. "Stenos" Greek word for Narrow https://www.biblehub.com Accessed September 2020

ness path that He is on. The broad path is the path that people use that are comfortable in their sinful behavior. They don't want to leave the broad path because of the sin that they are involved in. They are comfortable being outside of the will and the plans of God for their life. But being a born-again believer, we must stay on the narrow path that leads to eternal life and heaven. Choose you today who you will serve, Jesus or the enemy Satan? We cannot serve both of them. Only one, but you make the choice. Will it be heaven or hell?

DECLARATIONS

I will stay on the narrow path that leads to eternal life in heaven.

I will not follow the path of the world on the broad path.

I will continue to be sold out to Christ and live a life of righteousness.

I am the righteousness of God in Christ Jesus.

I will present my body as a living sacrifice, holy, and acceptable for that is my reasonable service.

I will accept Jesus as my Lord and Savior and live for Him.

April 19th

Matthew 28:18 (AMPC) says, "Jesus approached and, breaking the silence, said to them. All authority (all power of rule) in heaven and on earth has been given to Me."

Authority in the Merriam Webster Dictionary is power to influence or command thought, opinion, or behavior.[259] The Greek word for authority is "rabhah," meaning to be great or many.[260]

Jesus has power and authority over everything committed to Him that He redeemed by shedding His blood to redeem us back to God. Jesus purchased the church with His blood. The government is on His shoulders. He has power over all the angels, material world, devils, wicked men and His people.[261] Just mention of the name Jesus. Demons tremble at His name. Everything is subject to the voice and the will of God.

---

259. "Authority" Merriam-Webster.com 2019 https://www.merriam-webster.com Accessed September 2020
260. "Rabhah" Greek word for Authority https://www.biblehub.com Accessed September 2020
261. Matthew 28:18 Matthew Henry's Concise Commentary https://www.biblehub.com Accessed September 2020

PRAYER:

Father God, in the name of Jesus, I come to You today to thank You for being sin for us, suffering, bleeding, dying and rising again on the third day with all power in the palm of Your hand. I know that without Your sacrifice, I could not have a chance to live a life that God wants me to live in Him here on earth as well in heaven in Jesus' name. Lord, thank You for giving me the right to the tree of life by Your sacrifice. Lord, I thank You for loving us that much that You gave Your only begotten Son. Thank You that Jesus is sitting at the right hand of the Father interceding for me and the rest of His people, in Jesus' name. Lord, thank You that I am now walking from victory because I sit in heavenly places with You in Jesus' name. Amen.

April 20th

*D*EUTERONOMY 31:6 (AMPC) STATES, "Be strong, courageous, and firm, fear not nor be in terror before them, for it is the Lord your God Who goes with you, He will not fail you or forsake you."

Forsake in the Merriam Webster Dictionary is to renounce or turn away from entirely.[262] The Greek word for forsake is to leave behind, abandon, leave in the lurch, or desert.[263]

Be strong in God. He will not fail or leave you. God will not leave you to your own devices but will always be present to help you to be successful with the tasks that He assigned. God's presence is always with us. Sometimes you can reach out in front of you and feel His presence continually. If you draw nigh to God, He will draw nigh to you. Continue to have faith in God and trust Him to work everything out for you. You do not have to walk in fear when you know how much God loves you because perfect love casts out fear. With the perfect love of

---

262. "Forsake" Merriam-Webster.com 2019 https://www.merriam-webster.com Accessed October 2020
263. "Egkataleipo" Greek word for Forsake https://www.biblehub.com Accessed October 2020

God in your life, there is no reason for you to be fearful about anything that may arise. God is there for us whenever we need Him. Just call out to Him. He will come and rescue from your trials and struggles and help you to walk in perfect peace.[264]

DECLARATIONS

I am standing on the promises of God and I will not let go of them.

God didn't give me the spirit of fear, but He gave me power, love, and a sound mind to keep moving forward in Him.

I cast out the spirit of fear off of my life right now in Jesus' name.

If God be for us, then who can be against us.

I will walk in faith because faith and fear cannot cohabitate together.

I decree and declare that the enemy is a liar and the truth cannot be found in him.

---

264. Deuteronomy 31:6 Benson Commentary https://www.biblehub.com Accessed October 2020

April 21st

Psalm 149:4 (AMPC) says, "For the Lord takes pleasure in His people; He will beautify the humble with salvation and adorn the wretched with victory."

Adorn in the Merriam Webster Dictionary is to enhance the appearance of especially with beautiful objects.[265] The Greek word for adorn is "kosmeo," meaning to order, arrange, decorate, or deck.[266]

New mercies continually demand new songs of praise, upon the earth and in heaven. And the children of Zion have not only to bless the God who made them, but to rejoice in Him, as having created them in Christ Jesus unto good works, and formed them saints as well as men. The Lord takes pleasure in us and we should rejoice in Him. Let His saints employ their waking hours upon their beds in songs of praise. The Lord loves us and approves our conduct as long as it is rooted in Him. God gives

---

265. Adorn" Merriam-Webster.com 2019 https://www.merriam-webster.com Accessed October 2020

266. "Kosmeo" Greek word for Adorn https://www.biblehub.com Accessed October 2020

favor to His saints. All of this should add to their joy and fill their hearts with gladness.[267]

PRAYER:

Father God, in the name of Jesus, I come before You today with a song of praise in my heart. Lord, I honor and praise You because of the Love that You have for me. Lord, I praise You with my whole heart. I honor Your majesty and glory forever more, in Jesus' name. Lord, You are mighty and gracious. I want You to have Your way in my life like never before, in Jesus' name. Lord, send Your Shekinah Glory to live in my home and to surround me daily with Your Presence, in Jesus' name. Lord, move mightily in my life from this day forth, in Jesus' name. Lord, remove everything in me and my life that doesn't line up with Your Word, in Jesus' name. Amen.

---

267. Psalm 149:4 Matthew Henry's Concise Commentary https://www.biblehub.com Accessed October 2020

April 22nd

ROMANS 8:32 (AMP) SAYS, "He who did not withhold or spare (even) His own Son but gave Him up for us all, will He not also with Him freely and graciously give us all (other) things?"

Withhold in Merriam Webster is to refrain from granting, giving, or allowing.[268] The Greek word for withhold is "tereo," meaning to watch over or to guard.[269]

God loves us so much that He gave His only begotten Son so that we would have a right to the tree of life through Jesus. Every sin that we could ever commit was placed on Jesus, so now we do not have to continue in sin. All we have to do is accept Jesus and allow His Spirit to come and live within our spirit to have someone to lead and guide us. After knowing how much God loves us and what He sacrificed for us, we shouldn't want to continue in sin. I know that we live in an imperfect world, but we are children of God. If we continue to renew our minds

---
268. "Withhold" Merriam-Webster.com 2019 https://www.merriam-webster.com Accessed October 2020
269. "Tereo" Greek word for Withhold https://www.biblehub.com Accessed October 2020

with the Word of God then that is what will come out of us. It will make us not want to continue in sin and stay apart from Jesus, but to live a holy and righteous lifestyle before a gracious and merciful God.

DECLARATIONS

God, thank You for sending Your Son to give us a right to the tree of Life.

I thank Jesus for His sacrifice because it has redeemed me back to God by the shedding of His blood.

Thank You, Jesus, for Your blood that has washed me white as snow.

I can live again in eternity because I have accepted the finished works of Jesus on the cross.

Lord, thank You for saving and giving me the Holy Spirit.

I will not let sin or anything else separate me from the love, peace, mercy, and grace of God.

April 23rd

Hebrews 13:8 (AMPC) states, "Jesus Christ (the Messiah) is (Always) the same, yesterday, today, (yes) and forever (to the ages)."

Messiah in the Merriam Webster Dictionary is the expected King and deliverer of the Jews, Jesus, a leader of hope.[270] The Greek word for Messiah is "Messias," meaning the Anointed One, Jesus.[271]

God is the same in the Old Testament as He is today. God will be the same to His people forever. The Good News of the Gospel doesn't change. It remains the same. God is still equally merciful, powerful, and all-sufficient. He still feeds the hungry, encourages the trembling, and welcomes repenting sinners. He still rejects the proud and self-righteous, and teaches all He saves to love righteousness and to hate iniquity. All believers should seek to have their hearts established in simple dependence on free grace, by the Holy Spirit, which will comfort

---

270. "Messiah" Merriam-Webster.com 2019 https://www.merriam-webster.com Accessed October 2020
271. "Messias" Greek word for Messiah https://www.biblehub.com Accessed October 2020

their hearts, and render them proof against delusions. Christ is both our altar and our sacrifice; he sanctifies the gift.[272] God will not change. He is a God that cannot lie. God is good to everyone who puts their trust and hope in Him.

PRAYER:

Father God, in the name of Jesus, I come before You today acknowledging that You are the same yesterday, today and forever more. I realize that every miracle and healings that are recorded in the Bible are available for us today. Lord, increase my faith in You and Your Word to start believing You to help me through some trials that I am enduring. Lord, thank You for always being there for me, even when I didn't notice You. I remember when You rescued me from the life of sin and gave me a firm foundation to stand on in Your Word. You said in Your Word that if anyone needs wisdom, they are to ask You for it. Well, Lord I am Your child and I need wisdom so I can make the right decisions at the right time. I also want to be in the right timing with You for my life, so I will not get ahead of you. Lord, open my ears so I can hear You better. Remove anything that is sent by the enemy to block my hearing in Jesus' name. Lord, I thank You for making a new creature out of me and for moving me closer in Your presence in Jesus' name. Amen.

---

272. Hebrews 13:8 Matthew Henry's Concise Commentary https://www.biblehub.com Accessed October 2020

April 24th

DEUTERONOMY 7:12 (AMPC) STATES, "And If you hearken to these precepts and keep and do them, the Lord your God will keep with you the covenant and the steadfast love which He swore to your fathers."

Hearken in the Merriam Webster Dictionary is to give respectful attention, or to bring to mind something in the past. [273] The Greek word for hearken is "enotizomai," which means to give ear, to hearken, or to listen to. [274]

We are in danger of having fellowship with the works of darkness if we take pleasure in fellowship with those who do those works. Whatever brings us into a snare, brings us under a curse. [275] Many times once we come into the knowledge of God's Word, then we have been informed of the truth. We are to read and study it so it can enter our hearts so we won't sin

---
273. "Hearken" Merriam-Webster.com 2019 https://www.merriam-webster.com Accessed October 2020
274. "Enotizomai" Greek word for Hearken https://www.biblehub.com Accessed October 2020
275. Deuteronomy 7:12 Matthew Henry's Concise Commentary https://www.biblehub.com Accessed October 2020

against God. When you go deeper in the Word, you will lay a lot of the things down and not do them anymore, because it is contrary to the things of God. The Word comes to convict but not to destroy us. It grows us up so we can become like Jesus instead of the old man who was born in sin and shapen in iniquity. God wants to mature in Him so He can use us mightily for His Kingdom. While you are growing in God, the people that you use to hang around with will become smaller. You don't need to keep hanging around people who are habitually sinning because instead of you converting them, they will most likely start converting away from God. God will remove the ones that don't need to be in your circle and replace them with people going the same route you are headed in God. It is alright when people walk out of your life, because we do outgrow people, especially if you want to be totally sold out to God.

Declarations

I will not fall into the snares of the enemy because I am rooted and grounded in the love of Jesus.

I will not let what used to hold me in a snare to hold me down any longer.

I decree and declare that Jesus is the head of my life.

I decree and declare that I will stay rooted and grounded in the Word of God all the days of my life.

April 24th

Satan, I renounce you and all your evil ways, traps, plots, and ploys. I cover myself and my family under the blood of Jesus.

I plead the blood of Jesus over my mind, heart, spirit, soul, and body from this day forward, in Jesus' name.

April 25th

Psalm 32:10 (AMPC) says, "Many are the sorrows of the wicked, but he who trusts in, relies on, and confidently leans on the Lord shall be compasses about with mercy and with loving-kindness."

Lean in the Merriam Webster Dictionary is to cast's one weight to one side for support, to rely for support or inspiration.[276] The Greek word for leans is "diichurizomai," meaning to lean upon, or affirm confidently.[277]

God teaches by His Word and guides with secret intimations of His will. David gives a word of caution to sinners. The reason for this caution is that the way of sin will certainly end in sorrow. Here is a word of comfort to the saints. They may see that a life of communion with God is far the most pleasant and comfortable.[278] It is better to commune with God daily than to be alone with no one to back you up in this life. Those that

---
276. "Leans" Merriam-Webster.com https://www.merriam-webster.com Accessed October 2020
277. "Diischurizomai" Greek word for Leans https://www.biblehub.com Accessed October 2020
278. Psalm 32:10 Matthew Henry's Concise Commentary https://www.biblehub.com Accessed October 2020

April 25th

have Christ in their lives are not alone when something comes against them. All they have to do is cry out to God and He will send them help in the time of trouble. The sinner who keeps snubbing his nose at God and keeps refusing Jesus is alone. They have to face the troubles and trials without the Lord's help. Many people believe that they don't need God and that everything they do is done in their own strength. But this is not true because it takes God to wake us up every day, give us oxygen to breathe, and the strength to get dressed without assistance. When people think like this, we know that the enemy has them under his control and have them blinded to the fact that Jesus is the answer to all their problems. Many people go for years not having an intimate relationship with God. Unfortunately ,some leave this world still not believing in Him. The only thing that a believer can do is tell sinners the Word of God and pray for them to get delivered and saved before they leave this world without God. When you are a believer, it bothers you to see people walking around without knowing the true nature of God. Sometimes they refuse or reject you because they don't want to hear the truth. As long as the seed is sown, God will send someone else to water it and He will give the increase. So have faith in God to do the impossible in your loved one's lives.

PRAYER:

Father God, in the name of Jesus, I will trust You and lean on You for Your mercy and loving-kindness. Lord, I realize that I have to stay rooted and grounded in You and Your Word so I can continue to move forward in You God. Lord, I pray for my unsaved loved ones because Your Word declares that many are the sorrows of the wicked. If they don't know You or refuse to accept You, as their Lord and Savior, then they will not have You to back them up in their trials. Lord, open up their eyes and hearts right now to have a better chance in getting to know You for themselves. Lord, we know that they cannot be made righteous by their parents' relationship with Christ, but need their own intimate relationship with Christ first and foremost. Lord, pull on the strings of their hearts so they will stop running from You and give their lives totally to You right now in Jesus' name. Lord, we thank You for intervening in their lives in Jesus' name. Amen.

April 26th

Isaiah 40:29 (AMPC) states "He gives power to the faint and weary, and to him who has no might He increases strength (causing it to multiply and making it to abound)."

Weary in the Merriam Webster Dictionary is exhausted in strength, endurance, vigor, or freshness.[279] The Greek word for weary is "kamno," which means to become weary, sickness, spent, or ready to collapse.[280]

Where God has begun a good work in you, He is faithful to bring it to completion. He will help those who are in humble dependence on Him and not themselves. God wants us to depend on Him to bring our future to pass instead of trying to make it happen on our own. When we try to make things happen, weariness sets in. God wants us to trust and rest in Him. In His timing, it will all come to pass in our lives. In the meantime, study the word, read you some books and take some classes to

---

279. "Weary" Merriam-Webster.com https://www.merriam-webster.com Accessed October 2020
280. "Kamno" Greek word for Weary https://www.biblehub.com Accessed October 2020

help prepare you for your glorious future in God. God wants us to invest in ourselves, so we can be taught the things, methods that we need to know to move forward in the destiny where He is calling.

DECLARATIONS

Lord, Your Word declares, "Let the weak say they are strong, so I am getting stronger in You every day."

Lord, help me to not grow weary and have patience in Your timing in my life.

Lord, I will find rest in You for my weary soul.

Lord, you have begun a good work in me and You will bring it to completion in Your timing, in Jesus' name.

Lord, I am totally dependent on You for everything that I need in my life.

Lord, I will lay my agenda and will down for Yours, in Jesus' name.

April 27th

Isaiah 54:17 (AMP) says, "But no weapon that is formed against you shall prosper, and every tongue that shall rise against you in judgment you shall show to be wrong. This (peace, righteousness, security, triumph over opposition) is the heritage of the servants of the Lord (those in whom the ideal servant of the Lord is reproduced); this is the righteousness or the vindication which they obtain from Me (this is that which I impart to them as their justification) says the Lord."

Vindication in the Merriam Webster Dictionary is justification against denial or censure, or defense.[281] The Greek word for vindication is "ekdikeo," which means to avenge, give justice over, defend, or vindicate.[282]

No weapon formed against you shall prosper. The enemy will try to form it, but it will not come to anything. No instrument of war, sword, spear, persecution, or torture made by the

---

281. "Vindication" Merriam-Webster.com https://www.merriam-webster.com Accessed October 2020
282. "Ekdikeo" Greek word for Vindication https://www.biblehub.com Accessed October 2020

smith (blacksmith) will have any prosperity. It may be permitted for a time to appear to prosper but will not have any final success. No one will be able to injure you by words or accusations. If controversy shall rise, and someone accuses you of deceit, you will be able to convince them of error and the truth will come forth. The inheritance which awaits those who serve God is truth and victory. It is the protection of God in all times of trouble, his friendship in all periods of adversity, complete victory in all contests with error. Justification and vindication come from God and this is a part of our inheritance.[283]

PRAYER:

Father God, in the name of Jesus, I come to You today to thank You for Your protection from the enemy and all of his lies. Isaiah 54:17 says, "That no weapon formed against me shall be able to prosper." So, Lord I can depend on You to see me through the difficulty that I am facing right now, in Jesus' name. I cast down every fiery dart of the enemy that is sent to derail me from my destiny, in Jesus' name. Lord, I thank You for Vindicating me when my enemies set out to destroy me. You have erected a hedge of protection around my family and I. I cover my family and me with the blood of Jesus. Nothing by any means shall hurt or come against us as long as we stay rooted and grounded in Your Word. Lord, everything that I have decreed and declared in this prayer will come to pass from this day forward, in Jesus' name. Amen.

---

283. Isaiah 54:17 Barnes Notes on the Bible https://www.biblehub.com Accessed October 2020

April 28th

1 Chronicles 16:11 (AMPC) says, "Seek the Lord and His strength, yearn for and seek His face and to be in His presence continually!"

Yearn in the Merriam Webster Dictionary is to feel tenderness and compassion.[284] The Greek word for yearn is "orego," which means to stretch out, to reach after, or to yearn for.[285]

This is King David's Song of thanks after bringing the Ark of the Covenant back to Jerusalem and placing it inside the tent David had pitched for it. They had offered burnt and peace offerings before God. The ark was the place that the presence of God rested. God is all about the heart of man and our spiritual growth process. The more we grow in God, the more we find it is Him that we inquire of and require as vital to our needs. Our strength can be found in God.[286] In the presence of God is

---

284. "Yearn" Merriam-Webster.com 2019 https://www.merriam-webster.com Accessed October 2020
285. "Orego" Greek word for Yearn https://www.biblehub.com Accessed October 2020
286. 1 Chronicles 16:11 https://www.keystonevictoria.com Accessed October 2020

fullness of joy. "Lord, we long for Your presence every day in Jesus' name. Amen."

DECLARATIONS

I will seek You every day for supernatural strength to make it through my trials and storms.

I know that all of my help comes from the Lord, who created heaven and earth.

Lord, I will continue to seek Your face for everything that I need.

I will continue to move toward the light of Your Word from this day forward in Jesus' name.

Lord, I thank You for Your strength because it is amazing and what I need to make a move forward.

Lord, You said that You would supply our every need according to Your riches in glory by Christ Jesus.

April 29th

Psalm 16:11 (AMPC) says, "You will show me the path of life; in Your presence is fullness of joy, at Your right hand there are pleasures forevermore."

Pleasures in the Merriam Webster Dictionary is a source of delight or joy.[287] The Greek word for pleasures is "hedone, " which means a pleasure, a strong desire, or passion.[288]

Psalm 16 warms the hearts of all weary wanderers, as David joyfully displays his compelling confidence in His Lord, and writes of his utter trust in the God of salvation. Such praise is founded on the sure knowledge that the Lord is not only our protection, through all the changing scenes of this life, but that death, which is man's greatest enemy will finally be conquered. David demonstrated a living faith in the Lord because his trust was in God. He was not alarmed, by the arrows that fly by day, nor terrors that stalk at night despite the distressing dangers

---
287. "Pleasures" Merriam-Webster.com 2019 https://www.merriam-webster.com Accessed October 2020
288. "Hedone" Greek word for Pleasures https://www.biblehub.com Accessed October 2020

that he faced, including in his own death. David's knowledge and understanding of the character of God, brought him an inner peace that only comes from the Lord.[289]

PRAYER:

Father God, in the name of Jesus, thank You for reminding me that in Your presence is fullness of joy and in Your right hand are pleasures forevermore, in Jesus' name. Lord, I know that You are my protection in this life and the afterlife because You have the keys to death and the grave. To be absent from the body is to be present with You. Lord, I realize that I can now have peace in my heart regardless of whatever trials or storms come at me. Lord, keep my mind on You and Your word instead of the troubles of this world. You have everything under control in this world and in my life, in Jesus' name. Lord, I place all of my cares at Your feet and leave them there, never to pick them up again. Many times, I have worried or lost sleep about situations that I have no control over, but now I will give them over to You because You know how to work them out better than me. Lord, I know without a shadow of a doubt that You will always have my best interest at heart regardless if I agree or not. From now on, I will come into agreement with what You and Your Word say about me and not what my flesh says. Thank You, Lord, for listening and strengthening me today, in Jesus' name. Amen.

---

289. Psalm 16:11 https://www.dailyverse.knowing-jesus.com Accessed October 2020

April 30th

John 4:18 (AMPC) states, "There is no fear in love (dread does not exist), but full grown (complete, perfect) love turns fear out of doors and expels every trace of terror! For fear brings with it the thought of punishment, and (so) he who is afraid has not yet grown into love's complete perfection)."

Perfected love is described on www.conformingtojesus.com as to live according to God's Commandments, which is the fulfillment of the Law, because when we do so we don't hurt ourselves and we don't hurt others.[290]

When we are surrounded by family and friends who live in this type of love, there is no fear because this perfect love that God describes and commands us to live by in His Word, drives out any fear, anxiety, and worry. As we know, we can fully trust Him and those who are committed to following Him. We know that God is faithful and that those who seriously follow Him are the same, and they love their neighbor as themselves.

---

290. "Perfected love" https://www.conformingtoJesus.com Accessed October 2020

Whoever fears has not been made perfect in this kind of love. Fear is a punishment for those who live with it. They were hurt by someone who lived according to the world's ways and not God's ways. A broken heart arbors fear!

A person with a broken heart expects and fears God's punishment. They are hurting because they think that God doesn't love them and wants to inflict pain on them. This is not true. A broken heart will lie and convince the individual that God doesn't care about them. They think if God doesn't care, then nobody else will either. They live in hopelessness and always expect something bad to happen. People with a broken heart will look for love in all the wrong places. They search for worldly love to heal their hearts. But only the love of Jesus can fix their hearts and not the false love of the world. This is the nature of the broken heart without perfect love. If this sounds like you, then there is help for you? In God, we will find perfect love because He is righteous and faithful. His perfect love will heal our hearts and drive out fears. It doesn't happen overnight. It will take time, a faithful walk with God and little by little He will heal us. We will receive strength and empowerment from it.[291]

DECLARATIONS

Lord, help me love people the way You love and care for them in Jesus' name.

Lord, help me to love people past their issues and meet them where they are, in Jesus' name.

---

291. 1 John 4:18 https://www.conformingtoJesus.com Accessed October 2020.

April 30th

Lord, help me to start loving myself and everything that You made me to be, in Jesus' name.

Lord, Your Word declares that You are the healer of the brokenhearted. Please heal my heart in Jesus' name.

Lord, I give You my broken-heart, so that You can make me over again and I can become whole and healed.

Lord, I surrender my life, hurt, pain, past traumas, wounds, and broken-heart to You so You can save me and make me a new creature in Christ today in Jesus' name.

May 1st

MARK 11:24 (AMPC) SAYS, "For this reason I am telling you, whatever you ask for in prayer, believe (trust and be confident) that it is granted to you, and you will (get it)."

Granted in the Merriam Webster Dictionary is to bestow or transfer formally.[292] The Greek word for granted is "doreomai," meaning give, grant, or donate.[293]

We need faith to believe that when we pray to God about a matter, He will answer our prayers. We have to trust God to come through for us. Many times, we have to wait on God's timing before certain things happen. When we are playing the waiting game, we have to keep encouraging ourselves everyday with God's Word and praying out our needs unto Him. God is faithful and will rescue us when we need Him! I believe that when I pray for someone or a particular area in my life, my prayers will be answered by God.

---
292. "Granted" Merriam-Webster.com 2019 https://www.merriam-webster.com Accessed October 2020
293. "Doreomaj" Greek word for Granted. https://www.biblehub.com Accessed October 2020.

May 1st

Prayer purifies the heart, removes mountains of corruption, and makes them plain before the grace of God. One greatest errand to the throne of grace is to pray for the pardon of our sins; and care about this ought to be our daily concern. Have faith in God or confidence in God to accomplish the things that seem the most difficult to accomplish by us. God can do whatever you think is impossible in your life. God can handle everything concerning me in a blink of an eye.[294]

PRAYERS:

Father God, in the name of Jesus, thank You for teaching us how to pray effectively by bombarding heaven with our requests. Lord, I trust You with everything that concerns me. I know that You will work things out in my best interest, in Jesus' name. Lord, I know that You can do the impossible in our lives. Lord, thank You for protecting me when I didn't see the danger, in Jesus' name. Lord, thank You for all the prayers You have answered in my life and the prayers that I am waiting for You to answer, in Jesus' name. Lord, thank You for moving mountains and opening doors in my life, in Jesus' name. Amen.

---

294. Mark 11:24 Matthew Henry's Concise Commentary https://www.biblehub.com Accessed October 2020

May 2nd

2 Timothy 2:15 (AMPC) says, "Study and be eager and do your utmost to present yourself to God approved (tested by trial), a workman who has no cause to be ashamed, correctly analyzing and accurately dividing (rightly handling and skillfully teaching) the Word of Truth."

Study in the Merriam Webster Dictionary is an application in a particular field or to a specific subject, paying close attention to, or examination.[295] The Greek word for study is "meletao," meaning to care for, practice, study, ponder, practice, or plan.[296]

An article on www.dailyverse.knowing-jesus.com talks about the Word of God being the focus of our study and not wise philosophies or the limited scope of mortal man's understanding, but God-breathed Scripture is His inerrant Word of Truth. Through the study of the Bible, we should make every effort to discover the beautiful gems of wisdom found within

---

295. "Study" Merriam-Webster.com 2019 https://www.merriam-webster.com Accessed October 2020.
296. "Meletao" Greek word for Study https://www,biblehub.com Accessed October 2020

May 2nd

its pages. Indeed, it is the Spirit of truth that has been sent to guide us into all truth. That truth is to be discovered within the pages of the wonderful revelation of God's plans and purposes that have been given to man. We are to rightly divide the Word of truth, accurately handle the content, correctly learn and teach all that has been revealed to man in God's Word. We should not take the Scriptures out of context nor twist them to mean something else.[297] The Word of God is true all by itself. We should not add to it or take away from it.

DECLARATIONS

I will study God's Word to show myself approved.

I will study and get God's Word in my heart, so I will not sin against Him.

I will not be deceived when someone twists the Word of God because I will study and search out the Scriptures after a sermon.

Lord, give me a better understanding of Your Word in Jesus' name.

Lord, download any information that I may need for the journey because I cannot make it without You.

---

297. 2 Timothy 2:15 https://www.dailyverse.knowing-jesus.com Accessed October 2020

May 3rd

LUKE 6:36 (AMPC) SAYS, "So be merciful (sympathetic, tender, responsive, and compassionate) even as your Father is (all these)."

Sympathetic in the Merriam Webster Dictionary is given to, marked by, or arising from sympathy, compassion, friendliness, and sensitivity to others' emotions.[298] The Greek word for sympathetic is "sumpathes" which means sympathizing, compassionate, suffering or feeling like another.[299]

According to www.dailyverse.knowing-jesus.com, as children of God, we are required to follow Christ's example and be imitators of Him. Jesus is the Holy One of Israel, and we are called to be holy, just as He is holy. We are instructed to be perfect in understanding, thoroughly furnished for every good work. We are to be faultless, wanting nothing, and joined together as one in understanding, with the mind of Christ in the unity of the Spirit. We are set apart for the service of Christ and

---

298. "Sympathetic Merriam-Webster.com 2019 https://wwmerriam-webster.com Accessed October 2020.
299. "Sympathes" Greek word for Sympathetic https://www.biblehub.com Accessed October 2020

May 3rd

commanded to walk the way He desires. We are to be merciful because our Father is merciful, sympathetic, tender, responsive, forgiving, and full of compassion.[300]

PRAYER:

Father God, in the name of Jesus, thank You for having mercy on me and not giving me what I deserved when I was in the world of sin. I am grateful for having a praying mother and grandmother. They prayed that one day I would give my life to You. Lord, thank You for Your compassion, sympathy, and forgiveness. Thank You for not holding sin against me. You gave me a chance to repent and get in right standing with You. Lord, I can follow Your footsteps and have the same mercy on someone else. Lord, thank You for helping me treat people the way You commanded, in Jesus' name. Lord, thank You for Your grace that helps me move and feel the same way about Your people like You in Jesus' name. Lord, thank You for Your mercy and grace that has kept me and has given me Your unmerited empowerment to live a victorious life, in Jesus' name. Amen.

---

300. Luke 6:36 https://www.dailyverse.knowing-jesus.com Accessed October 2020

May 4th

1 John 2:1 (AMPC) says, "My Little children, I write you these things so that you may not violate God's law and sin. But if anyone should sin, we have an advocate (One Who will intercede for us) with the Father (it is) Jesus Christ (the all) righteous (upright, just, who conforms to the Father's will in every purpose, thought, and action."

Advocate in the Merriam Webster Dictionary is one who pleads the cause of another before a judicial or tribunal court.[301] The Greek word for advocate is "parakletos," meaning called to one's aid, intercessor, consoler, comforter, helper, or Paraclete.[302]

We have an advocate with the Father; One who has undertaken, and is fully able to plead on behalf of everyone who applies for pardon and salvation in His name, depending on His pleading for them. He is Jesus, the Savior, and the Christ, the Messiah, and the Anointed. He alone is the Righteous One,

---
301. "Advocate" Merriam-Webster.com 2019 https://www.merriam-webster.com Accessed October 2020.
302. "Paraletos" Greek word for advocates https://www.biblehub.com Accessed October 2020.

May 4th

Who received His nature from sin, and as our surety perfectly obeyed the law of God, and so fulfilled all righteousness. The Gospel when rightly understood and received, sets the heart against all sin, and stops the allowed practice of it. At the same time, it gives blessed relief to the wounded consciences of those who have sinned.[303]

DECLARATIONS

Lord, I will not practice sin. But if I do, I know that I have an Advocate with the Father through Christ Jesus.

Jesus is the atoning sacrifice for our sins, and not only for ours but also for the sins of the world.

I have been crucified with Christ and I no longer live, but Christ lives in me.

In Him, we have redemption through His blood, forgiveness of sins, in accordance with the riches of God's grace.

And once made perfect, He became the source of eternal salvation for all who obey Him.

For this reason, Christ is the mediator of a new covenant, that those who are called may receive the promised eternal inheritance.

---

303. Luke 6:36 Matthew Henry's Concise Commentary https://www.biblehub.com Accessed October 2020

May 5th

Psalm 85:2 (AMPC) says, "You have forgiven and taken away the iniquity of Your people, You have covered all their sin. Selah (pause, and calmly realize what that means)!"

Iniquity in the Merriam Webster Dictionary is corruption, immorality, a wicked act or thing.[304] The Greek word for iniquity is "pomeria," meaning wickedness or iniquities.[305]

God's remission of punishment, and restoration of His people to favor, was a full indication that He had forgiven their iniquity and covered their sins. The favor of God is the fountain of happiness to nations, as well as to particular persons. When God forgives sin, He covers it; and when He covers the sin of His people, He covers it all. In compassion to us, that is why Christ is our intercessor and He has stood before the Father, and He has turned away His anger from us. When we accept Jesus as our Lord and Savior, then we are then reconciled back

---

304. "Iniquity" Merriam-Webster.com 2019 https://www.merriam-webster.com Accessed October 2020
305. "Poneria" Greek for Iniquity https://www.biblehub.com Accessed October 2020.

May 5th

to God as if we have never sinned through justification and salvation.[306]

PRAYER:

Father God, in the name of Jesus, thank You for sending Jesus to suffer and die on the cross for me. I realize that You put all of my sins and the sins of the world on Him. Lord, thank You that now, by His blood, I can be saved and adopted back into the sonship through His sacrifice. Lord, thank You for forgiving our sins and having Jesus sit at Your right-hand, making intercession for me when I err and ask for help. Lord, thank You for covering all of our iniquities, sins and turning Your anger away from us in Jesus' name. Lord, I now accept the finished works of Jesus so that I can now be reconciled back to God through Your sacrifice on the cross. I can start to live a life that is pleasing to You God by surrendering to You, in Jesus' name. Thank You for coming to live in me and saving me from death, hell, and destruction, in Jesus' name. Amen.

306.. 1 John 2:1, Matthew Henery's Concise Commentary https://ww.biblehub.com Accessed October 2020.

May 6th

1 Peter 5:8 (AMPC) says, "Be well balanced (temperate, sober of mind), be vigilant and cautious at all times; for the enemy of yours, the devil, roams around like a lion roaring (in fierce hunger), seeking someone to seize upon and devour."

Temperate in the Merriam Webster Dictionary is keeping or held within limits, not extreme or excessive, mild.[307] The Greek word for temperate is "sophron," meaning of sound mind, self-controlled, sober-minded, modest, or chaste.[308]

The whole design of Satan is to devour and destroy souls. He is always contriving to determine whom he may ensnare to eternal ruin. We plainly must be sober, to govern both the outward and the inward man by the rules of temperance. To be vigilant; suspicious of constant danger from this spiritual enemy, watchful and diligent to prevent his designs. Be steadfast and solid, by faith.[309] We must not be ignorant of Satan's

---
307. "Temperate" Merriam-Webster.com 2019 https://merriam-webster.com Accessed October 2020
308. "Sophran" Greek for the word Temperate. https://www.biblehub.com Accessed October 2020
309. 1 Peter 5:8 Matthew Henry's Concise Commentary https://www.biblehub.com

May 6th

devices against us. The enemy hates God's people because he got kicked out of heaven and never can return. He is trying to stop you from getting in. His job is to kill, steal, and destroy, but we have God's protection as long as we stay underneath His umbrella.

DECLARATIONS

I will be mentally alert and self-controlled because the enemy goes around like a roaring lion seeking those that he can devour.

I will not relax or let my guard down spiritually because of the enemy's tricks.

The devil is the false accuser and slanderer of God's people. God is more powerful than anything that He created and that includes the devil.

I will resist the enemy and he will flee from me.

I can call on and count on God to strengthen me when the enemy comes at me like a flood. God will lift up a standard against him.

The enemy is a liar and the truth is not in him.

May 7th

Proverbs 3:13 (AMP) says, "Happy (blessed, fortunate, enviable) is the man who finds skillful and godly Wisdom, and the man who gets understanding (drawing it forth from God's Word and life's experiences)."

An article from www.teachinghumblehearts.com states that Godly wisdom is innocent, gentle, reasonable, peace-loving, impartial and sincere. It is full of mercy and willing to yield to others. It leads to godliness and peaceful relationships with others.

Our lives are the results of all the choices we make. It takes wisdom to ensure that our choices come together to end up at the narrow gate of eternal life, not the wide gate to eternal destruction. To find the path to the narrow gate, we need to seek wisdom and guidance from God. He will show us the way. Godly wisdom could result in us bringing many others with us to the narrow gate. You can recognize wise people in your life.

May 7th

They bring a sense of calm and peace wherever they go. They are quick to go to God for wisdom.[310]

PRAYER:

Father God, in the name of Jesus, I come to You today asking that You give me the wisdom to continue to make the right decisions. Lord, with Your wisdom, I will always make the right choices for myself and others. Lord, help me to always consult You before I make any major decisions in my life so I can be at peace. Lord, Your word declares that Godly wisdom is full of mercy and peacefulness. I know that I can go to sleep at night without wondering if I have made the right decision in a matter in Jesus' name. Lord, when other people come to me for advice, help me to give them godly wisdom instead of my opinion or worldly wisdom so their promises can be fulfilled by You. Lord, I thank You for making me wise and humbled, in Jesus' name. Amen.

---

310. Proverbs 3:13, https://www.teachinghumblehearts.com Accessed October 2020.

May 8th

EPHESIANS 2:19 (AMPC) SAYS, "Therefore you are no longer outsiders (exiles, migrants, and aliens, excluded from the rights of citizens), but you now share citizenship with the saints (God's own people, consecrated and set apart for Himself); and You belong to God's (own) household."

Citizenship in the Merriam Webster Dictionary is defined as membership in a community.[311] The Greek word for citizenship is "politeia," citizen, body, polity, or franchise.[312]

The church is compared to a city, and every converted sinner is free of it. It is also compared to a house, and every converted sinner is a part of the family; a servant and a child in God's house. The church is also compared to a building, founded on the doctrine of Christ; delivered by the prophets of the Old Testament, and the apostles of the New Testament. God dwells in all believers now. They become the temple of God through the

---

311. "Citizenship" Merriam-Webster.com 2019 https://www.merrian-webster.com Accessed October 2020
312. "Poloteia" Greek word for Citizenship https://www.biblehub.com Accessed October 2020

May 8th

working of the blessed Spirit. Let us then ask if our hopes are fixed on Christ, according to the doctrine of His Word? Have we devoted ourselves as holy temples of God through Him? Are we habitations of God by the Spirit? Let us take heed not to grieve the Holy Comforter, the Holy Spirit.[313]

DECLARATIONS

I am a Kingdom citizen and I will walk and demonstrate the Kingdom of God in my life, marriage, business, or church.

I have been adopted into the Kingdom of God because of the sacrifice that Jesus has done on the cross at Calvary.

When I show up at a place, the kingdom of God shows up because I am a glory carrier.

Lord, continue to prune and get the negative things out of me to produce more fruit.

Every promise over my life will come to pass and manifest in the present and the future in Jesus' name.

I will walk in the Spiritual authority You have given me from this day forward in Jesus' name.

---

313. Ephesians 2:19 Matthew Henry's Concise Commentary https://www.biblehub.com Accessed October 2020

May 9th

Psalm 119:64 (AMP) says, "The earth, O Lord, is full of Your mercy and loving-kindness, teach me Your statutes."

Statutes in the Merriam Webster Dictionary is a law enacted by the legislative branch of a government.[314] The Greek word for statutes is "nomos," meaning that which is assigned, law, divine laws, or the Pentateuch.[315]

This is the expression of a heart full of love for the Word of God. In the Psalmist's state of mind, the goodness of God is seen everywhere. The best preparation for seeing evidence that God is good is a heart full of love. Then the proof of that love springs up on every side. As when we truly love a friend, we find constant proof of His excellency of character. Lord, I desire to see more of Your laws (precepts). Your goodness to

---

314. "Statutes" Merrian-Webster.com 2019 https://www.merriam-webster.com Accessed October 2020
315. "Nomos" Greek word for Statutes https://www.biblehub.com accessed October 2020.

May 9th

me is widespread around me, which leads me to want to see more of You.[316]

PRAYER:

Father God, in the name of Jesus, I thank You for Your unconditional love. Your love is everlasting. I can see it and experience it every day, in Jesus' name. Your love is so contagious. I can now then transfer that same love over to other people. Lord, thank You that Your love doesn't change even when I miss the mark. Your love is so amazing that You woo me back into right standing with You when I get off track. Lord, I praise Your name and Worship You in Spirit and in truth for the blessings You have given my family and me in Jesus' name. Lord, I desire to see more of Your precepts. Help me to understand them, so that my life can align with Your Word in Jesus' name. Amen.

---

316. Psalm 119:64, Barnes Notes on the Bible https://www.biblehub.com Accessed October 2020.

May 10th

Psalm 94:18-19 (AMPC) says, "When I said, My foot is slipping, Your mercy and loving-kindness, O Lord, held me up. 19. In the multitude of my (anxious) thoughts within me, Your comforts cheer and delight my soul!"

Multitude in the Merriam Webster Dictionary is defined as a great number, or the state of being many.[317] The Greek word for multitude is "ochlos," which means a crowd, mob, the common people, or many.[318]

There is a rest remaining for the people of God after the days of their adversity, which shall not last always. He that sends the trouble, will send the rest. The psalmist found succor and relief only in the Lord, when all earthly friends failed. We are beholden, not only to God's power, but to His pity, for spiritual supports; and if we have been kept from falling into sin, or shrinking from our duty, we should give Him the glory,

---

317. "Multitude" Merriam-Webster.com 2019 https://www.merriam-webster.com Accessed October 2020
318. "Ochlos" Greek word for Multitude https://www.merriam-webster.com Accessed October 2020

May 10th

and encourage our brethren. We must look to the great and precious promises of the Gospel. The world's comforts give little to the soul, when hurried with melancholy thoughts; but God's comforts bring that peace and pleasure which the smiles of the world cannot give, and which the frowns of the world cannot take away. God is His people's refuge, to whom they may flees, in whom they are safe, and may be secure.[319]

DECLARATIONS

Lord, no matter what I am going through in my life and body, I will keep my eyes on You, Jesus.

Lord, send Your Supernatural Joy to hit my life like never before in Jesus' name.

I will walk in the peace that passeth all understanding in every area of my life in Jesus' name.

Lord, I thank You for comforting me when I need comfort from the cares of the world.

I will not walk-in doubt or unbelief, but I will walk in mustard seed faith in Jesus' name.

---

[319]. Psalm 94:18-19 Matthew Henry's Concise Commentary https://www.biblehub.com Accessed October 2020.

May 11th

EPHESIANS 2:10 (AMPC) SAYS, "For we are God's (own) handiwork (His workmanship), recreated in Christ Jesus, (born anew) that we may do those good works which God predestined (planned beforehand) for us (taking paths which He prepared ahead of time), that we should walk in them (living the good life which He prearranged and made ready for us to live)."

Handiwork in the Merriam Webster Dictionary is defined as work done personally.[320] The Greek word for handiwork is "poiema," meaning a form, framing, or purpose.[321]

God calls us His workmanship or His artwork. We are crafted with skill and a purpose by God. Specifically, we are created in Christ Jesus for good works. Good works do not give us salvation, but they are absolutely meant to be the result of it. God prepared what He wanted us to do for Him long ago. He has already planned what He wants us to do with our lives. We

---

320. "Handiwork" Merriam-Webster.com 2019 https://www.merriam-webster.com Accessed October 2020
321. "Yetser" Greek word for Handiwork https://www.biblehub.com Accessed October 2020.

May 11th

do not need to copy what someone else has done or is doing. He has a unique plan for each of us to serve Him in this world. His includes certain spiritual gifts and the work of the Holy Spirit to lead us in service to Him. Paul repeatedly emphasizes that salvation is accomplished based on grace through faith. Good works, human efforts, and our best intentions will never be enough to earn salvation. Every person is marked with sin, both deliberate and accidental, and for this reason, we deserve to be separated from God. Only through His mercy and grace can we be saved, leaving no room for bragging. This also means that all who are saved, Jew and Gentiles alike, are part of the same spiritual family. There is no cause for hostility between believers, we are all unworthy, and all saved by the same kindness of God.[322]

Prayer:

Father God, in the name of Jesus, thank You for giving me the gift of salvation. I know that I really don't deserve being saved but by Your grace and mercy, You chose to forgive me for everything that I have ever done in Jesus' name. Lord, I know that I cannot be saved in my own merit, but only by the sacrifice of Jesus. I now have a right to be saved from sin and have a new life in Jesus Christ. Lord, thank You for sacrificing Yourself for me so I can have a right to be all that I can be in You. I know that I cannot brag about any good deeds that I have done because they will not count for salvation. Salvation can only come through having an intimate relationship with You, Jesus. My righteousness is found in Jesus only and not in myself. My own righteousness is as filthy rags. I will receive righteousness

---

322. Ephesian 2:10 https://www.bibleref.com Accessed October 2020

through You Jesus because of the finished works You did on Calvary's cross. Lord, I thank You for making my life new all over again, in Jesus' name. Amen.

May 12th

*P*ROVERBS 2:11 (AMP) SAYS, "Discretion shall watch over you, understanding shall keep you."

Discretion in the Merriam Webster Dictionary is defined as the quality of having or showing discernment or good judgment, or the quality of being discreet.[323] The Greek word for discretion is "huparcho," which means to be in possession of, begin, go first, to be ready or at hand.[324]

Wisdom gives you an understanding as you study the Word. For the gospel makes a man wise and discreet in the business of salvation, and in his conduct and deportment; and the discretion it gives him will put him upon his guard, and direct him to watch against every error, and every false way. Wisdom gives good counsel and the gospel is full of it. If heeded, it is a means of preservation of the saints. The Bible can keep you from walking in evil if you apply it. A just thought shall preserve (keep)

---
323. "Discretion" Merriam-Webster.com 2019 https://www.merriam-webster.com Accessed October 2020
324. Huparcho" Greek word for Discretion. https://www.biblehub.com Accessed October 2020

you and help you from walking in sin and missing the mark in your life again.[325]

DECLARATIONS

Lord, You said in Your Word that if anyone needs wisdom they are to ask You.

Lord, give me a double dose of wisdom so I can continue to make the right decisions.

Lord, take my discernment to another level in You, so I can know who is for me and who is against me.

I will never get caught in any scandal that would tarnish my name or ministry.

Lord, I will pay attention to every red flag You give me about a person or organization in Jesus' name.

Lord, I will walk in integrity in every area of my life because I represent holiness and righteousness.

---

325. Proverbs 2:11 https://www.biblestudytools.com Accessed October 2020

May 13th

Isaiah 33:22 (AMPC) says, "For the Lord is our Judge, the Lord is our Lawgiver, the Lord is our King, He will save us."

Lawgiver in the Merriam Webster Dictionary is defined as ones who gives a code of laws to people.[326] The Greek word for Lawgiver is "nomothetes," meaning lawgiver.[327]

We have all we need and desire in God. For He is our Judge. The Lord Christ, who has all judgment committed to Him by the Father, who will judge His people, right their wrongs, and avenge their injuries.

The Lord is our Lawgiver, who has enacted wholesome laws for His church, writes them on their hearts, and puts His Spirit within them, to enable them to keep them.

---

326. "Law Giver" Merriam-Webster.com 2019 https://www.merriam-webster.com Accessed October 2020
327. "Nomothetes" Greek word for Law Giver https://www.biblehub.com Accessed October 2020.

The Lord is our King of saints, King of Zion, made so by His Father, owned by His church, under whose government it is in safety. He will save us from all of our sin, and from all enemies, with an everlasting salvation.[328]

PRAYER:

Father God, in the name of Jesus, I come to You today to thank You for being everything that I need all wrapped up into one. Lord, You are my Judge and You will right all of my wrongs when people have mistreated or misused me. You will avenge and vindicate me when someone tries to cheat me out of something that rightfully belongs to me. Lord, You are my Lawgiver because the Bible is the truth and it is given to me as a road map to follow. Lord, You are my King because the government was placed on Your shoulders so You would govern Your Kingdom. Lord, thank You for salvation, and forgiving me from my sins, and saving me from my enemies. Lord, through Your blood, I can now have eternal life and everlasting salvation by serving You all through eternity in Jesus' name. Amen.

---

328. Isaiah 33:22 Gill's Exposition of the Entire Bible https://www.biblehub.com Accessed October 2020

May 14th

Colossians 3:23-24 (AMPC) says, "Whatever may be your task, work at it heartily (from the soul), as (something done) for the Lord and not for men. 24. Knowing (with all certainty) that it is from the Lord (and not from men) that you will receive the inheritance which is your (real) reward. (The One Whom) you are actually serving (is) the Lord Christ (the Messiah)."

Task in the Merriam Webster Dictionary is a usually assigned piece of work often to be finished within a certain time.[329] The Greek word for task is "ergon," meaning work, labor, action, or employment.[330]

Whatever you are assigned to do, do it whole heartily unto God and not unto men. If you do it without complaining, God will reward you. You must serve Christ whole heartily while you are here on this earth. Obey Him even if it is uncomfortable. Speak what He is telling you to say without shrinking back. The Word of God must go forth. God will use every one of His

---
329. "Task" Merriam-Webster.com 2019 https://www.merriam-webster.com Accessed October 2020

330. "Ergon" Greek word for Task https://www.biblehub.com Accessed October 2020

people that are available to turn this world upside down for His glory in Jesus' name. We all have a job. We must get busy doing what He has called us to do. There shouldn't be any excuses when God says to move or go higher and deeper in Him. God needs all of us to step up and be who He has called us to be. It is time out for the same excuses over and over because someone else is tied to us making it to our destinies in God.

DECLARATIONS

Lord, everything that I do in my walk with You is for Your glory and not man's.

Lord, I will not continue to make excuses for why I can't move forward toward my destiny in You.

Lord, help me to become who You are calling me to be.

Lord, give me back my zeal and passion, so I can serve You with Joy and gladness.

Lord, I know that You will see my labor of love and reward me accordingly to Your will.

Lord, thank You for peace and the hedge of protection that You have on my life.

May 15th

PSALM 119:160 (AMPC) STATES, "The sum of Your word is truth (the total of the full meaning of all Your individual precepts); and every one of Your righteous decrees endures forever."

Decrees in the Merriam Webster Dictionary is defined as a foreordaining will, to command or enjoin by or as if by decree.[331] The Greek word for decrees is "dogma," meaning an opinion, a public decree, or ordinance.[332]

God has been ever faithful, and the principles of His government will ever continue to be worthy of confidence. God's Word is nothing but the truth. From the beginning of Genesis to the end of Revelation, every Word written in the Bible is true and ordained by God. These Words were given by the Holy Spirit to the writers of the Bible. Romans 3:4 states, "Of course not! Even if everyone else is a liar, God is true." As the Scrip-

---

331. "Decrees" Merriam-Webster.com https://www.merriam-webster.com Accessed October 2020

332. "Dogma" Greek for Decrees https://www.biblehub.com Accessed October 2020

tures say about Him, "You will be proved right in what you say, and you will win your case in court."[333]

PRAYER:

Father God, in the name of Jesus, thank You for giving us the Bible to pattern our life after because I know that every Word in it is true. Lord, help me to apply Your Word to every situation that arises so I can live a life that is pleasing unto You. Every Word in the Bible was given to the writer by the Holy Spirit. So every Word is life to those that hear it and receive it by faith, in Jesus' name. Lord, thank You for Your life-giving Word, in Jesus' name. When we pray Your Word, You are obligated to answer our prayers, in Jesus' name. I will speak things into existence by declaring Your Word over my life, in Jesus' name. Your Word declares that I can have what I say when asking in faith, in Jesus' name. Amen.

---

333. Psalm 119:160, Jamieson-Fausset Brown Bible Commentary https://www.biblehub.com Accessed October 2020.

May 16th

Psalm 121:1-2 (AMPC) states, "I will lift up my eyes to the hills (around Jerusalem, to sacred Mount Zion and Mount Moriah) From whence shall my help come? 2. My help comes from the Lord, Who made heaven and earth."

Lift in the Merriam Webster Dictionary is defined as to raise from a lower to a higher position, or elevate.[334] The Greek word for lift is "hupsoo," meaning to lift or raise up, to exalt, or uplift; to set on high.[335]

We are to look to God for our help because He is always there when we cry out to Him in any situation that arises. If we rely on friends, they may not be there when we need them. We can't rely on our family members because they may not have what we need. We cannot rely on our jobs or careers because we could lose it and not have an income to pay our bills. The only person that we can depend on for everything that con-

---
334. "Lift" Merriam-Webster.com 2019 https://www.merriam-webster.com Accessed October 2020
335. "Hupsoo" Greek word for Lift, https://www.biblehub.com Accessed October 2020

cerns us is God. Jehovah Jireh is our provider. He will supply our needs according to His riches in glory in Christ Jesus. Jesus is the answer to every problem in the world today.

DECLARATIONS

I will look to the hill from which comes my help because my help comes from God.

God is the God of the impossible. What is impossible with man is possible with God.

Lord, You are the lifter of my head.

Lord, I know that nothing that I could ever go through is too hard for You.

Lord, I lay all of my burdens and problems at Your feet and leave them there.

God, I thank You in advance for manifesting the harvest, breakthrough, and suddenly in my life in Jesus' name.

May 17th

Romans 10:9 (AMPC) states, "Because if you acknowledge and confess with your lips that Jesus is Lord and, in your heart, believe (adhere to, trust in, and rely on the truth) that God raised Him from the dead, you will be saved."

Saved in the Merriam Webster Dictionary is defined as delivered from sin and from spiritual death, or rescued from eternal punishment.[336] The Greek word for saved is "sozo," meaning to save, heal, preserve, rescue, or deliver us out of danger.[337]

Paul is giving full assurance that God's gracious offer of salvation by grace through faith in Christ's finished work is wide open to both the Jews and the Gentiles. He gave the assurance to both Israel and the nations: that if you confess with your mouth, "Jesus is Lord, and believe in your heart that God raised Him from the dead, you will be saved." Only the blood of the Messiah can pay the price for our sins, not our own righteousness. We don't need to jump through legalistic hoops to achieve

---
336. "Saved" Merriam-Webster.com 2019 https://www.merriam-webster.com October 2020
337. "Sozo" Greek word for Saved https://www.biblehub.com Accessed October 2020

salvation. Salvation can be obtained through Jesus and Him alone. All you have to do is receive the finished works of Jesus and you can be born again. Jesus died for our sins but was raised from the dead. If you can confess Jesus as the Lord, God of Abraham, Isaac and Jacob and believe in your heart that the Messiah was raised from the dead, you would be saved from death and eternal damnation.[338]

PRAYER:

Father God, in the name of Jesus, Romans 10:9 says, "That if I confess with my mouth that Jesus is Lord and believe in my heart that God raised Him from the dead that I would be saved from death, hell and eternal damnation." Lord, I believe and receive Jesus as Lord. I believe that God raised Him from the dead on the third day with all power in the palm of His hands. Lord, thank You for saving me, living inside me, and giving me Your divine nature, in Jesus' name. Lord, make a new creature out of me. I lay down the old man and pick up the new man as I continue to grow in the knowledge of You. Lord, have Your way in my life and remove anything that doesn't represent You. Now I can walk on the narrow path so I can make it to heaven one day. Thank You for Your peace, love, joy, strength, and comfort in Jesus' name. Amen.

---

338. Romans 10:9 https://www.dailyverse.knowing-jesus.com Accessed October 2020. "Stick" Merriam-Webster.com 2019 https://www.merriam-webster.com Accessed October 2020

May 18th

Proverbs 18:24 (AMP) says, "The man of many friends (a friend of all the world) will prove himself a bad friend, but there is a friend who sticks closer than a brother."

Sticks in the Merriam Webster Dictionary is to attach by or as if by causing to adhere to a surface.[339] The Greek word for sticks is "kollo," meaning to glue, cling, or paste.[340]

Christ Jesus will never forsake those who trust and love Him. May we be friends to others, for our Master's sake. Having loved His own, which were in the world, He loved them unto the end; and we are his friends if we do whatever He commands.[341]

DECLARATIONS

---

339. "Stick" Merriam-Webster.com 2019 https://www.merriam-webster.com Accessed October 2020
340. ."Kollo" Greek word for Sticks https://www.wordhippo.com Accessed Octob3er 2020
341. Proverbs 18:24 Matthew Henry's Concise Commentary https://www.biblehub.com Accessed October 2020

There is a friend that sticks closer than any brother and His name is Jesus.

I am a friend of Jesus because I am obedient to His word and do what He commands.

Jesus will stay with me in the midst of the storm and bring me through to the other side of it.

God is sending me real covenant friends who will love me and speak life over me.

God is going to send someone that is not threatened by my ministry or success to help me.

Lord, send faithful people to help me get to my next level in You.

May 19th

Psalm 91:4 (AMPC) says, "(Then) He will cover you with His pinions and under His wings shall you trust and find refuge; His truth and His faithfulness are a shield and a buckler."

Buckler in the Merriam Webster Dictionary is one that shields and protects.[342] The Hebrew word for buckler is "socherah," meaning a buckler.[343]

God will cover us under His feathers as birds do their young, who cannot cover themselves. They do this for a tender regard to them, whereby they both keep warm, and protect them from those that would hurt them. This represents the helpless state of the children of God, who are like young birds, weak and unable to defend themselves. The warmth and comforted souls have protection under His powerful and gracious presence. He comforts us during our tribulations and defends us from our enemies. His faithfulness is to preserve His saints for His King-

---
342. "Buckler" Merrian-Webster.com 2019 https://www.merriam-webster.com Accessed October 2020
343. "Socherah" Hebrew word for Buckler https://www.biblehub.com Accessed October 2020

dom and glory. Jesus and the Word is the truth. His person, blood, righteousness, and salvation are a shield and buckler around the saints to secure them from ruin and destruction. It is the shield which faith quenches the temptation of Satan.[344]

PRAYER:

Father God, in the name of Jesus, Psalm 91:4 (NLT) says, "He will cover you with his feathers, He will shelter you with his wings. His faithful promises are your armor and protection." Lord, I thank You for keeping me covered under Your wings where I can take refuge from the storms. Lord, I stand on Your Word because Your Word is truth and life to me forever and always, in Jesus' name. Lord, Your Word declares that You will protect me from my enemies and anyone that tries to misuse or mistreat me. Lord, I thank You for sacrificing Your life for me on Calvary's Cross so that my sins could be washed away by Your blood, in Jesus' name. Lord, thank You for blocking the attempts of Satan because he is trying to destroy my life. Thank You, Jesus, for giving me the abundant life when I surrendered, got saved, and renewed in Your blood, in Jesus' name. Amen.

---

344. Psalm 91:4 Gill's Exposition of the Entire Bible https://www.merriam-webster.com Accessed October 2020

May 20th

Psalm 23:5 (AMPC) states, "You prepare a table before me in the presence of my enemies. You anoint my head with oil, my (brimming) cup runs over."

Brimming in the Merriam Webster Dictionary is defined as containing or seeming to contain the greatest quantity or number possible, running over.[345] The Greek word for brimming is "gemizontas," meaning overflow, boil over, top up, bubble over, or run over.[346]

This is a Psalm of David and it talks about God being our faithful God, our merciful and gracious Savior, our good and caring Shepherd, who keeps, protects, and provides for us, through all the changing scenes of our lives. He is the One who upholds and protects; Who blesses and comforts, Who bountifully provides good things for us, in the presence of our enemies. He is the One Who intercedes for us in heavenly places.

---
345. "Brimming" Merriam-Webster.com 2019 https://www.merriam-webster.com Accessed October 2020
346. "Gemizontas" Greek word for Brimming https://www.biblehub.com Accessed October 2020

Our loving God supplies all of our needs, according to His riches in glory, through Christ Jesus our Savior. Though we may be afflicted on all sides, pressured, perplexed and persecuted for righteousness sake, we have not been forgotten or abandoned by our Heavenly Lord.[347]

DECLARATIONS

Thank You, Lord for preparing a table before me in the presence of my enemies.

Lord, Your Word declares that You would make my enemies my footstool in Jesus' name.

Lord, thank You for Your hedge of protection that surrounds my family and me like a shield.

You have anointed my head with oil and my cup is running over in Jesus' name.

Thank You, Lord for being with me through the thick and thin in my life and never leaving.

Lord, thank You for interceding for me and supplying my every need according to Your riches in glory in Christ Jesus.

---

347. Psalm 23:5 https://www.dailyverse.knowing-jesus.com Accessed October 2020

May 21st

Luke 11:13 (AMPC) says, "If you then, evil as you are, know how to give good gifts (gifts that are to their advantage) to your children, how much more will your heavenly Father give the Holy Spirit to those who ask and continue to ask Him!"

Gifts in the Merriam Webster Dictionary are defined as to endow with some power, quality or attribute.[348] The Greek word for gift is "charisma," a gift of grace, a free gift, and undeserved favor.[349]

Observe what to pray for; we must ask for the Holy Spirit, not only as necessary for prayer, but all spiritual blessings are included in Him. For by the influences of the Holy Spirit, we are brought to know God and ourselves, to repent, believe in, and love Christ. We are made comfortable in this world, and meet for happiness in the next. All of these blessings our heavenly Father is more ready to bestow on every one who asks for them, than an indulgent parent is to give food to a hungry child.

---

348. "Gifts" Merriam-Webster.com 2019 https://www.merriam-webster.com Accessed October 2020
349. "Charisma" Greek for Gifts https://www.biblehub.com Accessed October 2020

And this is the advantage of the prayer of faith, that it quiets and establishes the heart in God.[350]

PRAYER:

Father God, in the name of Jesus, I come before You today to ask for the Holy Spirit to come into my spirit right now, in Jesus' name. Lord, You said in Your Word that He is a gift and that we can pray to receive Him, in Jesus' name. Lord, send Your Holy Spirit to fall on me from the top of my head to the soles of my feet in Jesus' name. Saturate my heart and life with Your supernatural presence, in Jesus' name. Lord, You said if I would ask for the gifts that You would bestow them on me. Lord, send all the gifts that are assigned to my life and ministry right now, in Jesus' name. Lord, help those gifts increase in me, so I can use them for Your glory, in Jesus' name. Lord, fill me up until I overflow. Let my cup overflow and spill over so I can live a life that is pleasing unto You. Lord, continue to help me be all that I can and more so You can get the glory out of my life and ministry in Jesus' name. Lord, I receive the filling of the Holy Ghost that You have placed in my spirit today. I will continue to read Your word, pray, fast, and worship to remain in Your presence all the days of my life in Jesus' name. Amen.

---

350. Luke 11:13 Matthew Henry's Concise Commentary https://www.biblehub.com Accessed October 2020

May 22nd

John 14:27 (AMP) "Peace I leave with you, My (own) peace I now give and bequeath to you. Not as the world gives do I give to you. Do not let your hearts be troubled, neither let them be afraid. (Stop allowing yourselves to be agitated and disturbed; and do not permit yourselves to be fearful and intimidated and cowardly and unsettled.)"

Bequeath in the Merriam Webster Dictionary is to give or leave by will, to hand down, or transmit.[351] The Greek word for bequeath is "hupolimpano," meaning to leave behind, or inheritance.[352]

Jesus is talking to His disciples in the Scripture above. He stated that He would give them a legacy, the gift of peace. This peace is more than a meaningless sound or a wish. He repeats it with empathy. "My" and "speaks" is an actual possession which He imparts to them. "Peace on earth" was the angels' message

---
351. ."Bequeath" Merriam-Webster.com 2019 https://www.merriam-webster.com Accessed October 2020
352. "Hupolimpano" Greek word for Bequeath https://www.biblehub.com Accessed October 2020

when they announced His birth. "Peace to you" was His own greeting when He returned victorious from the grave. He is our peace and this peace was the farewell gift to the disciples because He was returning to sit at the right hand of the Father in heaven. The peace that the world gives is temporal, but the peace that Jesus gives is everlasting. We can have peace in the midst of the storms. Jesus will keep us in perfect peace when our minds are stayed on Him. Peace is a person and His name is Jesus, our Prince of peace. It is a gift so all we have to do is ask for His peace and He will give it to you.[353]

DECLARATIONS

I will not let my heart be troubled or be afraid, but I will put my total trust in You Lord.

Lord, I receive Your perfect peace because my mind is stayed on You.

I will not be agitated and disturbed about anything because God has everything in my life under control.

I will let Jesus take the wheel in my life because He knows what is best for me.

I will not walk in fear or be intimidated because these are the tricks of the enemy.

---

353. John 14:27 Ellicott's Commentary for English Readers https://www.biblehub.com Accessed October 2020

May 22nd

I will walk in boldness and confidence of God instead of walking cowardly and unsettled.

May 23rd

DEUTERONOMY 13:4 (AMP) SAYS, "You shall walk after the Lord your God and (reverently) fear Him, and keep His commandments and obey His voice, and you shall serve Him and cling to Him."

Reverently in the Merriam Webster Dictionary is expressing or characterized by reverence or worshipful.[354] The Greek word for reverently is "eulabeia," meaning caution, fear of God, or piety.[355]

We are to walk after the laws and rules that He has given, both with respect to their moral and civil conduct, and His religious worship. We are to fear Him and keep His commandments through reverential affection for Him. We will fear Him because He is God and we wouldn't want to do anything to hurt or displease Him. We will obey His voice because there is a purpose for His directives. Everything that He commands has a purpose to help build you and others to move forward in the

---

354. "Reverently" Merriam-Webster.com https://www.merriam-webster.com Accessed October 2020
355. "Eulabeia" Greek word for Reverently https://www.biblehib.com Accessed October 2020

May 23rd

calling on our lives. We shall serve Him and cleave (cling) to Him because we know that God has everything for our journey in Him. We should stay in close contact with God in every area of our lives. We shall worship Him in Spirit and in truth.[356]

PRAYER:

Father God, in the name of Jesus, Deuteronomy 13:4 (NLT) says, "Serve only the Lord your God and fear him alone. Obey his commands, listen to his voice, and cling to him." Lord I will only serve You for the rest of my life. And if I should ever stumble, I know that I can repent and get back in right standing with You. Lord, help me to stay on the right track and to obey You. Lord, I put You first in my life and reverence You. I do not want to do anything to grieve the Holy Spirit. Let everything that comes before my eye and ear gates be pure in Jesus' name. Lord, continue to make and mold me like the clay on the potter's wheel. Make me into Who You want me to be in You. Lord, I am thanking You in advance for what is getting ready to happen in my life, in Jesus' name. Amen.

---

356. Deuteronomy 13:4 Gill's Exposition of the Entire Bible https://www.biblehub.com Accessed October 2020

May 24th

Proverbs 17:19 (AMP) says, "He who loves strife and is quarrelsome loves transgression and involves himself in guilt; he who raises high his gateway and is boastful and arrogant invites destruction."

Quarrelsome in the Merriam Webster Dictionary is apt or disposed to quarrel in an often-petty manner, or contentious.[357] The Greek word for quarrelsome is "machomai," meaning to fight, or strive.[358]

If we keep a clear conscience and a quiet mind, we must shun all excitement to anger. A man who affects a style of living above his means goes way to ruin.[359] We must bridle our tongue, walk in the wisdom of God, and not say everything that comes to our mind to say. We do not need to grieve the Holy Spirit with our words, especially if it doesn't line up with holiness and righteousness in God. Strife leads to confusion, which

---

357. "Quarrelsome" Merriam-Webster.com 2019 https://www.merriam-webster.com Accessed October 2020
358. "Machomai" Greek word for Quarrelsome https://www.biblehub.com Accessed October 2020
359. Proverbs 17:19 Matthew Henry's Concise Commentary https://www.biblehub.com Accessed October 2020

May 24th

comes from Satan, the father of confusion. He uses people to get you to act out of character. We must hold our peace and talk to God about the matter. He will vindicate us instead of you trying to avenge yourself. Walk in forgiveness and keep short accounts because anger that is not dealt with turns to bitterness, hatred, strife and many other negative things. It is best to forgive the person so you can keep a pure heart and clean hands before God. Walking in forgiveness frees you up to move forward in your walk with God.

DECLARATIONS

I will not let strife make a victim out of me, but I will move forward in forgiveness.

I will not argue and be petty about things that are beyond my control.

Anger does not produce the righteousness of God in any way.

I will be a peacemaker regardless of how someone else approaches me.

I love what God loves (righteousness, doing what is right) and I hate what God hates (confusion, strife, arguing, sin) according to the Word of God.

Lord, I repent for allowing myself to be drawn out of character by some demonized people.

I will study to be quiet and not try to get the last word in during a confrontation.

May 25th

Psalm 19:14 (AMPC) says, "Let the words of my mouth and the meditation of my heart be acceptable in Your sight, O Lord, my (firm, impenetrable) Rock and my Redeemer."

Impenetrable in the Merriam Webster Dictionary is incapable of being penetrated or pierced.[360] The Greek word for impenetrable is ""astathmitos," meaning impenetrable or imponderable (impossible to access)[361]

"Lord, let all my doings only be righteous. Let the door of my lips be kept. I will utter or think anything evil. Allow the contents of my heart to be purged of anything that is not like You. Lord, You are my strength and Redeemer (deliverer) from sin, death, danger or unrighteousness."[362]

PRAYER:

---
360. "Impenetrable" Merriam-Webster.com 2019 https://www.merriam-webster.com Accessed October 2020
361. "Astathmitos" Greek word for Impenetrable https://www.biblehub.com Accessed October 2020
362. Psalm 19:14 Pulpit Commentary https://www.biblehub.com Accessed October 2020

The 180-Days of Communing with God Daily Devotional

Father, I come before You today to ask that Your will be done in my life. I will meditate on Your word day and night so I will not sin against You. Lord, I will meditate on a Scripture every day until it gets deep in my heart. Lord, purify my mouth, mind, and heart so I can live a righteous and holy lifestyle before You. Help me not to run to evil or do anything that would separate me from Your presence in Jesus' name. Lord, I thank You for Your joy because it is my strength. I thank You for Your supernatural strength that You have given me. Lord, thank You for the peace that passeth all understanding that will guide my heart through Christ Jesus. I will walk away from any unrighteousness and not take the bait of Satan when he tries to lure me away from my first love, who is Jesus, my deliverer. Amen.

May 26th

Psalm 37:4 (AMP) says, "Delight yourself also in the Lord, and He will give you the desires and secret petitions of your heart."

Petitions in the Merriam Webster Dictionary is to make a request to someone, something asked or requested.[363] The Greek word for petitions is "enteuxis," supplication, prayers, intercession, or petitions.[364]

Matthew 6:33 states that if you seek ye first the Kingdom of God and His righteousness then all other things will be added unto you." If we totally surrender to God, live for Him, obey Him and walk uprightly, then we would eat the good of the land. We wouldn't want anything because Jesus would supply our every need and give us our hearts' desires. The blessings of God will run us down and overtake us. We will experience an overflow. An abundance will come so rapidly that we wouldn't have time to catch our breaths. We have to totally depend on Him for everything. God delights in blessing His children that

---

363. "Petitions" Merriam-Webster.com 2019 https://www.merriam-webster.com Accessed October 2020
364."Enteuxis" Greek word for Petitions https://www.biblehub.com Accessed October 2020

obey Him and walk in their callings. He will not withhold anything from you.

DECLARATIONS

If I am obedient and walk uprightly, I will eat the good of the land and never lack anything.

Lord, I will serve You with my whole heart, mind, and soul in Jesus' name.

Jesus, I am going to seek You for everything that I need in my life.

Lord, everything that is on my heart will come to pass in my lifetime here on earth.

Lord, I love the time that I get to spend with You during my quiet time.

Let the words of my mouth be accepted in thy sight O, Lord, my strength and redeemer in Jesus' name.

May 27th

Proverbs 2:7 (AMPC) says, "He hides away sound and godly Wisdom and stores it for the righteous (those who are upright and in right standing with Him); He is a shield to those who walk uprightly and in integrity."

Integrity in the Merriam Webster Dictionary is defined as firm adherence (faithful) to a code of especially moral or artistic values, incorruptibility (incapable of corruption).[365] The Greek word for integrity is "adiaphthoria," meaning soundness, purity, or integrity.[366]

Those who earnestly seek heavenly wisdom will never complain that they have lost their labor; and the freeness of the gift does not do away the necessity of our diligence. Let them seek, and they shall find it; let them ask, and it shall be given them. Observe who are thus favored. They are the righteous, on whom the image of God is renewed, which consists in righ-

---
365. "Integrity" Merriam-Webster.com 2019 https://www.merriam-webster.com Access October 2020
366. "Adiaphthoria" Greek word for Integrity https://www.biblehub.com Accessed October 2020

teousness. If we depend upon God, and seek Him for wisdom, He will enable us to keep the paths of judgment.[367] An old cliché says, "You are too heavenly minded that you are no earthly good," is not correct. This Scripture above clearly states that to be heavenly minded is a good thing. We are to seek heavenly wisdom from God so we can make the best decisions in life. Colossians 3:2 (NLT) says, "Think about the things of heaven, not the things of earth." Think about the inheritance that is reserved in heaven. Take your heart and mind off from everything that is opposite to heavenly things. Christians should not neglect spiritual things for carnal or fleshly things.

PRAYER:

Father God, in the name of Jesus, Proverbs 2:7 (AMP) says, "That You hides away sound and godly Wisdom and stores it for the righteous (those who are upright and in right standing with Him)." Lord, I seek You today for wisdom so that I can make the best decisions in Jesus' name. Lord, remind me always to consult You with every major decision that would affect my future. I always want to be pleasing in Your sight and want my life to line up with Your will, in Jesus' name. To be heavenly minded is a good thing, especially if I am seeking You for the best in every situation that arises, in Jesus' name. Lord, help me to always be in right standing with You, in Jesus' name. Amen.

---

367. Proverbs 2:7 Matthew Henry's Concise Commentary https://www.biblehub.com Accessed October 2020

May 28th

MATTHEW 5:16 (AMP) SAYS, "Let your light shine before men that they may see your moral excellence and your praiseworthy, noble, and good deeds and recognize and honor and praise and glorify your Father Who is in heaven."

Moral Excellence in the Merriam Webster Dictionary is defined as the quality of doing what is right and avoiding what is wrong or virtue.[368] The Greek word for moral excellence is "arete," meaning moral goodness, virtue, uprightness, or a gracious act.[369]

Let your light so shine that men may see your good works and praise God for sending Jesus into the world. They might embrace the faith that you have shown and walked in. They may want to imitate your holy example by being moved to love and serve God and glorify Him with their lives.[370] Let your holy

---
368. "Moral Excellence" Merriam-Webster.com 2019 https://www.merriam-webster.com Accessed October 2020
369. "Arete" Greek word for Moral Excellence https://www.biblehub.com Accessed October 2020
370. Matthew 5:16 Benson Commentary https://www.biblehub.com Accessed October 2020

life, your pure conversation, and your faithful instructions be seen everywhere. Demonstrate that you are a real Christian and let everything that you do lead people back to God so that He can get the glory.[371]

James 1:22 (AMPC) says, "But be doers of the Word (obey the message), and not merely listeners to it, betraying yourselves (into deception by reasoning contrary to the Truth)."

Doers in the Merriam Webster Dictionary is defined as one that takes an active part.[372] The Greek word for doers is "poietes," meaning a maker, doer, carrier out, or performer.[373]

The Scripture above tells us to be doers of the Word instead of hearing it and not doing anything with it. We need to apply God's Word by studying it and getting it deep down in our hearts so we can be transformed by it. Mark 4:15 (NLT) states the seed that fell on the footpath represents those who hear the message, only to have Satan come at once and take it away. We have to be careful and not let the voice of the enemy steal the Word that will change our lives. We must meditate on the Word of God daily and believe Him at His Word because He can do anything but fail.

DECLARATIONS

---

371. Matthew 5:16 Barnes Nots on the Bible https://www.biblehub.com Accessed October 2020
372. "Doers" Merriam-Webster.com 2019 https://www.merriam-webster.com Accessed October 2020
373. "Poietes" Greek word for Doer https://www.biblehub.com Accessed October 2020

May 28th

Lord, I will let my light shine so that people can see You in me.

Lord, I will live a holy and righteous lifestyle, so that I will not cause anyone to stumble in their walk with You.

Lord, let my good deeds shine a light to God instead of me.

Lord, let my light burn bright in dark places, so people can be led to Jesus.

Lord, help me to not walk in fear and hide my light because my light is needed this season.

Lord, Your word declares that faith without works is dead, so I will use my faith to let my light shine bright.

PRAYER:

Father God, in the name of Jesus, I come before You today to ask You to help me retain Your spoken Word so the enemy can't steal it from me. Daily I will meditate on Your Word, so it can get down in my heart and spirit, so the Holy Spirit will have something to bring to my remembrance when I need it. Lord, forgive me for the times that I didn't study the Word like I should. I realize now how important it is to study daily. One thing about the enemy is, he doesn't take a day off and neither should I. Lord, I will apply the Word to every area of my life, so that I can continue to grow closer to You in Jesus' name. Lord, help me be fruitful in my walk with You and do everything You command me to do for Your glory, in Jesus' name. Greater is He that is within us than he that is in the world. Lord, there is nobody greater than You in Jesus' name. Amen.

May 29th

Psalm 119:114 (AMPC) says, "You are my hiding place and my shield; I hope in Your word."

Hiding place in the Merriam Webster Dictionary is a place where someone is hidden or can be hidden.[374] The Hebrew word for Hiding place is "mistar," meaning a secret place or a hiding place.[375]

God is our hiding place. Psalm 91:1 (NLT) says, "Those who live in the shelter of the Most High, will find rest in the shadow of the Almighty." When we are under the umbrella of God, we are safe from the storms of life and He protects us. He has a hedge of protection that surrounds all of His children like a shield and the enemy may form the weapon but it will not prosper. We are walking with victory because we are victorious in Jesus. He is our source and guide. He will release angels to encamp around His children to keep us safe from harm. So, regardless of what we think or feel, there are more with us than

---
374. "Hiding Place" Merriam-Webster.com 2019 https://www.merriam-webster.com Accessed October 2020
375. "Mistar" Hebrew word for Hiding place htps://www.biblehub.com Accessed October 2020

those against us. As long as we stay under the covering of Jesus, we will be safe and secure.

DECLARATIONS

Regardless of what the enemy throws at me, I am victorious in Christ Jesus.

I will continue to dwell in the shelter of the Almighty God.

There is rest for my weary soul in the shadow of God. I thank You for Your supernatural strength.

Lord, I can lay all of my cares and worries at Your feet, so I can rest in knowing that You are taking care of everything in my life.

Lord, You are my shield and buckler that keeps me covered from the storms of life.

I am leaning and depending on God. I will not fall apart when things don't go the way I want them to.

May 30th

Psalm 119:10 (AMP) "With my whole heart have I sought You, inquiring for and of You and yearning for You; Oh, let me not wander or step aside (either in ignorance or willfully) from Your commandments."

Yearning in the Merriam Webster Dictionary is a tender or urgent longing.[376] The Greek word for longing is "orego," meaning to stretch out, to reach after, or to yearn for.[377]

We are to guard our hearts and keep it pure as we seek the Lord wholeheartedly. We must be devoted and holding nothing back when we seek after the Lord. In Luke 15:8-9, a woman lost a precious coin and she diligently searched her whole house until she found it. We are to search for the Lord like we are searching for hidden treasure. Pray and ask Him to keep you on the path of righteousness so you won't wander away from His commandments. It is easy to get distracted. Many times the en-

---

376."Yearning" Merriam-Webster.com 2019 :https//www.merriam-webster.com Accessed October 2020

377."Orego" Greek word for Yearning https://www.biblehub.com Accessed October 2020

emy sends distractions to get us off course. We must keep our focus on the Lord. We need to store God's Word in our hearts so we won't sin against Him.[378]

In the book, "The Power of a Parent's Blessing," parents need to bless their children weekly. Many times the children are only used to being disciplined or corrected throughout the week. Take at least one day on the weekend to speak blessing over them. This will be a good time to start the weekly blessing. Many Jewish families are doing it over their children. Most of their children have become very successful. Here are a few examples of how to get started:

1. Have a meal together with everyone gathered around the dinner table.

2. After the meal, initiate a time of repentance and blessing. No one can receive blessings when carrying an emotional wound from the one seeking to bless them. Address any offenses, perceived or real. Look into Your child's eyes so you can discern any offenses or unhealed emotional wounds. If you discern any offense or emotional trauma, distance yourself from your child. Repentance is needed. Seek repair by acknowledging the offense and repenting for hurting them.

3. Bless each family member. Here is an example of a blessing over your children:

<u>May the Lor</u>d protect and defend you.

---

378. Psalm 119:10 https://www.astudyinginpsalm119.blogspot.com Accessed October 2020

May 30th

May He always shield you from shame.
May God grant you and bless you with long lives.
May you be like Ruth and Like Esther (girl).
May you be like Issac and Joseph (boy).
May you be deserving of praise.
Strengthen them, O 'Lord.
May the Lord preserve you from pain.
Favor them, Oh Lord, with happiness and peace.
May God give you spouses that will love and care for you.
Oh Lord, hear our prayer, Amen.

The family blessing extends beyond your children. It is also included for your spouse. It only takes a few minutes every day to do it with your spouse. Face each other with your eyes open because you need to look into each other's eyes to convey blessing not only in words but also with your facial expressions.

Here are several examples that will help you get started. Both of you declare the blessing on each other.

1. Repenting- if God shows you that you have wounded or sinned against your spouse in the previous 24 hours.
2. Thanking God for your spouse (acknowledging the qualities you appreciate about him/her).
3. Pronouncing the blessing over your spouse daily.
4. May Your heart always be at peace.
5. May your mind always be alert and learning.
6. May your strength match the length of your days.
7. May God keep you in His love at all times.

8. I bless your spiritual life, that you may continue to worship God in spirit and truth.

9. May the Lord bless you and keep you.

10. May the Lord's face shine upon you and be gracious to you.

You are speaking life into their present and future. Additionally, you are expressing the deep love that you have for them and showing that your family is a priority above all obligations.[379]

PRAYER:

Father, in the name of Jesus, I come today to seek You diligently with all of my heart, mind and soul. Lord, I will seek You while You may be found. I need Your presence in my life every day. I need You for everything that concerns my family and I. Lord, I admit that distractions get me off balance, but You always send Your Word by Your servants to help me get back on track, in Jesus' name. Lord, I am yearning for more of You, in Jesus' name. Lord, send Your fire to stir me up and get my zeal back for You, in Jesus' name. The more I seek You, the more I can hear You. It is vital that I hear from You in this season, in Jesus' name. Lord, help me to not wander from Your commandments, in Jesus' name. Amen.

---

379. . The Power of a Parent's Blessing by Craig Hill Accessed October 2020

May 31st

1 Peter 2:9 (AMPC) says, "But you are a chosen race, a royal priesthood, a dedicated nation, (God's) own, purchased, special people, that you may set forth the wonderful deeds and display the virtues and perfections of Him Who called you out of darkness into His marvelous light,"

Dedicated in the Merriam Webster Dictionary is devoted to a cause, ideal, or purpose, or zealous.[380] The Greek word for dedicated is "egkainia," meaning dedication or renewal.[381]

Lola Hardaway states in her book, "Tricked into Sickness," that the Spirit of Might is one of the seven spirits of God. As you read the Word of God, it is being embedded into your mind and spirit. You are pouring the Spirit of Might into your very own spirit, the real you. You are becoming more like God and empowering your spirit to develop more into the likeness of His Spirit. The more you pour God's Word into yourself, the more of His power you receive. Now the Spirit of Holiness be-

---

380. "Dedicated" Merriam-Webster.com 2019 https://www.merriam-webster.com Accessed October 2020
381. "Egkainia" Greek word for Dedicated https://www.biblehub.co, Accessed October 2020

comes more profound in you. Now you are in a place where only Godliness resides because His Spirit has been infused into yours. No more fears, doubts, and compromise. Only God because God is love. You are now totally embodied with love, and it becomes a robust of love. All of God's Word is pure and real. Now, it's all interlocked within you, ready to move forward and demonstrate God to the world. It is no longer you but the Christ in you. The Word in you impregnates you, and when brought forth, it enables you to do exactly what Jesus did and more.[382]

PRAYER:

Father God, in the name of Jesus, I bring Your Word back to You. 1 Peter 2:9 says, "But ye are a chosen generation, a royal priesthood, a holy nation, a peculiar people; that ye should shew forth the praises of him who has called you out of darkness into his marvelous light." Lord, I now understand why I haven't fit in because You have made me to be unique or peculiar. You have lifted up a standard against being mediocre in my walk with You. Lord, You have made me to stand out and be a demonstrator of Your Word and Your grace in Jesus' name. Lord, Your Word is pure and real. I will continue to move forward in You. Your Word declares that we have the same power that raised Jesus from the dead living on the inside of us. So, we will do greater works than Jesus while He walked on this earth. Amen.

---

382. Tricked Into Sickness by Loa Hardway Accessed October 2020

June 1st

Psalm 119:30 (AMPC) says, "I have chosen the way of truth and faithfulness. Your ordinances have I set before me."

Ordinances in the Merriam Webster Dictionary is defined as an authoritative decree or direction, order.[383] The Greek word for ordinances is "dikaioma," meaning a righteous deed, a thing pronounced by God to be righteous, and instance of perfect righteousness.[384]

Christ is the way and truth. He is the true way to God and to eternal happiness. To choose Him is to choose the good part, which shall never be taken away. When the choice is made, not by the free will of man, as left to itself, but under the influence and by the direction of the Spirit and grace of God. "I will look to study Your Word continually and get it in my spirit so I will not sin against You. Your Word is a lamp unto my feet and light unto my path. That light is the way to righteousness. I will walk

---
383. "Ordinances" Merriam-Webster.com 2019 https://www.merriam-webster.com Accessed October 2020
384. "Dikaiomai" Greek word for Ordinances https://www.biblehub.com Accessed October 2020

worthy of the calling of God on my life and apply His Word so I can please Him.[385]

DECLARATIONS

The Holy Spirit is the Spirit of truth, and He will lead and guide me in all truth.

I will stay on the narrow path to Jesus and eternal life.

Jesus is the way, truth and Life. No man comes to the Father unless they come through Jesus.

I will live in the truth of the Word every day of the year.

I will keep pursuing and chasing God because I need Him and He is the only one that can help me.

I know that God is moving and working things out for my family and me in the background, in Jesus' name.

---

385. Psalm 119:30 https://www.study.light.org Accessed October 2020

June 2nd

Psalm 91:6 (AMPC) says, "Nor of the pestilence that stalks in darkness, nor of the destruction and sudden death that surprise and lay waste at noonday."

Pestilence in the Merriam Webster Dictionary is defined as a contagious or infectious epidemic disease that is virulent and devastating.[386] The Greek word for pestilence is "loimos," meaning plagues, pestilence, or a pest.[387]

When we are abiding in the secret place with God, He will protect us from the deadly pestilence. God is the One that is protecting us from COVID-19. We are decreeing and declaring His word over ourselves and our families. Great security is promised to the believers in the midst of danger from sicknesses and diseases. Some may even be creeping around in the night, but God will protect and keep us covered. God will dispatch His angels to stand around your bedside to protect you. He who fully

---
386. "Pestilence" Merriam-Webster.com 2019 https://www.merriam-webster.com Accessed October 2020
387. ."Loimos" Greek word for Pestilence https://www.biblehub.com Accessed October 2020

puts their trust in God should not be afraid. God is our protector. We don't have anything to worry about. Continue to follow the rules of the government and wear your masks when you go into crowded places. Jesus was whipped with Thirty nine lashes for every sickness and disease in existence . Also, taking communion is a remedy for the COVID-19. When you eat the bread, you are taking healing in your body and when you drink the juice, it represents His blood. His blood redeemed us back to God. We can accept Jesus's finished works on the cross.

1 Corinthians 11:25 (NLT) says, "In the same way, he took the cup of wine after supper saying, 'This cup is the new covenant between God and his people---an agreement confirmed with my blood. Do this in remembrance of me as often (frequently, many times) as you drink it.'"

PRAYER:

Father God, in the name of Jesus, we come before You today to thank You for watching out for Your people during the pestilence in Jesus' name. Lord, send Your warring angels to surround and fight for me so I don't get sick from COVID-19 or any other contagious diseases, in Jesus' name. Lord, I pray Psalm 91 or the prayer of protection over myself, my family, and any other person susceptible to contracting this disease. Lord, cover us under the blood of Jesus so nothing evil can come near our dwelling. You will give Your angels charge over us to keep us in all of thy ways. Lord, if we may have some symptoms of the disease, we cast down, bind all of the symptoms and send them back to the abyss in Jesus' name. Satan, the

June 2nd

blood of Jesus, is against you. You will not attack the children of God's bodies with any symptoms or illnesses in Jesus' name. I loose the healing virtue of Jesus to saturate everyone from the top of their heads to the soles of their feet in Jesus' name. Lord, send Your Holy Ghost fire to burn up all traces of the virus out of their bodies and lungs in Jesus' name. I decree and declare healing to all of their bodies in Jesus' name. Amen.

June 3rd

Job 8:7 (AMP) says, "And though your beginning was small, yet your latter end would greatly increase."

Latter in the Merriam Webster Dictionary is defined as situated or occurring nearer to the end of something than to the beginning.[388] The Greek word for latter is "husteros," meaning later, last, or latter.[389]

The Scripture above talks about when you might not have enough money to do anything that you need when starting small. You were robbing Peter to pay Paul, as the old cliché would say. You never really have enough of anything, but you have been faithful to God and living a life that is pleasing to Him. Now God wants to reward you for your faithfulness to Him. He wants to bless everything that you put your hand to. He wants to give you double for your trouble. You will have double in every area of your life. Your barns will be filled. You

---
388. "Latter" Merriam-Webster.com 2019 https://www.merriam-webster.com Accessed October 2020
389. "Husteros" Greek word for Latter https://www.biblehub.com Accessed October 2020

will have blessings chasing you down from everywhere. You will know that without a shadow of a doubt, God is doing it and not yourself. God will give you witty ideas, inventions, and new streams of income to make the extra finances that you will need so your home will be blessed. He will give you more than enough. You will have an overflow to bless others and other ministries. God will wait until you are older to even use you for ministry. Everyone needs to know that they are never too old for God to use them for His glory. God will use everything that you have ever gone through in your life. Nothing shall be wasted. He will use it all. You experienced what you went through for an eternal purpose and He will get the glory out of it.

DECLARATIONS

Lord, Your Word declares that my latter shall be greater than my beginning.

Lord, thank You for letting me know that everything that I have gone through in my life was for a purpose.

I will not continue to dwell on my age because You can use me at any age for Your glory.

There will be glory after these trials and tribulations that I am going through right now.

I am getting ready to go from the land of not enough, just enough, to the land of more than enough.

I will not despise small beginnings because what is coming is going to blow my mind.

June 4th

Psalm 46:10 (AMPC) says, "Let be and be still, and know (recognize and understand) that I am God. I will be exalted among the nations! I will be exalted in the earth."

Recognize in the Merriam Webster Dictionary is defined as to acknowledge acquaintance with.[390] The Greek word for recognize is to know exactly, to recognize, discern, or come to know by directing my attention to him.[391]

This verse above has been a comfort to many believers in Christ. Jesus is the defense and our defender against the enemies of our souls. All who rest in Him find courage and strength. He is our refuge from the storms of life and our shelter in the midst of oppression. We are called to be still and to know that He is God. He will never fail. He will be glorified throughout the whole earth. God is the supreme creator of all and Commander of the armies of heaven. He redeems us by faith in the

---

390. "Recognize" Merriam-Webster.com 2019 https://www.merriam-webster.com Accessed October 2020
391. "Epiginosko" Greek for Recognize https://www.biblehub.com Accessed October 2020

shed blood of Christ, and will never leave us nor forsake us. We are to rest peacefully in the truth of His Word, and be still in His holy presence. We are to know in our heart, by faith with thanksgiving, that He is the Lord, our God who pardons all our iniquities and heals all our diseases. He redeems our life from the pit and crowns us with lovingkindness and compassion.[392]

PRAYER:

Father God, in the name of Jesus, I come to You today because Your Word declares for me to be still and know that You are God. I am going to be still and wait on You to move in my life. In the meantime, I will continue to study Your Word, pray, fast, worship, and prepare myself for the calling that is on my life. Lord, I ask that You would give me Your peace that passeth all understanding while I wait so I will not get anxious in my waiting in Jesus' name. Lord, I realize that peace is a precious gift that You give to Your people in Jesus' name. Lord, I will pray over my prophetic words and believe that in Your timing that they will be manifested in my life, in Jesus' name. Lord, thank You for sustaining me in the wilderness and in the desert. Lord, increase my faith in the waiting period of my life. Your Word declares that without faith, it is impossible to please God. Lord, I know that You have everything under control in my life and I do not have anything to worry about concerning it. I know that with You, I will have a future and an expected end in Jesus' name. Amen.

---

[392]. Psalm 46:10 https://www.dailyverse.knowing-jesus.com Accessed October 2020

June 5th

Matthew 5:9 (AMPC) says, "Blessed (enjoying enviable happiness, spiritually prosperous—with life-joy and satisfaction in God's favor and salvation, regardless of their outward conditions) are the makers and maintainers of peace, for they shall be called the sons of God!"

Enviable in the Merriam Webster Dictionary is defined as highly desirable.[393] The Greek word for enviable is "makarismos," meaning a declaration of blessedness.[394]

The Scripture above talks about people who are of a peaceable temper and endeavor to promote peace in others. Study to be quiet and be peaceable with all men. Don't sow seeds of discord between your fellow brothers or sisters in Christ. We should avoid contention and labor to extinguish it when it arises. We must handle our differences, restore peace whenever it is broken, and preserve it. We shall be owned by God as His

---
393. "Enviable" Merriam-Webster.com 2019 https://www.merriam-webster.com Accessed October 2020
394. "Makarismos" Greek word for Enviable https://ww.biblehub.com Accessed October 2020

genuine children, by reason of their great likeness to Him for He is the God of peace and love. If peacemakers are blessed, then woe to the peace breakers. The peacemakers are happy. They love, desire, and delight in peace.[395]

DECLARATIONS

I will be a peacemaker and I don't have to defend myself because God will defend me.

I will not get out of character by demonized people.

Blessed are the peacemakers because they will see God.

I will hold my peace and let the Lord fight my battles.

I will not allow my flesh to get the best of me and get me in trouble with God.

God will prepare a table before me in the presence of my enemies.

I will walk in agape love toward those who want to despitefully mistreat me.

---

395. Matthew 5:9 Benson Commentary https://www.biblehub.com Accessed October 2020

June 6th

Colossians 2:9-10 (AMPC) states, "For in Him the whole fullness of Deity (the Godhead) continues to dwell in bodily form (giving complete expression of the divine nature). 10. And you are in Him, made full and having come to fullness of life (in Christ you too are filled with the Godhead-Father, Son, and Holy Spirit—and reach full spiritual stature). And He is the Head of all rule and authority (of every angelic principality and power)."

Godhead in the Merriam Webster Dictionary is defined as divine nature or essence, God, the nature of God especially as existing in three persons.[396] The Greek word for Godhead is "theotes," meaning deity, or Godhead in the incarnated Christ.[397]

The fullness of the Godhead gives its complete expression of the divine nature in Christ. Jesus is the exact image of God and His fullness dwells in Him. This should trump everything.

---
396. "Godhead" Merriam-Webster.com 2019 https://www.merriam-webster.com Accessed October 2020
397. "Theotes" Greek word for Godhead https://www.biblehub.com Accessed October 2020

2 Corinthians 10:5 states, "we demolish arguments and every pretension that sets itself up against the knowledge of God, and we take captive every thought to make it obedient to Christ." We have been brought into the fullness of Christ, filled with Him living in us, so we will continue to experience this saturation. Christ is the head over every power and authority. If we hold onto His teachings, we are His disciples indeed. To be free, we have to know the truth and remain in it, which comes through renewing our minds in the Word of God and knowing His will concerning our lives. We have all been given the fullness in Christ through His divine nature.[398]

PRAYER:

Father God, in the name of Jesus, I thank You for Your divine nature that lives on the inside of me to lead and guide me in all truth. I will not adopt the world philosophies or any legalistic laws because they cloud the true concept of who You are, in Jesus' name. Lord, help me turn off anything that goes against Your Word concerning Your divine nature and the Godhead. I know that in Christ dwells ALL the fullness of the Godhead, and the fullness of God's nature dwells bodily within You Jesus also. I will not participate in legalistic traditions of men because they are foolish and are false teachings. I want to come into a true understanding of Christ because, in Him, I have been made complete. So, Father God, I thank You for this wonderful truth that Christ is all that I need. He is my complete sufficiency in all things, in Jesus' name. Amen.

---

398. Colossians 2:9-10 https://www.joblog.net Accessed October 2020

June 7th

PSALM 91:14 (AMPC) SAYS, "Because he has set his love upon Me, therefore will I deliver him; I will set him on high, because he knows and understands My name (has a personal knowledge of My mercy, love, and kindness—trusts and relies on Me, knowing I will never forsake him, no, never)."

Personal knowledge in www.thelawdictionary.org is the knowledge possessed by any individual. It is usually accumulated through observation or personal experiences.[399] The Greek word for personal knowledge is "gnosis," meaning doctrine, wisdom, knowledge, or knowledge gleaned first hand (personal).[400]

Those who rightfully know God will set their love upon Him. They, by prayer, constantly call upon Him. His promise is that He will in due time deliver the believer out of trouble, and in the meantime be with them in trouble. The Lord will manage all His worldly concerns, and preserve His life on earth, so long

---

399. "Personal Knowledge" https://www.thelawdictionary.org Accessed October 2020
400. "Gnosis" Greek word for Personal knowledge https://www.biblehub.com Accessed October 2020

as it shall be good for Him. For encouragement in this he looks unto Jesus. He shall live long enough until He has done the work He was sent to do, and is ready for heaven. Who would wish to live a day longer than God has some work to do, either by Him or upon Him?[401]

DECLARATIONS

By prayer and supplication, I will constantly call upon God to help in the time of trouble.

God, You are a life preserver because I will live a long and prosperous life doing everything that You have called me to do.

Because I rightfully know God, I will set my love upon Him daily in Jesus' name.

Lord, thank You for delivering me and setting me free from my enemies and the plots, plans, and ploys of Satan.

Lord, I understand and have personal knowledge of Your name and who You are to me.

Lord, thank You for never leaving or forsaking me, but being with me until the end of this world.

---

401. Psalm 91:14 Matthew Henry's Concise Commentary https://www.biblehub.com Accessed October 2020

June 8th

Psalm 91:9 (AMPC) says, "Because you have made the Lord your refuge, and the Most High your dwelling place."

Dwelling place in the Merriam Webster Dictionary is the place where someone lives.[402] The Greek word for dwelling place is "mone" meaning lodging, dwelling place, room, abode, or an abiding.[403]

Whatever happens, nothing shall hurt the believer. Though trouble and affliction befall, it shall come, not for his hurt, but for good. Though for the present it is not joyous but grievous.[404] Whatever the devil meant for evil, God will turn it around for your good. The enemy cannot stop anything in your life. He may cause delays but God will make sure you get where He is wanting to take you. The enemy cannot curse what or who God says is blessed. The only power the devil has over the believer

---
402. "Dwelling Place" Merriam-Webster.com 2019 https://www.merriam-webster.com Accessed October 2020
403. "Mone" Greek word for Dwelling Place https://www.biblehub.com Accessed October 2020
404. Psalm 91:9 Matthew Henry's Concise Commentary https://www.biblehub.com Accessed October 2020

is what they give him. He has no teeth. He has to gum everything. We have power over the enemy and he is under our feet. Pick up your feet. As an act of faith say, "Devil, you are under my feet where you are going to stay. I will not be intimidated by you any longer. God has me covered in the secret place and nothing by any means shall hurt me."

PRAYER:

Father God, in the name of Jesus, I need You to be my one and only dwelling place from the storms that are raging in my life. Lord, help me to stop worrying about things that I have no control over. Lord, it seems hard at times to give You all of my concerns, but I know if I want to have perfect peace, then I must release what is troubling me to You. There is no need for me to be up tossing and turning at night without efficient sleep because I am stressing about something that only You can fix in my life. Lord, You are my shelter from the storms in my life. Lord, I release all my fears to You about COVID-19. Psalm 91:10-11 says, "There shall no evil befall thee, neither shall any plague come nigh thy dwelling. 11. For He shall give His angels charge over thee, to keep thee in thy ways." These Scriptures reassure me that You have my whole household covered from the COVID-19. Lord, thank You for having Your angels to watch over my family and me to keep us safe and secure. Lord, I feel peace, joy, love when I am in Your refuge and I know that I don't have anything to fear as long as I am in You and You are in me in Jesus' name. Amen.

June 9th

John 8:36 (AMPC) says, "So if the Son liberates you (makes you free men), then you are really and unquestionably free."

Unquestionably in the Merriam Webster Dictionary is not questionable or indisputable.[405] The Greek word for unquestionably is "anamisvititos," meaning incontestable or absolute.[406]

If the Son sets you free, you will be free indeed. Freedom is the cry of every man, woman, boy, and girl. Jesus wants to set every one of us free. We have to come willingly and give our lives to Him. Expect the finished works that He did on the cross. You shall know the truth (Jesus) and the truth (Jesus) shall make you free. We must come into the realization of knowing the truth about the unique person and saving work of the Lord Jesus Christ as a firm belief, which is outlined in the God breathed Scriptures. Many have asked what must they do to be saved? You have to believe in the Lord Jesus Christ and you will be saved. Believe in Jesus for the forgiveness of

---

405. "Unquestionably Merriam-Webster.com 2019 https://www.merriam-webster.com Accessed October 202
406. "Anamfivolos" https://www.wordhippo.com Accessed October 2020

sins, the salvation of the soul, and life everlasting. Believing the truth will set you free. Every man is born dead in sin and everyone lives in the bondage to sin. We were slaves to sin and entrapped by it until we gave our lives to Jesus. The only way that we can be set free from the slavery of sin, Satan, death and the curse of the Law is to know Christ personally. Know Him as your personal Savior because He willingly died in our place to pay the price for sin. So, we can now be set free from the slavery of sin through a relationship with Jesus.[407]

DECLARATIONS

Through Jesus' sacrifice, I now can be made righteous through His finished work on the cross.

I take authority over every foul spirit that tries to come and oppress me. You have no legal right to attack my body in Jesus' name.

God is a God of love, power and authority.

I will walk in the authority that Jesus says that I have in Jesus' name.

I will praise and worship God and get in His presence so the harvest can hit my life like never before.

Lord, I thank You for ordering my footsteps and the hedge of protection that You have surrounding me.

---

407. John 8:36 https://www.dailyverse.knowing-jesus.com Accessed October 2020

June 10th

*P*ROVERBS 1:5 (AMPC) SAYS, "The wise also will hear and increase in learning, and the person of understanding will acquire skill and attain to sound counsel (so that he may be able to steer his course rightly)."

Counsel in the Merriam Webster Dictionary is advice given especially as a result of consultation.[408] The Greek word for counsel is "sumboulion," meaning a body of advisers, consultation, advice, resolution, or decree.[409]

In the Scripture above, Solomon gives his children a directive, which comes with this wisdom. Once one is wise and increases in knowledge, they now have a responsibility to pass that knowledge on. The ideal motivation of seeking wisdom is not so much obtaining it for ourselves, but attaining a position to guide others. Those who have the inherent responsibility to guide, or give "wise counsel." We should not bottle up our wis-

---
408.. "Counsel" Merriam-Webster.com 2019 https://www.merriam-webster.com Accessed October 2020
409. "Sumboulion" Greek word for Counsel https://www.biblehub.com Accessed October 2020

dom and hide it. We must train others to live wisely, especially dealing with our own children. We desperately want to be sure they do not make the same mistakes we did. We ask them to pay attention to our advice, which is based on a tough, or hard experience.[410]

PRAYER:

Father God, in the name of Jesus, James 1:5 (NLT) says, "If you need wisdom, ask our generous God, and he will give it to you. He will not rebuke you for asking." Lord, I am asking that you will give me godly wisdom to make the right decisions in my life. I want to help as many people make the right decisions in their life so they won't go through the same hardships that I went through. Lord, help my children to understand that I do not want them to follow in my footsteps. That is why I try to warn them of the pitfalls before they get to them. Most of the time, my child kicks against the advice so I will in turn step back and let them go through the same things that I experienced. Lord, help them to take and receive sound doctrine from wise people who are Holy Spirit filled. Lord, I thank You for the gift of godly wisdom instead of worldly wisdom. Godly wisdom is sound counsel and worldly wisdom is a counsel of foolish things, in Jesus' name. Amen.

---

[410]. Proverbs 1:5 https://www.bibleref.com Accessed October 2020

June 11th

Proverbs 1:33 (AMPC) says, "But whoso hearkens to me (Wisdom) shall dwell securely and in confident trust and shall be quiet, without fear or dread of evil."

Wisdom in the Merriam Webster Dictionary is ability to discern inner qualities and relationships, insight, a wise attitude, belief, or course of action.[411] The Greek word for wisdom is "sophia," meaning wisdom, insight, skill (human or divine), or intelligence.[412]

Peace and safety, or fear and destruction? Lady Wisdom offers you a good life. It is astounding to see how men's lives differ by their foolish choices and God's judgment. Peace and protection are precious; they can be yours starting today. The choice is yours. God offers you wisdom in His word. If you ignore or reject it, He will laugh and mock you when you fear and calamities come, and they both will come. He will desert you

---

411. Wisdom" Merriam-Webster.com 2019 https://www.merriam-webster.com Accessed October 2020
412.. "Sophia" Greek word for Wisdom https://www.biblehub.com Accessed October 2020

and not hear your cries, even when you pray to Him for help according to Proverbs 1:24-32. If you love and exalt wisdom, God will bless you with tranquility (peace). Consequences for foolishness are hard. Choose wisdom! Peace is precious and it is a good life. It is happiness, calm, peace, safety and it is gotten only one way but through two doors. 1. Wisdom, only those who fear God and keep His commandments, which is true in wisdom, will have peace. 2. The blessed results of right decisions and God's supernatural favor.[413]

DECLARATIONS

If anybody needs wisdom, let them ask of God, who gives it to them generously.

I will choose to read the Word of God for the wisdom that I need on a particular matter.

Peace is a gift. Do not let anyone or anything steal it from you.

In peace, there is calm, happiness, safety and all of these can only be gotten from a personal relationship with Jesus.

When you walk in obedience to God, you will walk in peace and safety in Him.

I will stay in the precious will of God because that is the right thing to do, in Jesus' name.

---

413. Proverbs 1:33 https://www.letgodbetrue.com Accessed October 2020

June 11th

In God and in the secret place the enemy cannot come inside the glory.

June 12th

Isaiah 41:10 (AMPC) says, "Fear not (there is nothing to fear), for I am with you; do not look around you in terror and be dismayed, for I am your God. I will strengthen and harden you to difficulties, yes, I will help you; yes, I will hold you up and retain you with My (victorious) right hand of rightness and justice."

Retain in the Merriam Webster Dictionary is to keep possession or use, to hold secure and intact.[414] The Greek word for retain is "krateo," meaning to be strong, rule, or hold fast.[415]

"Fear not" appears in the Bible 366 times. One for each day of the year. Plus one for leap year. The words of encouragement are spoken to us by the Creator of the Universe. He is the One who tells His children not to fear, nor to be discouraged, because He is our God and that should be sufficient. We should simply take Him at His Word. Faith in His Word is what God desires for us all. We are warned that unless we trust His Word,

---

414. "Retain" Merriam-Webster.com 2019 https://www.merriam-webster.com Accessed October 2020
415. "Krateo" Greek word for Retain https://www.biblehub.com Accessed October 2020

June 12th

we can't please Him. God is gracious to us because He knows that the cares of this life have us in doubt and, sometimes, discouragement. Christ is our righteousness; our ever-present help in the time of trouble. Christ's grace is always sufficient for all our needs. He is our covering, and if God be for us then who can be against us? Christ and you are more than the majority on any given day of the week.[416]

PRAYER:

Father God, in the name of Jesus, Your Word declares that You did not give us the spirit of fear, but of power and love and a sound mind. Lord, I do realize that the enemy is trying to get me to doubt what You have spoken over my life. Lord, I will continue to study and read Your Word so that my faith can start to build up in Jesus' name. Lord, I believe but help my unbelief as well in Jesus' name. Lord, You are our righteousness and an ever-present help in the time of trouble. Lord, I know that You love me without a shadow of doubt, because You sent Your Son to die for me so that I could have a right to be redeemed back to God in Jesus' name. Lord, You said in Your Word that Your grace was sufficient. It was my strength in the time of weakness. You also said in Your Word to let the weak say they are strong, and I am strong in You Lord. Thank You for taking me from strength to strength, from faith to faith, and from glory to glory, in Jesus' name. Amen.

---

416. Isaiah 41:10 https://www.dailyverse.knowing-jesus.com Accessed October 2020

June 13th

Proverbs 17:3 (AMP) says, "The refining pot is for silver and the furnace for gold, but the Lord tries the hearts."

Refining in the Merriam Webster Dictionary is to free (something, such as metal, sugar, oil) from impurities or unwanted material.[417] The Greek word for refining is "puroo," meaning to set on fire, to burn, or refined.[418]

God takes His people through a refiner's fire to purify us. When the storms of life come and turn up the heat on us, then everything that is not good falls off and leaves the polished, purified renewed spirit. Man looks at our outer appearance but God looks and tries our hearts. God wants His people to have pure hearts and clean hands. We are to walk in love with all people showing His love so the world would believe that God sent Jesus. The refiner's fire will get lying, hatred, unforgiveness, bitterness, and many other negative emotions out of our

---

417. "Refining Merriam-Webster.com 2019 https://www.merriam-webster.com Accessed October 2020
418. "Puroo" Greek word for Refining https://www.biblehub.com Accessed October 2020

hearts. So, we can give other people the same grace that God has given us.

DECLARATIONS

I will continue to go through the refiner's fire, so that I can come out as pure gold.

O' create in me a clean heart and renew a right spirit in me.

I will have clean hands and a pure heart, and will not lift up my soul to that which is false and does not swear deceitfully.

Blessed are the pure in heart, for they shall see God.

"For thou, O God, hast proved us, thou hast tried, as silver is tried.

June 14th

Proverbs 17:17 (AMPC) says, "A friend loves at all times, and is born, as is a brother, for adversity."

Adversity in the Merriam Webster Dictionary is a state or instance of serious or continued difficulty or misfortune.[419] The Greek word for adversity is "sugkakoucheomai," meaning to endure adversity with(pass), or suffer ill-treatment with.[420]

A real friend loves his friend in prosperity and adversity. He is more than a friend in time of need. He is a brother, as affectionate and as trusty as one connected by the closet ties of relationship. Crisis tests a friend as fire is to gold.[421] Jesus is a friend that sticketh closer than any brother. He will be with us in prosperity and adversity. Jesus is with us all the time as long as we are with Him, serving, praising, worshipping, and reading His Word. Jesus will never leave us. He will be with us until the

---

419. "Adversity" Merriam-Webster.com 2019 https://www.merriam-webster.com Accessed October 2020
420. "Sugkakoucheomai" Greek word for Adversity https://www.biblehub.com Accessed October 2020
421. Proverbs 17:17 Matthew Henry's Concise Commentary https://www.biblehub.com Accessed October 2020

June 14th

end of this age. True friends don't just walk off from you when things are going bad in your life, but they will help you get back on your feet so both of you can have more than enough to live off of and teach you how to keep prospering so you can get out of poverty.

PRAYER:

Father God, in the name of Jesus, I come to You today to thank You for being a friend that will stick closer to me than any brother. Lord, thank You for giving me ideas and witty inventions to have regular income coming into my home. I can continue to sow seed into the Kingdom of God in Jesus' name. Lord, Your Word declares that You give seed to the sower and bread to the eater. Lord, I thank You for teaching me about being a good steward over my finances, so I don't end up eating all of my seed instead of sowing it. Lord, thank You for the favor that You have placed on my life. I can now start being successful in new ventures because Your stamp of approval is on everything that I set my hand to do, in Jesus' name. Your Word declares that everything that I put my hand to do would prosper and be a good source of income for family and me in Jesus' name. Amen.

June 15th

Philippians 2:6 (AMPC) says, "Who, although being essentially one with God and in the form of God (possessing the fullness of the attributes which make God God), did not think this equality with God was a thing to be eagerly grasped or retained."

Essentially in the Merriam Webster Dictionary is in essence, fundamentally used to identify or stress the basic or essential character or nature of a person or thing or to say that a description is basically true or accurate.[422] The Greek word for essentially is "ouiastika," which means essentially.[423]

Notice the two natures of Christ: His Divine nature and human nature. Who being in the form of God, partaking the Divine nature, as the eternal and only-begotten Son of God. His human nature herein He became like us in all things except sin. Thus low, of His own will, He stooped from the glory. He had life with the Father before the world. Christ's two states, of humiliation and exaltation, are noticed. Christ not only took upon

---

422. "Essentially" Merriam-Webster.com 2019 https://www.merriam-webster.com Accessed October 2020
423. "ousiastika" Greek word for Essentially https://www.biblehub.com Accessed October 2020

June 15th

Himself the likeness and fashion, or form of a man, but of one in a low state; not appearing in splendor. His whole life was a life of poverty and suffering. The lowest step was His dying the death of the cross. The death of a malefactor (commits a crime) and a slave; exposed to public hatred and scorn. The exaltation of Christ's human nature, in union with the divine. At the name of Jesus, not the mere sound of the word, but the authority of Jesus, all should pay solemn respect. It is to the glory of God the Father, to confess that Jesus Christ is Lord. For it is His will that all men should honor the Father.[424]

DECLARATIONS

Jesus has given us His greatest and most precious promises, so that through them, we may participate in His divine nature.

I will escape the world's corruption caused by human desires, if I cling to the promises of God.

His divine power has given to us all things that pertain to life and godliness.

Eye has not seen, nor ear heard, nor have entered into the heart of man the things which God has prepared for those who love Him.

We are the children of God. Therefore, the world does not know us.

---

424. Philippians 2:6 Matthew Henry's Concise Commentary https://www.biblehub.com Accessed October 2020

June 16th

Hebrew 12:11 (AMPC) says, "For the time being, no discipline brings joy, but seems grievous and painful; but afterwards it yields a peaceable fruit of righteousness to those who have been trained by it (a harvest of fruit which consists in righteousness-in conformity to God's will in purpose, thought, and action, resulting in right living and right standing with God)."

Discipline in the Merriam Webster Dictionary is control gained by enforcing obedience or order, or self-control.[425] The Greek word for discipline is "paideuo," chastening, chastisement, instruction, or nurture.[426]

The Father of our souls never willingly grieves nor afflicts His children. It is always for our profit. Our whole life here is a state of childhood, and imperfect as to spiritual things. Therefore we must submit to the discipline of such a state. When we come to a perfect state, we shall be fully reconciled to all

---

425. "Discipline" Merriam-Webster.com https://www.merriam-webster.com Accessed October 2020
426. "Paideia" Greek word for Discipline https://www.biblehub.com Accessed October 2020

June 16th

God's chastisement of us now. God's correction is not condemnation. The chastening may be borne with patience, and greatly promote holiness. Let us then learn to consider the afflictions brought on us by the malice of men, as corrections sent by our wise and gracious Father, for our spiritual good.[427]

PRAYER:

Father God, in the name of Jesus, I come before You today asking that You give me Your Supernatural Strength to continue to go through this trial that I am going through right now. Lord, You said that You wouldn't put more on us than we were able to bear Lord, this load has gotten really heavy and I don't know if I can take it anymore. I need You to come to my rescue and lift this load off me. I realize that what I am dealing with is because I disobeyed You. I chose to do it my way instead of how You instructed, so now I am being chastened by You. Lord, forgive me for doing things in my own strength instead of waiting on You to move and position me. Lord, I know this lesson is a hard one, but I just need You to help me make it through it. I want to learn my lesson the first time so that I do not have to repeat the process again, in Jesus' name. Lord, thank You for forgiving me and giving me another chance to get Your instructions right this time, in Jesus' name. Thank You for the fruit that is produced out of the chastisement that will last me a lifetime, in Jesus' name. Amen.

---

427. Hebrew 12:11 Matthew Henry's Concise Commentary https://www.biblehub.com Accessed October 2020

June 17th

Psalm 92:13 (AMPC) says, "Planted in the house of the Lord, they shall flourish in the courts of our God."

Planted in the Merriam Webster Dictionary is to put or set in the ground for growth.[428] The Greek word for planted is "neophutos," meaning newly planted.[429]

Those that are planted in the house of the Lord shall flourish and produce much fruit. Planted people are like seeds planted in fertile soil. They will grow with the proper nutrients, water, sun and grow and rapidly produce after its own kind. Christians who are planted in the house of God after pruning will produce an overabundance of fruit. Everything that they put their hand to shall prosper because they put God first in their lives. They will not only produce for one season but for multiple seasons. They have sought first the kingdom of God and His righteousness and all other things will be added unto them.

---
428. "Planted" Merriam-Webster.com 2019 https://www.merriam-webster.com Accessed October 2020
429. "Neophutos" Greek word for Planted https://www.biblehub.com Accessed October 2020

June 17th

DECLARATIONS

I will flourish in the courts of the Lord, and produce more fruit.

I have been planted and will continue to grow in the house of the Lord.

Lord, prune me so that I can continue to produce more fruit season after season.

I will seek first the Kingdom of God and His righteousness so all other things will be added unto me.

Everything that I put my hands to do will prosper because I put God first in my life.

June 18th

John 8:36 (AMPC) says, "So if the Son liberates you (makes you free men, then you are really and unquestionably free."

Liberates in the Merriam Webster Dictionary is defined as to free something, such as a country) from domination by foreign power.[430] The Greek word for liberates is "eleutheroo," meaning to make free, to exempt (from liability), or liberate.[431]

Freedom is the cry of every man, woman, boy, and girl. Jesus proclaimed, "If the Son makes you free, you will be free indeed. You should know and the truth shall make you free." Jesus is the Word that was made flesh and dwelled among us. So those that not only know who Jesus is have received the finished works of Jesus and have Him as their Lord and Savior are the ones that are free indeed. There is a difference between knowing Him and serving Him with all of your heart, mind, and soul. Many people do not trust the shed blood of Jesus as a payment for

---

430. "Liberates" Merriam-Webster.com 2019 https://www.merriam-webster.com Accessed October 2020
431. "eleutheroo" Greek word for Liberates https://www.biblehub.com Accessed October 2020

June 18th

their sins. When we don't mix the truth of who Jesus is with the faith in our hearts, we cannot be set free by that fact. To be truly saved, we have to believe in the Lord Jesus Christ and you can then be saved. For example, look at the jailer when Paul and Silas were in the Roman jail. After prayer, praise and worship went on and the earthquake shook their bands loose. The jailer asks them, "What must He do to be saved?" He was told the same thing that was stated above. The jailer was simply set free from bondage by just knowing and believing in the Lord Jesus Christ, knowing Him as Lord and Savior and believing the finished work of Christ. So now the jailer was set free from just knowing and believing and putting it into action.[432] WOW! This is Powerful!!

PRAYER:

Father God, in the name of Jesus, John 8:36 (NLT) says, "So if the Son sets you free, you are truly free." According to this Scripture, I became free when I received You and accepted You as my Lord and Savior. I believed and accepted Your finished works on the cross at Calvary. Lord, I repent for running from You for nearly half of my life because I didn't fully understand Your Word. Lord, thank You for sending a mentor in my life to teach me and help me understand Your Word better after I gave my life to You. I know all the promises that You have laid out for me, by reading and studying Your Word. Thank You for the Holy Ghost, who also has been teaching and comforting me when I ask Him for answers. Lord, I am free from the Law and eternal damnation. I now have You as my Lord and Savior and

---

432. John 8:36 https://www.dailverse.knowing-jesus.com Accessed October 2020

all I have to do is listen for the voice of God to lead and guide me on the right path to take in Jesus' name. Amen.

June 19th

Galatians 5:13 (AMPC) says, "For you, brethren, were(indeed) called to freedom; only (do not let your) freedom be an incentive to your flesh and an opportunity or excuse (for selfishness), but through love you should serve one another."

Incentive in the Merriam Webster Dictionary is something that incites or has a tendency to incite to determination or action.[433] The Greek word for incentive is "erethisma," meaning incentive. [434]

We are not under the Law, but under grace. We were not born under the Law, which was given to the pre-Cross Israel. We have been saved by grace, during this Post-Cross, church dispensation. The incredible freedom we received in Christ, released us from the recurring need to offer daily sacrifices to God. It freed us from the annual obligations to have our sins covered for another year by the insufficient blood of bulls and

---
433. "Incentive" Merriam-Webster.com 2019 https://www.merriam-webster.com Accessed October 2020
434. "Erethisma" Greek word for Incentive https://www.biblehub.com Accessed October 2020

goats. Having been saved through our faith in Christ, for ALL our sins, we are to put off our old former ways. We are to live by faith and walk in spirit and truth. Sadly, many have abused the wonderful freedom we have in Christ during this dispensation of the grace of God. Some seek to turn the wonderful freedom we have in the Lord Jesus, into an opportunity to indulge in sin. Some allow the lust of the flesh, the lust of the eye, and the pride of life to dominate their mind-catapulting them into an ungodly, carnal lifestyle, that is detrimental to our spiritual growth, disastrous to our Christian witness, and dishonoring to the lovely Lord Jesus, who bought us with His own blood.[435]

DECLARATIONS

I will live by faith and we are to walk in the spirit and truth.

I will seek the wonderful freedom that I have in Christ Jesus to walk holiness and righteousness.

I will not allow the lust of the flesh, the lust of the eye, or the pride of life to dominate my mind.

I will not let my good be evil spoken of or destroy my Christian witness.

I will not dishonor the Lord Jesus by not walking in the freedom that He has given me.

---

435. Galatians 5:13 https://www.dailyverse.knowing-jesus.com Accessed October 2020

June 19th

Lord, thank You for purchasing me with Your shed blood and for taking on You my past, present, and future sin.

I will not be distracted by what is going on around me, but I will continue to walk in the peace of God.

June 20th

John 15:7 (AMPC) says, "If you live in Me (abide vitally united to Me) and My words remain in you and continue to live in your hearts, ask whatever you will, and it shall be done for you."

Abide in the Merriam Webster Dictionary is defined as to endure without yielding, withstand, to continue in a place, or sojourn.[436] The Greek word for abide is "meno," meaning to stay, abide, remain, wait, or wait for.[437]

If we abide in Christ and His Words remain in our hearts, we can ask God whatever we need from Him. As long as it is in His will, God will do it for you. When we pray in Jesus' name, we will have whatever we ask. Faith works by love. When we love God, we obey His Word. There is nothing that God wouldn't do for us. If His teaching abides with us to control our thoughts and ideas, it remains in us as our guide and inspiration. The believer in Christ should be full of the Word of God and be in

---

436. "Abide" Merriam-Webster.com 2019 https://www.merriam-webster.com Accessed Ocbtober 2020
437. "Meno" Greek word for Abide https://www.biblehub.com Accessed October 2020

June 20th

constant communion with Christ. They will not act upon their own will but the will of the Father.[438]

PRAYERS:

Father, in the name Jesus, Your Word declares that if we abide in You, and Your Words abide in me, then I shall ask and it shall be done. Lord, Your Word remains in my heart. I will continue to study and read it to get it down further in my heart. God, I love You and want to be obedient to Your Word and live a life that is pleasing unto You in Jesus' name. I know that every day that I pray or declare I will end the prayer in Jesus' name. I know that Jesus is the only way that you can get to God. I will hide the Word in my heart so I will not sin against You. God You are my rock and upon You, I can stand, not to worry about sinking further into despair. You are my hope in a hopeless situation in Jesus' name. Lord, let Your will be done on earth as it is in Heaven in Jesus' name. Amen.

---

438. John 15:7 Pulpit Commentary https://www.biblehub.com Accessed October 2020

June 21st

*P*SALM 91:7 (AMPC) SAYS, "A thousand may fall at your side, and ten thousand at your right hand, but it shall not come near you."

Thousand in the Merriam Webster Dictionary is defined as a number equal to 10 times 100, or a very large number.[439] The Greek word for thousand is "chilia," meaning thousand.[440]

No matter how many wicked falls around thee, on the right hand and the left hand, you will have nothing to fear. You will be safe. You may feel assured of divine protection. Your mind may be calm through a sense of such guardianship, and your very calmness will conduce to your safety. It is true that others, beside the dissipated (overindulging in sensual pleasures), vicious (cruel or violent), and debased (reduced in value), may be the victims; but the great law is that temperance (self-control), soberness (Seriousness), virtue (High moral standards), cleanliness (being clean), and that regard to comfort and health

---

439. ."Thousand" Merriam-Webster.com 2019 https://www.merriam-webster.com Accessed October 2020
440. "Chilia" Greek word for Thousand https://www.biblehub.com Accessed October 2020

June 21st

to which religion (Jesus) and virtue (high moral standards) prompt, constitute a marked security. The righteous are in such safety that they only see the calamity.[441] This includes the flu, COVID-19, West Nile Virus, etc. All of these are classified as plagues and pestilence. According to the Word of God, the righteous are protected and safe from these things. So even if the righteous contract these diseases, Jehovah Rapha can heal them. They will recover from these illnesses and diseases. God is our protector. So we have to stay up under the blood of Jesus while we are under it and not get out of position.

DECLARATIONS

A thousand shall fall at my side, and ten thousand at my right side.

≈

The plague or pestilence shall not come near me.

I will continue to stay under the blood of Jesus so nothing by any means shall harm me.

No weapon that is formed against me shall prosper.

The weapon may form, but it will not prosper in my life.

Having communion with Jesus will help keep us safe from sicknesses and diseases.

---

441. Psalm 91:7 Barnes Notes on the Bible https://www.biblehub.com Accessed October 2020

June 22nd

PSALM 138:2 (AMPC) SAYS, "I will worship toward Your holy temple and praise Your name for Your loving-kindness and for Your truth and faithfulness; for You have exalted above all else Your name and Your word and You have magnified Your word above all Your name!"

Worship in the Merriam Webster Dictionary is defined as to honor or show reverence for as a divine being or supernatural power.[442] The Greek word for worship is "proskuneo," meaning to do reverence, I go down on my knees, do obeisance(respect) to, or worship.[443]

When we can praise God with our whole heart, we need not be unwilling for the whole world to witness our gratitude and joy in Him. Those who rely on His loving-kindness and truth through Jesus Christ, will ever find Him faithful to His Word. If He spared not His own Son, how shall he not with Him freely

---

442. "Worship" Merriam-Webster.com 2019 https://www.merriam-webster.com Accessed October 2020
443. "Proskuneo" Greek word for Worship https://www.biblehub.com Accessed October 2020

June 22nd

give us all things? God gives us strength in our souls, bears the burdens, resists the temptations, and does the duties of an afflicted state. He strengthens us to keep hold of Himself by faith, and to wait with patience for the event. We are bound to be thankful.[444]

PRAYER:

Father God, in the name of Jesus, I come to You today in worship to thank You for Your loving-kindness and for your truth. Your Word declares that we shouldn't be ashamed to praise You with our whole heart and let the world know how much You mean. Lord, You are faithful to Your Word. Daniel 2:20 declares, "Praise be to the name of God for ever and ever; wisdom and power are his." Lord, I will praise You for all the trials and storms You have seen me through 2020. Lord, I praise You for keeping me and my family covered under Your blood. Lord, I praise You that none of my family have COVID-19. Thank You that they haven't lost their jobs in the COVID-19 outbreak, in Jesus' name. Lord, I thank You for blessing my family and me with business opportunities that have really been sustaining us through this plague. Lord, I know it was Your grace and mercy that has brought us from February 2020 to the present date. Lord, You said in Your Word that Your grace was sufficient for us. It was strength that made us perfect in our weaknesses, in Jesus' name. Amen.

---

444. Psalm 138:2 https://www.biblehub.com Accessed October 2020

June 23rd

Psalm 34:10 (AMP) says, "The young lions lack food and suffer hunger, but they who seek (inquire of and require) the Lord (by right of their need and on the authority of His Word) none of them shall lack any beneficial thing."

Beneficial in the Merriam Webster Dictionary is defined as receiving or entitling one to receive advantage, use or benefit.[445] The Greek word for beneficial is "eudokia," meaning properly, what seems good or beneficial to someone, "Good pleasure"or God's good pleasure.[446]

The young lion represents our own power and self-sufficiency, doing things on our own without the guidance of the Holy Spirit or not even asking God about the situation. The earnest seeks after divine truth and righteousness and that can only be found in Jesus and in His Word.[447] Jesus said in His Word,

---
445. "Benefical" Merriam-Webster.com 2019 https://www.merriam-webster.com Accessed October 2020
446. "eudokia" Greek word for Beneficial https://www.biblehub.com Accessed October 2020
447. Psalm 34:10 MacLaren's Expositions https://www.biblehub.com Accessed October 2020

June 23rd

He would supply our every need, such as His riches in glory by Christ Jesus. He is the only reliable source that we have in this world that we can truly depend on. God wants us to come to Him and depend on Him for all of our needs or wants. He is often sitting and waiting for us to come to Him and ask Him for whatever we need. We tend to ask everybody else about it first. God wants us to put Him first and come to Him first with what we need before going to other people. If we need healing, Jesus is Jehovah Rapha. If we need our needs provided for, then He is Jehovah Jireh, our provider. It doesn't matter what we need. Jesus has the answer for it. Jesus wants to be Lord of our lives; won't you turn all of your problems over to Jesus today.

DECLARATIONS

I will not try to do everything in my own strength, but will lean on Jesus for everything instead.

I will seek the Lord so that I will not want for any good thing.

God will supply my every need according to His riches in Glory by Christ Jesus.

I will put God first in my life and ask Him to provide everything that I need for this journey.

God, You are my Jehovah Rapha. You are a healer of all my sicknesses and diseases.

Sickness cannot stay around or in my body when I plead the blood of Jesus over my body and mind.

June 24th

ACTS 3:20 (AMPC) SAYS, "And that He may send (to you) the Christ (the Messiah), Who before was designated and appointed for you—even Jesus."

Christ in the Merriam Webster Dictionary is defined as the Messiah, Jesus, the ideal truth that comes as a divine manifestation of God to destroy incarnate error.[448] The Greek word for Christ is "christos," meaning Jesus, the name of the Messiah, or the Anointed One.[449]

The absolute necessity of repentance is to be solemnly charged upon the consciences of all who desire that their sins may be blotted out, and that they may share in the refreshment which nothing but a sense of Christ's pardoning love can afford. Blessed are those who have felt this. It was not needful for the Holy Spirit to make known the times and seasons of these dispensations. These subjects are still left obscure. When sin-

---
448. "Christ" Merriam-Webster.com 2019 https://www.merriam-webster.com Accessed October 2020
449 . "Christos" Greek word for Christ https://www.biblehub.com Accessed October 2020

ners are convinced of their sins, they will cry to the Lord for pardon; and to the penitent, converted, and believing, times of refreshment will come from the presence of the Lord. In a state of trial and probation, the glorified Redeemer will be out of sight because we must live by faith in Him.[450]

PRAYER:

Father God, in the name of Jesus, I come before You today to thank You God for sending Jesus to come and give His life for me and the rest of the world. Through His sacrifice, He has redeemed me back to You and now it as if I have never sinned. Now when You look at me since I have been born-again You see Jesus. I have been indeed made perfect in Jesus through the Holy Spirit. We can come to Jesus by just crying out to Him when we have a need, that only He can fulfill. Lord, I know that as I am decreeing and declaring Your Word my faith has been increasing. You said in Your Word that faith comes by hearing; hearing the Word of God. So, I listen to the Word every chance that I get so my faith can remain strong in You. I know that we go from faith to faith by Your Word and our testimonies. So, I now can feel more comfortable telling my testimonies to someone who doesn't know You to encourage them to come to You in Jesus' name. Amen.

---

450. Acts 3:20 Matthew Henry's Concise Commentary https://www.biblehub.com Accessed October 2020

June 25th

2 Corinthians 6:18 (AMPC) says, "And I will be a Father to you, and you shall be My sons and daughters, says the Lord Almighty."

Father in the Merriam Webster Dictionary is defined as the first person of the Trinity.[451] The Greek word for Father is "pater," meaning a father, (Heavenly) Father, or elder.[452]

God will be a Father to the fatherless. A Father is a protector, counselor, and guide of His children. He instructs, provides, and counsels them in the time of need. No relation is more tender than this. God will be our friend, protector, guide, or counselor. He will cherish us. He will acknowledge us as His children. No higher honor can be conferred on mortals than to be adopted into the family of God, and to be permitted to call the Most High our Father. No rank is so elevated as that of being the sons and the daughters of the Lord Almighty.[453]

---

451. "Father" Merriam-Webster.com 2019 https://www.merriam-webster.com Accessed October 2020
452. "Pater" Greek word for Father https://www.Biblehub.com Accessed October 2020
453. 2 Corinthians 6:18 Barnes Notes on the Bible https://www.biblehub.com Accessed October 2020

DECLARATIONS

God, I thank You for being the Father that I never had in my life.

Thank You for loving me when I felt that I wasn't lovable to anyone else.

God, thank You for being my protector, friend, counselor and provider in Jesus' name.

God, You are a friend that sticks closer than any brother.

God, thank You for adopting me into Your family as Your child in Jesus' name.

Lord, You are the Most High God and I give You the glory and honor for Who You are in my life.

June 26th

Psalm 55:18 (AMPC) says, "He has redeemed my life in peace from the battle that was against me (so that none came near me), for they were many who strove with me."

Strove/Strive in the Merriam Webster Dictionary is defined as striving to denote serious effort or energy, endeavor, or contend to struggle in opposition.[454] The Greek word for strove/strive is "agonizomai," meaning to contend for a prize, struggle, striving, conflict, or warfare.[455]

In every trial, let us call upon the Lord, and He will save us. He shall hear us and not blame us for coming too often. David had many against him. He gives God glory, for it is He that raises us up friends and makes them faithful to us. There are more true Christians than fake ones. Believers have more real friends than false ones. We are to look to Christ for all of our help. We need to cast our burdens on the Lord and rest upon

---
454. "Strove/Strive Merriam-Webster.com 2019 https://www.merriam-webster.com Accessed October 2020
455. "Agonizomai" Greek word for Strove/Strive https://www.biblehub.com Accessed October 2020

His providence and promises because He will strengthen our spirits by His Spirit. He will never suffer the righteous to be moved or be shaken by any troubles, as to quit their duty to God or their comfort in Him.[456]

PRAYER:

Father God, in the name of Jesus, I come before You today to lay all of my cares at Your feet. You can take care of them better than I can in Jesus' name. Lord, when it seems like the whole world is against us, we can rest assured that You have our backs and will take care of us. There are more with us than against us. You will raise us up with covenant friends who will help us along the way. Lord, I will look to You for all of my help because it all comes from You, the Father of lights, in Jesus' name. Lord, I refuse to quit the path You have laid out for me regardless of who is for or against me in Jesus' name. Lord, thank You for sending Your Holy Spirit to strengthen my spirit for the journey I am on in my walk with You. Lord, I thank You for always being by my side through the thick and thin in Jesus' name. Amen.

---

456. Psalm 55:18 Matthew Henry's Concise Commentary https://www.biblehub.com Accessed October 2020

June 27th

Psalm 120:1 (AMPC) says, "IN MY distress I cried to the Lord, and He answered me."

Distress in the Merriam Webster Dictionary is defined as pain or suffering affecting the body, a bodily part, or the mind, or trouble.[457] The Greek word for distress is "stenochoria," meaning narrowness of space, difficulty, great distress, or anguish.[458]

The Psalmist was brought into great distress by a deceitful tongue. May every good man be delivered from lying lips. They had forged false charges against him. In this distress, he sought after God by fervent prayer. God can bridle their tongues. He obtained a gracious answer to His prayer.[459] Just like David in the Scripture above, people can be deceitful to us as well. They try to slander our names and talk bad about us to other people. We can follow David's example by crying out to God and

---

457. "Distress" Merriam-Webster.com 2019 https://www,merriam-webster.com Accessed October 2020
458. "Stenochoria" Greek word for Distress https://www.biblehub.com Accessed October 2020
459. Psalm 120:1 Matthew Henry's Concise Commentary https://www.biblehub.com Accessed October 2020

He will avenge us and fix the problem. We don't have to chase down anyone about anything that is said about us because God will be our vindicator. He knows the right things to do and say to get the matter resolved without us acting out of character. Prayer can change any situation that you come up against in your life. We know that since we are children of God, He hears our prayers. When we pray, He will answer us in His own timing. So, all we have to do is be patient and God will handle the situation. When we see our enemies going through, we need to be praying God's mercy for them instead of rejoicing over their calamities.

DECLARATIONS

Lord, I cried out to You in my distress and You came to my rescue in Jesus' name.

I will not be drawn out by people who are saying deceitful things about me.

God, You are my vindicator and I will let You handle the matter like only You can.

I will pray for my enemies and ask God to have mercy on them despite the things they have done to me.

In my distress, I cried out to the Lord, and He heard me.

Lord, bridle the tongues of the liars that have forged false charges against me.

June 28th

Isaiah 26:3 (AMP) says, "You will guard him and keep him in perfect and constant peace whose mind (both its inclination and its character) is stayed on You, because He commits himself to You, leans on You, and hopes confidently in You."

Guard in the Merriam Webster Dictionary is one assigned to protect or oversee another.[460] The Greek word for guard is "phroureo," meaning I guard, keep, as by a military guard.[461]

God will guard and keep us in perfect peace as long as our minds are stayed on Him. He wants us to look to Him and not our problems. When we look at our problems more than we do Him, we tend to get distracted and get off course. God will give us His Supernatural peace that no matter what is going on around us, we are calm, not nervous, or anxious about it. If we lay all of the cares of this world at His feet instead of carrying them in our hearts, we all would be better off. Through worry,

---
460. "Guard" Merriam-Webster.com 2019 https://www.merriam-webster.com Accessed October 2020
461. "Phroureo" Greek word for Guard https://www.biblehub.com Accessed October 2020

you can get high blood pressure and many other things that deal with worry. Depression comes from worrying about the situation more than thinking or looking to God for the answer and solution to the problem. God is our ever-present help in the time of troubles. He has us covered. All we have to do is cry out to Him. He will help us get through anything that we are going through in our lives. There is nothing in this world that God cannot handle. If we need protection, God will dispatch a band of angels to surround and cover us to keep us safe from harm and hurt.

PRAYER:

Father God, in the name of Jesus, I come to You today to give You all the cares of this world that are bothering me. I know that You want me to have Your perfect peace and the only way that I can have that is to give You all of my cares in Jesus' name. Lord, I give You my family who don't have a personal relationship with You yet. I know that in due time You will draw them by Your Spirit. Lord, I give You my career and not sure what my next move is. I trust You to lead me in the right direction. Lord, I give You everything that I am worried about that makes me go into depression. I know that if I give it to You, then I can be happy again with my life. Lord, I give You my children. It seems like they are living outside Your will. I know that You have told me that You are already working on their hearts for Your glory. Lord, I give You my finances. You said that You would supply my every need according to Your riches in glory by Christ. Lord, I now give You all of my bills. I know that You will find a way to pay all of them off so You can get the glory

June 28th

out of it. Lord, I thank You for being there for me to lay all of my troubles on so I can continue to walk in the peace that passeth all understanding in Jesus' name. Amen.

June 29th

*D*EUTERONOMY 31:6 (AMP) SAYS, "Be strong, courageous, and firm, fear not nor be in terror before them, for it is the Lord your God Who goes with you; He will not fail you or forsake you."

Courageous in the Merriam Webster Dictionary is defined as having or characterized by courage or brave.[462] The Greek word for courageous is "tharseo," meaning to be of good courage, good cheer, or am bold.[463]

Be strong in the Lord and in the power of His might. God is telling us to be strong in Him. We are not strong in our own ability, but we are strong because we depend on Him to be with us and help us through our trials and disappointments. God says do not be afraid of Your enemies because they can't hurt you. It doesn't matter what your enemies are thinking or trying to do to you either. It doesn't matter if you have 100 enemies. They can't do anything to harm you. The Word of God states

---

462. "Courageous" Merriam-Webster.com 2019 https://www.merriam-webster.com Accessed October 2020
463. "Tharseo" Greek word for Courageous https://www.biblehub.com Accessed October 2020

June 29th

that no weapon that is formed against you shall prosper. Every ditch that they try to dig for you, they will fall in it themselves. God is with us as long as we are obedient and living a holy and righteous lifestyle with a life of repentance when we have missed the mark. We will have complete victory because God is with us. No devil in hell can stop the plan of God for your life. God will remove your enemies from around you. They will flee from you seven ways. God will even make your enemies be your biggest supporters. They will be blessing you and don't even know why they are doing it. God is the only One that can make your enemies your footstool- something that you step up on to go higher!

DECLARATIONS

God, You said in Your Word that You would make my enemies my footstools.

I will be strong and courageous because God is with me.

Lord, according to Your Word, You will never leave or forsake me, but will be with me until the end of the world.

I am not in the world alone because Jesus is with me and leading me.

Though things may be hard at times, I refuse to give up.

All weapons that are formed against my entire family shall not prosper because God will lift up a standard against them.

June 30th

DEUTERONOMY 1:29-30 (AMP) SAYS, "Then I said to you, dread not, neither be afraid of them. 30. The Lord your God Who goes before you, He will fight for you just as He did for you in Egypt before your eyes."

Dread in the Merriam Webster Dictionary is defined as to feel extreme reluctance to meet or face.[464] The Greek word for dread is "deiliao," meaning to be cowardly to be timid, or fearful.[465]

God said, "Do not dread (be afraid) because I have already gone before you and prepared the way. Don't be afraid to move forward and something that God is telling you to do. He wouldn't have told you to do it, if it was beyond your ability. If you have an unbelieving heart then the enemy will place doubt in you. You will feel like you are not equipped or qualified to be doing what God is telling you to do for His kingdom. God is

---

464. "Dread" Merriam-Webster.com https://www.merriam-webster.com Accessed October 2020
465. "Deiliao" Greek word for Dread https://www.biblehub.com Accessed October 2020.

June 30th

very trust-worthy because He cannot lie. If He is telling you to do something be obedient and do it. Sometimes you have to do it in spite of your fear because fear is one of the enemy's scare tactics to keep you stuck from moving forward in God. Don't let the enemy paralyze you to stay in your comfort zone. He knows that if you ever overcome the fear and find out your true identity in God, you will be a sniper in the spirit. He knows that he will not have a chance to mess with you or your family because you will get into your war stance. He will have to run from you.

PRAYER:

Father God, in the name of Jesus, You said in Your Word not dread or be afraid of them because You have prepared the way before me. Lord, You also said in Your Word that You will never leave or forsake me, but You will be with me until the end of this world. I know with that promise, I do not have to back up from the enemy's threats in fear. Lord, I believe that You are with me and You are looking out for me, so I don't have anything to ever worry about. I cancel and veto the spirit of fear and timidity off my life and send it back to the pits of hell far from me in Jesus' name. I will walk in the authority that Jesus' shed blood has given me. I don't have to fear because You are with me. Lord, I thank You for making every crooked place straight and placing the spirit of boldness in me so that I can continue to move forward in You from this day forward, in Jesus' name. Amen.

About The Author

Dr. LaRose Angela Richardson is the wife of Richard Richardson and the mother of Satar Cowan. She has one granddaughter, Allara Cowan. She has lived in Southeast Georgia all of her life. In May 2016, she graduated with a Doctor's Degree in Theology from Crossland Christian University in Orlando, Florida. She is the co-author of "It Cost Me Everything" written by Prophetess Kimberly Moses. She also has two other books that she has written. The first one is "Waking in Total Freedom after Healing from Deep Inner Wounds," and the second one is "Prayers That Availeth Much." Her new book is "180 days of Communing with God Daily devotional." She has also started a blog this year under the name of Grace Ministries Walking in Freedom, which can be found at ministerrich0628.blogspot.com. Her ministry pages can be found on Facebook, "Grace Ministries" and "Walking in Freedom." You can go on those pages weekly and hear a LIVE word from the Lord. All the teachings are words of encouragement that will inspire and to help you move forward in ministry. She can be contacted on Facebook on her ministry pages or her personal page "Angela Richardson." You can also email her at ministerrich0628@gmail.com.

References

1. "Devotional" Merriam-Webster. Com 2019. https://www.merriam-webster.com Accessed July 2020.
2. "proskartereo" The Greek word for devotional. https://www.biblehub.com accessed July 2020
3. "Acknowledgement" https://www.biblehub.com accessed July 2020
4. "Yada" Hebrew word https://www.biblehub.com accessed July 2020.
5. "Wise" Merriam-Webster.com 2019. https://www.merriam-webster.com July 2020
6. "Sophos" Greek word https://www.biblehub.com accessed July 2020.
7. "Knock" Merriam-Webster.com 2019. https://www.merriam-webster.com accessed July 2020.
8. "Krouo" Greek word https://www.biblehub.com accessed July 2020.
9. "Believe" Merriam-Webster.com 2019. https://www.merriam-webster.com July 2020
10. "Pisteuo" Greek word https://www.biblestudytools.com July 2020.
11. "Law" Merriam-Webster.com https://www.merriam-webster.com accessed July 2020

12. "Nomos" Greek word for law https://www.biblehub.com accessed July 2020

13. "Will" Merriam-Webster.com 2019 https://www.merriam-webster.com accessed July 2020

14. "Thelema" Greek word for Will https://www.biblehub.com accessed July 2020

15. Matthew 6:10 Matthew Henry's Concise Bible Commentary & Barnes Notes on the Bible. https://www.biblehub.com accessed July 2020

16. "Laugh" Merriam-Webster.com 2019 https://www.merrriam-webster.com accessed July 2020

17. "Gelos" Greek word laugh https://www.biblehub.com accessed July 2020

18. "Weeping my do for a night but Joy comes in the morning article. https:/www.fromhispresence.com accessed July 2020

19. "Persistent" Merriam-Webster.com 2019 https://www.merriam-webster.com accessed July 2020.

20. "Anaideia" Greek for persistent https://www.biblehub.com accessed July 2020

21. "Fervent" Merriam-Webster.com 2019 https://www.merriam-webster.com accessed July 2020

22. "Zeo" Greek word for fervent https://www.biblehub.com accessed July 2020

23. "Encourage" Merriam-Webster.com 2019 https://www.merriam-webster.com accessed July 2020

24. "Parakaleo" Greek word for encourage https://www.biblehub.com accessed July 2020

25. "Cast" Merriam-Webster.com 2019 https://www.merriam-webster.com accessed July 2020

References

26. "Rhipto" Greek word for Cast https://www.biblehub.com accessed July 2020

27. "Good News" Merriam-Webster.com 2019 https://www.merriam-webster.com accessed July 2020

28. "evaggelin" Greek word for Good News https://www.biblehub.com accessed July 2020

29. "Foundation" Merriam-Webster.com 2019 https://www.merriam-webster.com accessed July 2020

30. "Themelios" Greek word for Foundation https://www.biblehub.com accessed July 2020

31. "Wait" Merriam-Webster.com 2019 https://www.merriam-webster.com accessed July 2020

32. "Perimeno" Greek word for Wait http://www.biblehub.com accessed July 2020

33. "Bless" Merriam-Webster.comn2019 https://www.merriam-webster.com accessed July 2020

34. "Makarios" Greek word for Bless https://www.biblehub.com accessed July 2020

35. "Hold" Merriam-Webster.com 2019 https://www.merriam-webster.com accessed July 2020

36. "Katecho" Greek word for hold https://www.biblehub.com accessed July 2020

37. "Joy" Merriam-Webster.com 2019 https://www.merriam-webster.com accessed July 2020

38. "Chura" Greek Word for Joy https://www.biblehub.com accessed July 2020

39. "Anger" Merriam-Webster.com 2019 https://www.merriam-webster.com accessed July 2020

40. "Orge" Merriam-Webster.com 2019 https://www.biblehub.com accessed July 2020

41. "Humility" Merriam-Webster.com 2019 https://www.merriam-webster.com accessed July 2020

42. "tapeinophrosune" Greek for Humility https://www.biblehub.com accessed July 2020

43. "Tongues" Merriam-Webster.com 2019 https://www.merriam-webster.com accessed July 2020

44. "Glossa" Greek for Tongues https://www.biblehub.com accessed July 2020

45. Benefits of Praying in Tongues by KCM.org Accessed July 2020

46. "Remain" Merriam-Webster.com 2019 https://www.merriam-webster.com accessed July 2020

47. "Meno" Greek word for Remain https://www.biblehub.com accessed July 2020

48. "Sanctification" Merriam-Webster.com 2019 https://www.merriam-webster.com accessed August 2020

49. "Hagiasmos" Greek word for Sanctification https://www.biblehub.com accessed August 2020

50. Hebrews 12:14 Matthew Henry Concise Commentary https://www.biblehub.com accessed August 2020

51. "Convinced" Merriam-Webster.com 2019 https://www.merriam-webster.com accessed August 2020

52. "Peitho" Greek word for convinced https://www.biblehub.com
Accessed August 2020

53. "Forgets" Merriam-Webster.com 2019 https://www.merriam-webster.com accessed August 2020

54. "epilanthanomi" https://www.biblehub.com accessed August 2020

References

55. Dailyverse.knowing-jesus.com , https://www.dailyverse.knowing-jesus.com accessed August 2020

56. "Steadfast" Merriam-Webster.com 2019 https://www.merriam-webster.com accessed August 2020

57. "Epilanthanomai" Greek word for Steadfast https://www.biblehub.com accessed August 2020

58. "Glory" Merriam-Webster.com 2019 https://www.merriam-webster.com accessed August 2020

59. "Doxa" Greek for Glory https://www.biblehub.com accessed August 2020

60. "Owe" Merriam-Webster.com 2019 https://www.Merriam-webster.com accessed August 2020

61. "Ophelio" Greek word for Owe https://www.biblehub.com accessed August 2020

62. "Benefit" Merriam-Webster.com 2019 https://www.merriam-webster.com accessed August 2020

63. "Ophelia" Greek Word for Benefit https://www.biblehub.com accessed August 2020

64. "Conformity" Merriam-Webster.com 2019 https://www.merriam-webster.com accessed August 2020

65. "Suschematizo" Greek word for Conformity https://www.biblehub.com accessed August 2020

66. "Accepting" Merriam-Webster.com 2019 https://www.merriam-webster.com accessed August 2020

67. "Dechomai" Greek for Accepting https://www.biblehub.com accessed August 2020

68. "Temple" Merriam-Webster.com 2019 https://www.merriam-webster.com accessed August 2020

69. "Naos" Greek word for Temple https://www.bbiblehub.com accessed August 2020

70. "Peace" Merriam-Webster.com 2019 https://www.merriam-webster.com accessed august 2020

71. "Eirene" Greek word for Peace https://www.biblehub.com accessed August 2020

72. "Joy" Merriam-Webster.com 2019 https://www.merriam-webster.com accessed August 2020

73. "Chara" Greek word for Joy https://www.biblehub.com accessed August 2020

74. "Suffer" Merriam-Webster.com 2019 https://www.merriam-webster.com accessed August 2020

75. "Pathema" Greek word for Suffer https://www.biblehub.com accessed august 2020

76. 1 Peter 4:16 Barnes Notes on the Bible https://www.biblehub.com accessed August 2020

77. "Whatever" Merriam-Webster.com 2019 https://www.merriam-webster.com accessed august 2020

78. "hostis" Greek for Whatever https://www.biblehub.com accessed August 2020

79. "Confirmed" Merriam-Webster.com 2019 https://www.merriam-webster.com accessed August 2020

80. "Bebaioo" Greek for Confirmed https://www.biblehub.com accessed august 2020

81. "Faith" Merriam-Webster.com 2019 https://www.merriam-webster.com accessed August 2020

82. "Pistis" Greek word for Faith https://www.biblehub.com accessed August 2020

83. "Destroying" Merriam-Webster.com 2019 https://www.merriam-webster.com August 2020

84. "Portheo" Greek word for Destroying https://www.biblehub.com accessed August 2020

References

85. "Understand" Merriam-Webster.com 2019 https://www.biblehub.com accessed August 2020

86. "Nous" Greek for Understand https://www.biblehub.com accessed August 2020

87. "Permanent" Merriam-Webster.com 2019 https://www.merriam-webster.com accessed August 2020

88. "Aparabatos" Greek for Permanent https://www.biblehub.com accessed August 2020

89. "Superabundantly" Merriam-Webster.com 2019 https://www.merriam-webster.com accessed August 2020

90. "Perisseuma" Greek for Superabundantly https://www.biblehub.com accessed August 2020

91. "Diligence" Merriam-Webster.com 2019 https://www.merrian-webster.com accessed August 2020

92. "Spoude" Greek word for Diligence https://www.biblehub.com accessed August 2020

93. "Precepts" Merriam-Webster.com 2019 https://www.merriam-webster.com accessed August 2020

94. "Entalma" Greek for Percepts https://www.biblehub.com accessed August 2020

95. "Boldly" Merriam-Webster.com 2019 https://www.merriam-webster.com Accessed August 2020

96. "Tolmao" Greek word for Boldly https://www.biblehub.com accessed August 2020

97. "Commandments" Merriam-Webster.com 2019 https://www.merriam-webster.com Accessed August 2020

98. "Entole" Greek for Commandments https://www.biblehub.com accessed August 2020

99. "Witness" Merriam-Webster.com 2019 https://www.merriam-webster.com Accessed August 2020.

100. "Martureo" Greek word for Witness. https://www.bible-tools.org Accessed August 2020.

101. "Consoles" Merriam-Webster.com 2019 https://www.merriam-webster.com August 2020.

102. "Paramutheomai" Greek word for Consoles. https://www.biblehub.com Accessed August 2020

103. "Strength" Merriam-Webster. Com 2019 https://www.merriam-webster.com August 2020.

104. "Ischus" Greek Word for Strength https://www.biblehub.com Accessed August 2020.

105. "Look" Merriam-Webster.com 2019 https://www.merriam-webster.com August 2020.

106. "Apoblepo" Greek word for Look https://www.merriam-webster.com August 2020

107. "Train" Merriam-Webster.com 2019 https://www.merriam-webster.com September 2020.

108. "Gumnazo" Greek word for Train https://www.biblehub.com September 2020

109. "Admonish" Merriam-Webster.com 2019 https://www.merriam-webster.com September 2020.

110. "Noutheteo" Greek word for Admonish https://www.biblehub.com September 2020

111. "Faults" Merriam-Webster.com 2019 https://www.merriam-webster.com August 2020

112. "Memphomai" Greek word for Faults https://www.biblehub.com September 2020

113. "Conclusion" Merriam-Webster.com 2019 https://www.merriam-webster.com September 2020

114. "Sumbibazo" Greek word for Conclusion https://www.biblehub.com September 2020.

References

115. "Hope" Merriam-Webster.com 2019 https://www.merriam-webster.com September 2020.

116. "Elpis" Greek word for Hope https://www.biblehub.com Accessed September 2020.

117. "Might" Merriam-Webster.com 2019 https://www.merriam-webster.com September 2020

118. "Ischus" Greek word for Might https://www.biblehub.com Accessed September 2020

119. "Exult" Merriam-Webster.com 2019 https://www.merriam-webster.com September 2020

120. "Agalliao" Greek word for Exult https://www.biblehub.com Accessed September 2020.

121. Zephaniah 3:17 Mattew Henry's Concise Commentary. https://www.bibblehub.com Accessed September 2020.

122. "Fervently" Merriam-Webster.com 2019 https://www.merriam-webster.com September 2020

123. "Zeo" Greek word for Fervently https://www.biblehub.com Accessed September 2020

124. "Salvation" Merriam-Webster.com 2019 https://www.merriam-webster.com Accessed September 2020

125. 'Soteria" Greek word for Salvation https://www.biblehub.com Accessed September 2020

126. "Inflexibility" Merriam-Webster.com 2019 https://www.merriam-webster.com Accessed September 2020

127. "Akamptos" Greek word for Inflexibility https://www.wordhippo.com Accessed September 2020

128. "Everlasting" Merriam-Webster.com 2019 https://www.merriam-webster.com September 2020

129. "Aionios" Greek word for Everlasting https://www.biblehub.com Accessed September 2020

130. "Indulge" Merriam-Webster.com 2019 https://www.merriam-webster.com Accessed September 2020

131. "Poreuomai" Greek word for Indulge https://www.biblehub.com Accessed September 2020

132. "Hedged" Merriam-Webster.com 2019 https://www.merriam-webster.com Accessed September 2020

133. "Phragmos" Greek word for Hedged https://www.biblehub.com Accessed September 2020

134. 2 Corinthians 4:8, Matthew Henry's Concise Commentary https://www.biblehub.com Accessed September 2020

135. "Anxious" Merriam-Webster.com 2019 https://www.merrian-webster.com Accessed September 2020

136. "Merimnao" Greek word for Anxious https://www.biblehub.com Accessed September 2020

137. Psalm 94:19, Matthew Henry's Concise Commentary https://www.biblehub.com Accessed September 2020

138. "Loving-Kindness" Merriam-Webster.com 2019 https://www.merriam-webster.com Accessed September 2020

139. "Storgiki Kalosyni" Greek word for Loving-Kindness https://www.wordhippo.com Accessed September 2020

140. "Temptation" Merriam Webster.com 2019 https://www.merriam-webster.com Accessed September 2020

141. "Peirzo" Greek word for Temptation https://www.biblehub.com Accessed September 2020

142. James 1:12 https://www.dailyverse.knowing-jesus.com Accessed September 2020

143. "Renewed" Merriam-Webster.com 2019 https://www.merriam-webster.com Accessed September 2020

144. "Anakainoo" Greek word for Renewed https://www.biblehub.com Accessed September 2020

References

145. 'Executes" Merriam-Webster.com 2019 https://www.biblehub.com Accessed September 2020

146. "Poieo" Greek for Executes https://www.Gospelhall.org Accessed October 2020

147. Psalm 103:6-7, Matthew Henry's Concise Commentary https://www.biblehub.com Accessed September 2020

148. "Rock" Merriam-Webster.com 2019 https://www.merriam-webster.com Accessed September 2020

149. "Petra" Greek word for Rock https://www.Thayer'sGreekLexicon Accessed September 2020

150. "Plans" Merriam-Webster.com 2019 https://www.merriam-webster.com Accessed September 2020

151. "Boule" Greek for Plans https://www.biblehub.com September 2020

152. "Exalt" Merriam-Webster.com 2019 https://www.merriam-webster.com Accessed September 2020

153. "Hupsoo" Greek word for Exalt https://www.biblehub.com September 2020

154. Isaiah 25:1, https://www.knowingjesus.com Accessed September 2020

155. "Covenant" Merriam-Webster.com 2019 https://www.merriam-webster.com Accessed September 2020

156. "Diatheke" Greek word for Covenant https://www.biblehub.com Accessed September 2020

157. "Instruct" Merriam-Webster.com 2019 https://www.merriam-webster.com Accessed September 2020

158. "Katecheo" Greek word for Instruct https://www.biblehub.com Accessed Spetember 2020

159. "Mediator" Merriam-Webster.com 2019 https://www.merriam-webster.com Accessed September 2020

160. "Mesistes" Greek word for Mediator https://www.biblehub.com Accessed September 2020

161. "Endued" Merriam-Webster.com 2019 https://www.merriam-webster.com Accessed September 2020

162. "Epistemon" Greek for Endued https://www.biblehub.com Accessed September 2020

163. "Unyielding" Merriam-Webster.com 2019 https://www.merriam-webster.com Accessed September 2020

164. "Aklines" Greek word for Unyielding https://www.biblehub.com Accessed September 2020

165. "Path" Merriam-Webster.com 2019 https://www.merriam-webster.com Accessed September 2020

166. "Tribos" Merriam-Webster.com 2019 https://www.merriam-webster.com Accessed September 2020

167. "Lord" Merriam-Webster.com 2019 https://www.merriam-webster.com Accessed September 2020

168. "Kyrios" Greek word for Lord https://www.biblehub.com Accessed September 2020

169. Psalm 145:9, Mattew Henry's Concise Commentary https://www.biblehub.com Accessed September 2020

170. "Near" Merriam-Webster.com 2019 https://www.merriam-webster.com Accessed September 2020

171. "Eggus" Greek for Near https://www.biblehub.com Accessed September 2020

172. Psalm 145:18-19 Matthew Henry's Concise Commentary https://www.biblehub.com Accessed September 2020

173. "Soul" Merriam-Webster.com 2019 https://www.merriam-webster.com Accessed September 2020

174. "Psche" Greek for Soul https://www.biblehub.com Accessed September 2020

References

175. "Bless" Merriam-Webster.com 2019 https://www.merriam-webster.com Accessed September 2020

176. "Makarios" Greek for Bless https://www.biblehub.com Accessed September 2020

177. "Invincible" Merriam-Webster.com 2019 https://www.merriam-webster.com Accessed September 2020

178. "Anikitos" Greek word for Invincible https://www.biblehub.com Accessed September 2020

179. Habakkuk 3:19, Matthew Henry's Concise Commentary https://www.biblehub.com Accessed September 2020

180. "Sufficient" Merriam-Webster.com 2019 https://www.merriam-webster.com Accessed September 2020

181. "Hikanos" Greek word for Sufficient https://www.biblehub.com Accessed September 2020

182. Matthew 6:34 Matthew Henry's Concise Commentary https://www.biblehub.com Accessed September 2020

183. "Sin" Merriam-Webster.com 2019 https://www.merriam-webster.com Accessed September 2020

184. "Hamartia" Greek word for Sin https://www.biblehub.com

185. Psalm 119:11 Matthew Henry's Concise Commentary https://www.biblehub.com Accessed September 2020

186. "Bond" Merriam-Webster.com 2019 https://www.merriam-webster.com Accessed September 2020

187. "Halusis" Greek word for Bonds https://www.biblehub.com Accessed September 2020

188. Psalm 107:13-14 Matthew Henry's Concise Commentary https://www.biblehub.com Accessed September 2020

189. "Master" Merriam-Webster.com 2019 https://www.merriam-webster.com Accessed September 2020

190. "Despotes" Greek for Master https://www.biblehub.com Accessed September 2020

191. "Unobtrusive" Merriam-Webster.com 2019 https://www.merriam-webster.com Accessed September 2020

192. "Tapeinos" Greek word for Unobtrusive https://www.wordhippo.com Accessed September 2020

193. James 3:13 Matthew Henry's Concise Commentary https://www.biblehub.com Accessed September 2020

194. "Perverse" Merriam-Webster.com 2019 https://www.merriam-webster.com Accessed September 2020

195. "Diastrepho" Greek word for Perverse. https://www.biblehub.com Accessed September 2020

196. Jeremiah 17:9 Matthew Henry's Concise Commentary https://www.biblehub.com Accessed September 2020

197. "Admonishing" Merriam-Webster.com 2019 https://www.merriam-webster.com Accessed September 2020

198. "Noutheteo" Greek word for Admonished https://www.biblehub.com Accessed September 2020

199. Colossians 1:28 Matthew Henry's Concise Commentary https://www.biblehub.com Accessed September 2020

200. "Assurance" Merriam-Webster.com 2019 https://www.merriam-webster.com Accessed September 2020

201. "Hupostasis" Greek word for Assurance https://www.biblehub.com Accessed September 2020

202. 1 John 5:14 Matthew Henry's Concise Commentary https://www.biblehub.com Accessed September 2020

203. 'Reliance" Merriam-Webster.com 2019 https://www.merriam-webster.com Accessed September 2020

204. "Exartisi" Greek word for Reliance https://www.biblehub.com Accessed September 2020

References

205. "Redeemer" Merriam-Webster.com 2019 https://www.merriam-webster.com Accessed September 2020

206. "Lutrotes" Greek for Redeemer https://www.biblehub.com Accessed September 2020

207. "Continually" Merriam-Webster.com 2019 https://www.merriam-webster.com Accessed September 2020

208. "Proskartereo" Greek word for Continually https://www.biblehub.com Accessed September 2020

209. "Prayer" Merriam-Webster.com 2019 https://www.merriam-webster.com Accessed September 2020

210. "Proseuchomai" Greek word for Prayer https://www.biblehub.com Accessed September 2020

211. Psalm 42:8 Matthew Henry's Concise Commentary https://www.biblehub.com Accessed September 2020

212. "Thoroughly Merriam-Webster.com 2019 https://www.merriam-webster.com Accessed September 2020

213. "Ekkathairo" Greek word for Thoroughly https://www.biblehub.com Accessed September 2020

214. "Self-Confident" Merriam-Webster.com 2019 https://www.merriam-webster.com Accessed September 2020

215. "Pepoithesis" Greek word for Self-Confident https://www.biblehub.com Accessed September 2020

216. Proverbs 29:11 Matthew Henry's Concise Commentary https://www.biblehub.com Accessed September 2020

217. "Stumble" Merriam-Webster.com 2019 https://www.merriam-webster.com Accessed September 2020

218. "Ptaio" Greek word for Stumble https://www.biblehub.com Accessed September 2020

219. Psalm 119:165 Pulpit Commentary https://www.biblehub.com Accessed September 2020

220. "Help" Merriam-Webster.com 2019 https://www.merriam-webster.com Accessed September 2020

221. "Sunantilambanomai" Greek word for Help https://www.biblehub.com September 2020'

222. "Deliverance" Merriam-Webster.com 2019 https://www.merriam-webster.com Accessed September 2020

223. "Soteria" Greek word for Deliverance https://www.biblehub.com Accessed September 2020

224. "Green" Merriam-Webster.com 2019 https://www.merriam-webster.com Accessed September 2020

225. "Prasinos" Greek word for Green https://www.biblehub.com Accessed September 2020

226. Psalm 52:8 Barnes Notes on the Bible https://www.biblehub.com Accessed September 2020

227. "Representatives" Merriam-Webster.com 2019 https://www.merriam-webster.com Accessed September 2020

228. "Presbeuo" Greek word for Representatives https://www.biblehub.com Accessed September 2020

229. Colossians 3:12 Matthew Henry's Concise Commentary https://www.biblehub.com Accessed September 2020

230. "Inclined" Merriam-Webster.com 2019 https://www.merriam-webster.com Accessed September 2020.

231. "Prosklisis" Greek word for Inclined https://www.biblehub.com Accessed September 2020

232. "Languishing" Merriam-Webster.com 2019 https://www.merriam-webster.com Accessed September 2020

233. "Astheneo" Greek word for Languishing https://www.biblehub.com Accessed September 2020

234. Jeremiah 31:25 Gill's Exposition of Entire Bible https://www.biblehub.com Accessed September 2020

References

235. "Intentional" Merriam-Webster.com 2019 https://www.merriam-webster.com Accessed September 2020

236. "Ek Protheseos" Greek for Intentional https://www.wordhippo.com Accessed September 2020

237. 1 Corinthians 13:1 Matthew Henry's Concise Commentary https://www.biblehub.com Accessed September 2020

238. "Finisher" Merriam-Webster.com 2019 https://www.merriam-webster.com Accessed September 2020

239. "Teleiotes" Greek for Finisher https://www.biblehub.com Accessed September 2020

240. Fire Merriam-Webster.com 2019 https://www.merriam-webster.com Accessed September 2020

241. "Pur" Greek word for Fire https://www.biblehub.com Accessed September 2020

242. "Hammer" Merriam-Webster.com 2019 https://www.merriam-webster.com Accessed September 2020

243. "Halmuth" Hebrew word for Hammer https://www.biblehub.com Accessed September 2020

244. Jeremiah 23:29 Ellicott's Commentary for English Readers https://www.biblehub.com Accessed September 2020

245. "Sweeter" Merriam-Webster.com 2019 https://www.merriam-webster.com Accessed September 2020

246. "Mathoq" Greek word for Sweeter https://www.biblehub.com Accessed September 2020

247. Psalm 119:103 Benson Commentary https://www.biblehub.com Accessed September 2020

248. "Reap" Merriam-Webster.com 2019 https://www.meriam-webster.com Accessed September 2020

249. "Therizo" Greek word for Reap https://www.biblehub.com Accessed September 2020

250. Psalm 126:5 Matthew Henry's Concise Commentary https://www.biblehub.com Accessed September 2020

251. "Forgive" Merriam-Webster.com 2019 https://www.merriam-webster.com Accessed September 2020

252. "Aphesis" Greek word for Forgive https://www.biblehub.com Accessed September 2020

253. "Skillful" Merriam-Webster.com 2019 https://www.merriam-webster.com Accessed September 2020

254. "Panourgos" Greek for Skillful https://www.biblehub.com Accessed September 2020

255. "Selfish" Merriam-Webster.com 2019 https://www.merriam-webster.com Accessed September 2020

256. "Eritheia" Greek word for Selfish https://www.biblehub.com Accessed September 2020

257. "Narrow" Merriam-Webster.com 2019 https://www.merriam-webster.com Accessed September 2020

258. "Stenos" Greek word for Narrow https://www.biblehub.com Accessed September 2020

259. "Authority" Merriam-Webster.com 2019 https://www.merriam-webster.com Accessed September 2020

260. "Rabhah" Greek word for Authority https://www.biblehub.com Accessed September 2020

261. Matthew 28:18 Matthew Henry's Concise Commentary https://www.biblehub.com Accessed September 2020

262. "Forsake" Merriam-Webster.com 2019 https://www.merriam-webster.com Accessed October 2020

263. "Egkataleipo" Greek word for Forsake https://www.biblehub.com Accessed October 2020

264. Deuteronomy 31:6 Benson Commentary https://www.biblehub.com Accessed October 2020

References

265. "Adorn" Merriam-Webster.com 2019 https://www.merriam-webster.com Accessed October 2020

266. "Kosmeo" Greek word for Adorn https://www.biblehub.com Accessed October 2020

267. Psalm 149:4 Matthew Henry's Concise Commentary https://www.biblehub.com Accessed October 2020

268. "Withhold" Merriam-Webster.com 2019 https://www.merriam-webster.com Accessed October 2020

269. "Tereo" Greek word for Withhold https://www.biblehub.com Accessed October 2020

270. "Messiah" Merriam-Webster.com 2019 https://www.merriam-webster.com Accessed October 2020

271. "Messias" Greek word for Messiah https://www.biblehub.com Accessed October 2020

272. Hebrews 13:8 Matthew Henry's Concise Commentary https://www.biblehub.com Accessed October 2020

273. "Hearken" Merriam-Webster.com 2019 https://www.merriam-webster.com Accessed October 2020

274. "Enotizomai" Greek word for Hearken https://www.biblehub.com Accessed October 2020

275. Deuteronomy 7:12 Matthew Henry's Concise Commentary https://www.biblehub.com Accessed October 2020

276. "Leans" Merriam-Webster.com https://www.merriam-webster.com Accessed October 2020

277. "Diischurizomai" Greek word for Leans https://www.biblehub.com Accessed October 2020

278. Psalm 32:10 Matthew Henry's Concise Commentary https://www.biblehub.com Accessed October 2020

279. "Weary" Merriam-Webster.com https://www.merriam-webster.com Accessed October 2020

280. "Kamno" Greek word for Weary https://www.biblehub.com Accessed October 2020

281. "Vindication" Merriam-Webster.com https://www.merriam-webster.com Accessed October 2020

282. "Ekdikeo" Greek word for Vindication https://www.biblehub.com Accessed October 2020

283. Isaiah 54:17 Barnes Notes on the Bible https://www.biblehub.com Accessed October 2020

284. "Yearn" Merriam-Webster.com 2019 https://www.merriam-webster.com Accessed October 2020

285. "Orego" Greek word for Yearn https://www.biblehub.com Accessed October 2020

286. 1 Chronicles 16:11 https://www.keystonevictoria.com Accessed October 2020

287. "Pleasures" Merriam-Webster.com 2019 https://www.merriam-webster.com Accessed October 2020

288. "Hedone" Greek word for Pleasures https://www.biblehub.com Accessed October 2020

289. Psalm 16:11 https://www.dailyverse.knowing-jesus.com Accessed October 2020

290. "Perfected love" https://www.conformingtoJesus.com Accessed October 2020

291. 1 John 4:18 https://www.conformingtoJesus.com Accessed October 2020.

292. "Granted" Merriam-Webster.com 2019 https://www.merriam-webster.com Accessed October 2020

293. "Doreomaj" Greek word for Granted. https://www.biblehub.com Accessed October 2020.

294. Mark 11:24 Matthew Henry's Concise Commentary https://www.biblehub.com Accessed October 2020

References

295. "Study" Merriam-Webster.com 2019 https://www.merriam-webster.com Accessed October 2020.

296. "Meletao" Greek word for Study https://www,biblehub.com Accessed October 2020

297. 2 Timothy 2:15 https://www.dailyverse.knowing-jesus.com Accessed October 2020

298. "Sympathetic Merriam-Webster.com 2019 https://ww-merriam-webster.com Accessed October 2020.

299. "Sympathes" Greek word for Sympathetic https://www.biblehub.com Accessed October 2020

300. Luke 6:36 https://www.dailyverse.knowing-jesus.com Accessed October 2020

301. "Advocate" Merriam-Webster.com 2019 https://www.merriam-webster.com Accessed October 2020.

302. "Paraletos" Greek word for advocates https://www.biblehub.com Accessed October 2020.

303. Luke 6:36 Matthew Henry's Concise Commentary https://www.biblehub.com Accessed October 2020

304. "Iniquity" Merriam-Webster.com 2019 https://www.merriam-webster.com Accessed October 2020

305. "Poneria" Greek for Iniquity https://www.biblehub.com Accessed October 2020.

306. 1 John 2:1, Matthew Henery's Concise Commentary https://ww.biblehub.com Accessed October 2020.

307. "Temperate" Merriam-Webster.com 2019 https://merriam-webster.com Accessed October 2020

308. "Sophran" Greek for the word Temperate. https://www.biblehub.com Accessed October 2020

309. 1 Peter 5:8 Matthew Henry's Concise Commentary https://www.biblehub.com Accessed October 2020

310. Proverbs 3:13, https://www.teachinghumblehearts.com Accessed October 2020.

311. "Citizenship" Merriam-Webster.com 2019 https://www.merrian-webster.com Accessed October 2020

312. "Poloteia" Greek word for Citizenship https://www.biblehub.com Accessed October 2020

313. Ephesians 2:19 Matthew Henry's Concise Commentary https://www.biblehub.com Accessed October 2020

314. "Statutes" Merrian-Webster.com 2019 https://www.merriam-webster.com Accessed October 2020

315. "Nomos" Greek word for Statutes https://www.biblehub.com accessed October 2020.

316. Psalm 119:64, Barnes Notes on the Bible https://www.biblehub.com Accessed October 2020.

317. "Multitude" Merriam-Webster.com 2019 https://www.merriam-webster.com Accessed October 2020

318. "Ochlos" Greek word for Multitude https://www.merriam-webster.com Accessed October 2020

319. Psalm 94:18-19 Matthew Henry's Concise Commentary https://www.biblehub.com Accessed October 2020.

320. "Handiwork" Merriam-Webster.com 2019 https://www.merriam-webster.com Accessed October 2020

321. "Yetser" Greek word for Handiwork https://www.biblehub.com Accessed October 2020.

322. Ephesian 2:10 https://www.bibleref.com Accessed October 2020

323. "Discretion" Merriam-Webster.com 2019 https://www.merriam-webster.com Accessed October 2020

324. Huparcho" Greek word for Discretion. https://www.biblehub.com Accessed October 2020

References

325. Proverbs 2:11 https://www.biblestudytools.com Accessed October 2020

326. "Law Giver" Merriam-Webster.com 2019 https://www.merriam-webster.com Accessed October 2020

327. "Nomothetes" Greek word for Law Giver https://www.biblehub.com Accessed October 2020.

328. Isaiah 33:22 Gill's Exposition of the Entire Bible https://www.biblehub.com Accessed October 2020

329. "Task" Merriam-Webster.com 2019 https://www.merriam-webster.com Accessed October 2020

330. "Ergon" Greek word for Task https://www.biblehub.com Accessed October 2020

331. "Decrees" Merriam-Webster.com https://www.merriam-webster.com Accessed October 2020

332. "Dogma" Greek for Decrees https://www.biblehub.com Accessed October 2020

333. Psalm 119:160, Jamieson-Fausset Brown Bible Commentary https://www.biblehub.com Accessed October 2020.

334. "Lift" Merriam-Webster.com 2019 https://www.merriam-webster.com Accessed October 2020

335. "Hupsoo" Greek word for Lift, https://www.biblehub.com Accessed October 2020

336. "Saved" Merriam-Webster.com 2019 https://www.merriam-webster.com October 2020

337. "Sozo" Greek word for Saved https://www.biblehub.com Accessed October 2020

338. Romans 10:9 https://www.dailyverse.knowing-jesus.com Accessed October 2020

339. "Stick" Merriam-Webster.com 2019 https://www.merriam-webster.com Accessed October 2020

340."Kollo" Greek word for Sticks https://www.wordhippo.com Accessed Octob3er 2020

341. Proverbs 18:24 Matthew Henry's Concise Commentary https://www.biblehub.com Accessed October 2020

342. "Buckler" Merrian-Webster.com 2019 https://www.merriam-webster.com Accessed October 2020

343. "Socherah" Hebrew word for Buckler https://www.biblehub.com Accessed October 2020

344. Psalm 91:4 Gill's Exposition of the Entire Bible https://www.merriam-webster.com Accessed October 2020

345. "Brimming" Merriam-Webster.com 2019 https://www.merriam-webster.com Accessed October 2020

346. "Gemizontas" Greek word for Brimming https://www.biblehub.com Accessed October 2020

347. Psalm 23:5 https://www.dailyverse.knowing-jesus.com Accessed October 2020

348. "Gifts" Merriam-Webster.com 2019 https://www.merriam-webster.com Accessed October 2020

349. "Charisma" Greek for Gifts https://www.biblehub.com Accessed October 2020

350. Luke 11:13 Matthew Henry's Concise Commentary https://www.biblehub.com Accessed October 2020

351."Bequeath" Merriam-Webster.com 2019 https://www.merriam-webster.com Accessed October 2020

352. "Hupolimpano" Greek word for Bequeath https://www.biblehub.com Accessed October 2020

353. John 14:27 Ellicott's Commentary for English Readers https://www.biblehub.com Accessed October 2020

354. "Reverently" Merriam-Webster.com https://www.merriam-webster.com Accessed October 2020

References

355. "Eulabeia" Greek word for Reverently https://www.biblehib.com Accessed October 2020

356. Deuteronomy 13:4 Gill's Exposition of the Entire Bible https://www.biblehub.com Accessed October 2020

357. "Quarrelsome" Merriam-Webster.com 2019 https://www.merriam-webster.com Accessed October 2020

358. "Machomai" Greek word for Quarrelsome https://www.biblehub.com Accessed October 2020

359. Proverbs 17:19 Matthew Henry's Concise Commentary https://www.biblehub.com Accessed October 2020

360. "Impenetrable" Merriam-Webster.com 2019 https://www.merriam-webster.com Accessed October 2020

361. "Astathmitos" Greek word for Impenetrable https://www.biblehub.com Accessed October 2020

362. Psalm 19:14 Pulpit Commentary https://www.biblehub.com Accessed October 2020

363. "Petitions" Merriam-Webster.com 2019 https://www.merriam-webster.com Accessed October 2020

364. "Enteuxis" Greek word for Petitions https://www.biblehub.com Accessed October 2020

365. "Integrity" Merriam-Webster.com 2019 https://www.merriam-webster.com Access October 2020

366. "Adiaphthoria" Greek word for Integrity https://www.biblehub.com Accessed October 2020

367. Proverbs 2:7 Matthew Henry's Concise Commentary https://www.biblehub.com Accessed October 2020

368. "Moral Excellence" Merriam-Webster.com 2019 https://www.merriam-webster.com Accessed October 2020

369. "Arete" Greek word for Moral Excellence https://www.biblehub.com Accessed October 2020

370. Matthew 5:16 Benson Commentary https://www.biblehub.com Accessed October 2020

371. Matthew 5:16 Barnes Nots on the Bible https://www.biblehub.com Accessed October 2020

372. "Doers" Merriam-Webster.com 2019 https://www.merriam-webster.com Accessed October 2020

373. "Poietes" Greek word for Doer https://www.biblehub.com Accessed October 2020

374. "Hiding Place" Merriam-Webster.com 2019 https://www.merriam-webster.com Accessed October 2020

375. "Mistar" Hebrew word for Hiding place htps://www.biblehub.com Accessed October 2020

376. "Yearning" Merriam-Webster.com 2019 :https//www.merriam-webster.com Accessed October 2020

377. "Orego" Greek word for Yearning https://www.biblehub.com Accessed October 2020

378. Psalm 119:10 https://www.astudyinginpsalm119.blogspot.com Accessed October 2020

379. The Power of a Parent's Blessing by Craig Hill Accessed October 2020

380. "Dedicated" Merriam-Webster.com 2019 https://www.merriam-webster.com Accessed October 2020

381. "Egkainia" Greek word for Dedicated https://www.biblehub.co, Accessed October 2020

382. Tricked Into Sickness by Loa Hardway Accessed October 2020

383. "Ordinances" Merriam-Webster.com 2019 https://www.merriam-webster.com Accessed October 2020

384. "Dikaiomai" Greek word for Ordinances https://www.biblehub.com Accessed October 2020

References

385. Psalm 119:30 https://www.study.light.org Accessed October 2020

386. "Pestilence" Merriam-Webster.com 2019 https://www.merriam-webster.com Accessed October 2020

387."Loimos" Greek word for Pestilence https://www.biblehub.com Accessed October 2020

388. "Latter" Merriam-Webster.com 2019 https://www.merriam-webster.com Accessed October 2020

389. "Husteros" Greek word for Latter https://www.biblehub.com Accessed October 2020

390. "Recognize" Merriam-Webster.com 2019 https://www.merriam-webster.com Accessed October 2020

391. "Epiginosko" Greek for Recognize https://www.biblehub.com Accessed October 2020

392. Psalm 46:10 https://www.dailyverse.knowing-jesus.com Accessed October 2020

393. "Enviable" Merriam-Webster.com 2019 https://www.merriam-webster.com Accessed October 2020

394. "Makarismos" Greek word for Enviable https://ww.biblehub.com Accessed October 2020

395. Matthew 5:9 Benson Commentary https://www.biblehub.com Accessed October 2020

396 "Godhead" Merriam-Webster.com 2019 https://www.merriam-webster.com Accessed October 2020

397. "Theotes" Greek word for Godhead https://www.biblehub.com Accessed October 2020

398. Colossians 2:9-10 https://www.joblog.net Accessed October 2020

399. "Personal Knowledge" https://www.thelawdictionary.org Accessed October 2020

400. "Gnosis" Greek word for Personal knowledge https://www.biblehub.com Accessed October 2020

401. Psalm 91:14 Matthew Henry's Concise Commentary https://www.biblehub.com Accessed October 2020

402. "Dwelling Place" Merriam-Webster.com 2019 https://www.merriam-webster.com Accessed October 2020

403. "Mone" Greek word for Dwelling Place https://www.biblehub.com Accessed October 2020

404. Psalm 91:9 Matthew Henry's Concise Commentary https://www.biblehub.com Accessed October 2020

405. "Unquestionably Merriam-Webster.com 2019 https://www.merriam-webster.com Accessed October 2020

406. "Anamfivolos" https://www.wordhippo.com Accessed October 2020

407. John 8:36 https://www.dailyverse.knowing-jesus.com Accessed October 2020

408. "Counsel" Merriam-Webster.com 2019 https://www.merriam-webster.com Accessed October 2020

409. "Sumboulion" Greek word for Counsel https://www.biblehub.com Accessed October 2020

410. Proverbs 1:5 https://www.bibleref.com Accessed October 2020

411. "Wisdom" Merriam-Webster.com 2019 https://www.merriam-webster.com Accessed October 2020

412. "Sophia" Greek word for Wisdom https://www.biblehub.com Accessed October 2020

413. Proverbs 1:33 https://www.letgodbetrue.com Accessed October 2020

414. "Retain" Merriam-Webster.com 2019 https://www.merriam-webster.com Accessed October 2020

References

415. "Krateo" Greek word for Retain https://www.biblehub.com Accessed October 2020

416. Isaiah 41:10 https://www.dailyverse.knowing-jesus.com Accessed October 2020

417 "Refining Merriam-Webster.com 2019 https://www.merriam-webster.com Accessed October 2020

418. "Puroo" Greek word for Refining https://www.biblehub.com Accessed October 2020

419. "Adversity" Merriam-Webster.com 2019 https://www.merriam-webster.com Accessed October 2020

420. "Sugkakoucheomai" Greek word for Adversity https://www.biblehub.com Accessed October 2020

421. Proverbs 17:17 Matthew Henry's Concise Commentary https://www.biblehub.com Accessed October 2020

422. "Essentially" Merriam-Webster.com 2019 https://www.merriam-webster.com Accessed October 2020

423. "ousiastika" Greek word for Essentially https://www.biblehub.com Accessed October 2020

424. Philippians 2:6 Matthew Henry's Concise Commentary https://www.biblehub.com Accessed October 2020

425. "Discipline" Merriam-Webster.com https://www.merriam-webster.com Accessed October 2020

426. "Paideia" Greek word for Discipline https://www.biblehub.com Accessed October 2020

427. Hebrew 12:11 Matthew Henry's Concise Commentary https://www.biblehub.com Accessed October 2020

428. "Planted" Merriam-Webster.com 2019 https://www.merriam-webster.com Accessed October 2020

429. "Neophutos" Greek word for Planted https://www.biblehub.com Accessed October 2020

430. "Liberates" Merriam-Webster.com 2019 https://www.merriam-webster.com Accessed October 2020

431. "eleutheroo" Greek word for Liberates https://www.biblehub.com Accessed October 2020

432. John 8:36 https://www.dailverse.knowing-jesus.com Accessed October 2020

433. "Incentive" Merriam-Webster.com 2019 https://www.merriam-webster.com Accessed October 2020

434. "Erethisma" Greek word for Incentive https://www.biblehub.com Accessed October 2020

435. Galatians 5:13 https://www.dailyverse.knowing-jesus.com Accessed October 2020

436. "Abide" Merriam-Webster.com 2019 https://www.merriam-webster.com Accessed Ocbtober 2020

437. "Meno" Greek word for Abide https://www.biblehub.com Accessed October 2020

438. John 15:7 Pulpit Commentary https://www.biblehub.com Accessed October 2020

439."Thousand" Merriam-Webster.com 2019 https://www.merriam-webster.com Accessed October 2020

440. "Chilia" Greek word for Thousand https://www.biblehub.com Accessed October 2020

441. Psalm 91:7 Barnes Notes on the Bible https://www.biblehub.com Accessed October 2020

442. "Worship" Merriam-Webster.com 2019 https://www.merriam-webster.com Accessed October 2020

443. "Proskuneo" Greek word for Worship https://www.biblehub.com Accessed October 2020

444. Psalm 138:2 https://www.biblehub.com Accessed October 2020

References

445. "Benefical" Merriam-Webster.com 2019 https://www.merriam-webster.com Accessed October 2020

446. "eudokia" Greek word for Beneficial https://www.biblehub.com Accessed October 2020

447. Psalm 34:10 MacLaren's Expositions https://www.biblehub.com Accessed October 2020

448. "Christ" Merriam-Webster.com 2019 https://www.merriam-webster.com Accessed October 2020

449. "Christos" Greek word for Christ https://www.biblehub.com Accessed October 2020

450. Acts 3:20 Matthew Henry's Concise Commentary https://www.biblehub.com Accessed October 2020

451. "Father" Merriam-Webster.com 2019 https://www.merriam-webster.com Accessed October 2020

452. "Pater" Greek word for Father https://www.Biblehub.com Accessed October 2020

453. 2 Corinthians 6:18 Barnes Notes on the Bible https://www.biblehub.com Accessed October 2020

454. "Strove/Strive Merriam-Webster.com 2019 https://www.merriam-webster.com Accessed October 2020

455. "Agonizomai" Greek word for Strove/Strive https://www.biblehub.com Accessed October 2020

456. Psalm 55:18 Matthew Henry's Concise Commentary https://www.biblehub.com Accessed October 2020

457. "Distress" Merriam-Webster.com 2019 https://www,merriam-webster.com Accessed October 2020

458. "Stenochoria" Greek word for Distress https://www.biblehub.com Accessed October 2020

459. Psalm 120:1 Matthew Henry's Concise Commentary https://www.biblehub.com Accessed October 2020

460. "Guard" Merriam-Webster.com 2019 https://www.merriam-webster.com Accessed October 2020

461. "Phroureo" Greek word for Guard https://www.biblehub.com Accessed October 2020

462. "Courageous" Merriam-Webster.com 2019 https://www.merriam-webster.com Accessed October 2020

463. "Tharseo" Greek word for Courageous https://www.biblehub.com Accessed October 2020

464. "Dread" Merriam-Webster.com https://www.merriam-webster.com Accessed October 2020.

465. "Deiliao" Greek word for Dread https://www.biblehub.com Accessed October 2020.

Index

3

39 stripes, 223

5

5-Fold, 27

A

abandon, 241
abandoned, 306
Abba, 18, 25, 122, 123
abide, 46, 47, 70, 96, 97, 165, 378, 379
abiding, 46, 337, 351
ability, 58, 102, 118, 143, 158, 164, 231, 357, 398, 400
Abraham, 140, 150, 300
abundance, 319
abundant, 87, 120, 193, 304
acceptable, 146, 157, 167, 238, 317
accomplish, 94, 267
accountable, 106, 221
accusations, 180, 258

acknowledge, 3, 4, 129, 299, 343, 389
actions, 13, 42, 54, 117, 169
Adam, 16, 178, 191, 192
admirable, 75
admonish, 100, 109, 185
adoration, 118
Adorn, 243
advance, 13, 298, 313
advancements, 13
advantage, 61, 235, 307, 308, 384
adversity, 258, 284, 364
advice, 109, 185, 279, 355, 356
advocate, 156, 272
affairs, 24
affirm, 98, 252
affliction, 73, 100, 229, 351
afraid, 9, 35, 58, 172, 189, 206, 263, 309, 310, 338, 398, 400, 401
agape, 20, 49, 221, 346
age, 32, 106, 128, 140, 149, 341, 365
agenda, 110, 256
agendas, 110
agitated, 309, 310
agreement, 28, 187, 206, 262, 338
alarm, 136
alignment, 2, 3, 4, 14, 182
alive, 11, 136, 152, 226
alone, 22, 133, 145, 170, 172, 185, 190, 195, 210, 218, 252, 253, 272, 300, 313, 399
altar, 24, 248

Index

amazing, 87, 186, 223, 260, 283
ambition, 235
angels, 74, 153, 220, 239, 309, 327, 337, 338, 352, 396
anger, 39, 40, 49, 200, 201, 274, 275, 314, 315
Anger, 39, 315
angry, 33
anoint, 123, 305
anointed, 306
anointing, 141
antagonism, 39
anxiety, 188, 202, 263
anxious, 116, 134, 173, 184, 284, 344, 395
apply, 54, 64, 96, 289, 296, 324, 325, 336
approval, 62, 365
arc, 58
arguments, 81, 348
armor of God, 35, 36
arresting, 181
arrogance, 42, 43
ashamed, 23, 73, 74, 209, 268, 383
ashes, 17
ask, 4, 10, 12, 14, 16, 26, 30, 32, 34, 38, 39, 40, 43, 45, 46, 49, 66, 68, 72, 74, 76, 79, 82, 84, 86, 87, 89, 105, 107, 115, 119, 129, 133, 139, 148, 154, 158, 165, 176, 182, 184, 186, 187, 192, 201, 203, 215, 216, 221, 230, 233, 234, 235, 248, 266, 275, 281, 290, 307, 308, 310, 318, 321, 325, 329, 344, 356, 358, 373, 378, 379, 385, 394
assigned, 55, 141, 241, 282, 293, 308, 395
assignments, 96
assistance, 205, 253

437

assurance, 187, 299
attacks, 58
attempt, 138
attitude, 18, 19, 214, 357
attitudes, 54
attribute, 181, 307
author, 221, 222, 402
authority, 64, 82, 113, 213, 239, 281, 347, 348, 354, 367, 384, 401
avenge, 257, 291, 292, 315, 394

B

bait, 40, 191, 318
barns, 340
battlefield, 140
battles, 89, 180, 346
beacon, 23
beautiful, 47, 243, 268
beauty, 17
beginning, 2, 25, 164, 295, 340, 341
behavior, 39, 53, 213, 214, 238, 239
behaviors, 82, 176
belief, 78, 222, 353, 357
believe, 9, 10, 20, 27, 47, 51, 66, 86, 93, 94, 98, 135, 138, 145, 149, 201, 216, 223, 253, 266, 299, 300, 307, 324, 344, 353, 361, 362, 373, 401
believer, 25, 120, 238, 253, 349, 351, 378
bench, 70
benefits, 44, 169, 170

benevolent, 136, 220

best, 7, 15, 20, 24, 31, 32, 40, 55, 62, 66, 87, 94, 105, 129, 153, 174, 180, 188, 262, 267, 282, 287, 310, 315, 322, 346

better, 2, 8, 14, 22, 25, 35, 49, 60, 66, 90, 96, 105, 107, 108, 145, 159, 176, 228, 248, 252, 254, 262, 269, 373, 392, 395

beyond, 86, 221, 315, 331, 400

Bible, 13, 47, 55, 64, 71, 73, 154, 211, 218, 248, 258, 268, 283, 289, 292, 295, 296, 304, 313, 324, 360, 381, 389

birth, 117, 310

birthed, 19

bitter, 84

bitterness, 89, 315, 362

blackmail, 81

blame, 42, 112, 391

bless, 14, 16, 25, 33, 87, 130, 166, 169, 236, 243, 330, 331, 332, 340, 341, 358

blessed, 14, 33, 40, 87, 101, 116, 117, 161, 169, 273, 278, 281, 341, 346, 351, 358

block, 3, 4, 30, 153, 211, 248

blood, 35, 36, 40, 63, 66, 67, 68, 82, 89, 99, 107, 113, 133, 192, 221, 224, 226, 239, 246, 251, 258, 273, 275, 292, 299, 304, 338, 339, 344, 372, 375, 376, 377, 381, 383, 386, 396, 401

Blood of the Lamb, 158

bloodline, 99, 178, 226

blueprint, 206

boast, 235

bodies, 47, 67, 83, 84, 152, 163, 167, 339

Body of Christ, 20, 63, 208

bold, 93, 94, 398

boldly, 21, 93, 94, 191

boldness, 93, 187, 311, 401

bondage, 147, 209, 354, 373

book, 60, 87, 330, 333, 402

boundaries, 117

brass, 221

brave, 31, 398

bravery, 171

Bread of Life, 175

breakthrough, 29, 195, 211, 212, 230, 298

breakthroughs, 110

breathe, 46, 47, 136, 253

bridle, 201, 314, 393, 394

broad path, 237, 238

broken, 1, 36, 105, 177, 226, 264, 265, 345

brother, 301, 302, 364, 365, 390

brothers, 39, 55, 71, 220, 221, 345

building, 83, 186, 280

burden, 19, 124, 137

burdens, 24, 25, 35, 126, 137, 162, 298, 383, 391

business, 24, 112, 123, 151, 189, 197, 206, 281, 289, 383

businesses, 102, 135

busy, 55, 294

C

calamities, 229, 357, 394

calamity, 100, 381

calling, 14, 43, 56, 105, 140, 148, 203, 206, 208, 236, 256, 294, 313, 336, 344

calm, 10, 69, 196, 279, 358, 380, 395

Index

captive, 81, 348
career, 122, 396
careers, 24, 30, 297
careful, 11, 39, 76, 324
cares, 15, 24, 49, 100, 104, 148, 162, 168, 170, 173, 186, 262, 285, 328, 361, 392, 395, 396
cast out, 49, 190, 226, 242
cataracts, 184
chain breaker, 178
chair, 79
chances, 8, 152
changed, 54, 60
chaos, 24, 70
character, 28, 39, 63, 104, 128, 186, 262, 282, 315, 346, 366, 394, 395
charisma, 307
charitable, 220
chasing, 336, 341
chastisement, 368, 369
cheer, 134, 284, 398
children, 1, 23, 24, 25, 51, 70, 87, 102, 106, 107, 108, 113, 116, 121, 123, 142, 153, 158, 177, 243, 245, 270, 272, 303, 307, 319, 327, 330, 331, 339, 346, 355, 356, 360, 367, 368, 389, 394, 396
choice, 7, 107, 238, 335, 357
Christ, 2, 8, 9, 10, 20, 23, 27, 28, 47, 51, 52, 54, 57, 58, 59, 61, 65, 66, 68, 69, 70, 72, 73, 76, 79, 81, 82, 83, 84, 87, 93, 94, 100, 105, 109, 110, 113, 125, 130, 131, 133, 138, 146, 149, 155, 156, 157, 158, 172, 175, 178, 183, 185, 186, 187, 191, 195, 203, 208, 210, 214, 216, 217, 218, 221, 224, 229, 238, 243, 247, 248, 253,

254, 260, 265, 270, 272, 273, 274, 280, 281, 286, 287, 291, 293, 298, 299, 301, 306, 307, 318, 328, 334, 335, 343, 344, 345, 347, 348, 353, 354, 361, 366, 367, 373, 375, 376, 378, 379, 382, 385, 387, 391, 396

    Christ Jesus, 10, 70, 72, 82, 87, 133, 155, 156, 318

    Christian, 1, 28, 73, 138, 192, 233, 324, 376, 402

    Christlikeness, 53

    church, 7, 8, 21, 81, 83, 120, 144, 210, 239, 280, 281, 291, 292, 375

    churches, 42, 110

    circumspect, 53

    circumstances, 179, 187, 230

    citizen, 280, 281

    civil, 312

    clean, 34, 43, 60, 66, 68, 76, 84, 105, 111, 148, 176, 198, 315, 362, 363, 380

    cohabitate, 242

    coin, 329

    comfort, 22, 56, 100, 120, 183, 247, 252, 285, 300, 343, 380, 392, 401

    comfortable, 238, 252, 307, 388

    comforter, 100, 272

    command, 84, 91, 96, 196, 239, 295, 326

    Commander, 343

    commandments, 96, 151, 164, 171, 312, 329, 332, 358

    commands, 110, 153, 263, 301, 302, 312, 313

    commission, 21, 66, 135

    committed, 66, 76, 82, 97, 135, 239, 263, 291

    commune, 7, 252

    communion, 99, 252, 338, 379, 381

compassion, 142, 163, 164, 259, 270, 271, 274, 344
compassionate, 213, 270
compensate, 16
completion, 255, 256
comprehend, 86, 128, 129
concern, 10, 168, 235, 267
conclusion, 114, 222
condemn, 133, 203
confess, 27, 66, 112, 113, 135, 201, 216, 299, 300, 367
confidence, 9, 22, 51, 74, 78, 116, 172, 187, 189, 200, 210, 261, 267, 295, 311
confident, 51, 200, 266, 357
confirm, 75
conflict, 49, 391
conformity, 63, 368
confrontation, 316
confusion, 48, 49, 181, 314, 315
conquered, 171, 261
conquerors, 125
consecration, 48, 174
consequences, 2
console, 12, 100
consult, 36, 234, 279, 322
consultation, 355
contagious, 283, 337, 338
contaminated, 76
contempt, 120
contentions, 182
convict, 250
corner, 195, 230

corrupt, 183, 184

corruption, 213, 267, 274, 321, 367

costs, 51

counsel, 109, 147, 153, 174, 185, 200, 289, 355, 356

counselor, 12, 389, 390

counterintuitive, 54

courage, 22, 93, 343, 398

courageous, 31, 58, 241, 398, 399

course, 26, 58, 295, 330, 355, 357, 395

courts, 370, 371

covenant, 151, 204, 249, 273, 302, 338, 392

covering, 211, 275, 328, 361

COVID 19, 57

cowardly, 9, 309, 311, 400

creator, 128, 343

Creator, 128, 360

creature, 2, 25, 27, 28, 60, 66, 97, 103, 105, 110, 121, 127, 135, 143, 184, 201, 216, 248, 265, 300

crises, 3

crooked place, 401

cross, 28, 52, 105, 155, 222, 223, 246, 275, 281, 288, 338, 353, 354, 367, 373

crown of life, 139

crushed, 132

cry, 10, 114, 125, 135, 152, 160, 162, 165, 177, 211, 253, 297, 353, 372, 388, 396

cultures, 156

currency, 79, 86

curse, 33, 41, 249, 351, 354

cursing, 67

cymbal, 220

D

dabbling, 117
daily, 1, 7, 28, 47, 52, 53, 58, 69, 70, 92, 96, 105, 178, 244, 252, 267, 324, 325, 331, 350, 375
damnation, 65, 300, 373
danger, 93, 137, 230, 249, 267, 276, 299, 317, 337
Daniel, 18, 383
darkness, 65, 98, 99, 177, 249, 333, 334, 337
daughters, 70, 152, 389
David, 118, 159, 161, 189, 198, 227, 252, 259, 261, 262, 305, 391, 393
daytime, 196
Death, 2, 130
deceitful, 183, 184, 393, 394
deceived, 269
decision, 7, 188, 279, 322
decisions, 17, 203, 248, 279, 290, 322, 356, 358
declarations, 1
declare, 13, 48, 93, 94, 110, 119, 131, 216, 228, 230, 242, 250, 331, 339, 379
decree, 13, 94, 110, 131, 147, 207, 216, 228, 242, 250, 295, 335, 339, 355
deed, 21, 66, 135, 335
defend, 180, 194, 257, 303, 330, 346
defense, 132, 194, 257, 343
deity, 347
delight, 37, 71, 134, 144, 261, 284, 346

deliver, 122, 177, 178, 190, 215, 299, 349

deliverance, 39, 82, 110, 124, 192, 201, 207

delusions, 248

demonic spirit, 226

demonized, 315, 346

Demons, 239

demonstration, 54

depend, 29, 58, 62, 139, 186, 205, 255, 258, 297, 319, 322, 385, 398

depression, 217, 396

designed, 1

desire, 4, 54, 76, 116, 127, 130, 140, 144, 165, 166, 176, 235, 261, 282, 283, 291, 346, 387

desires, 12, 13, 24, 37, 71, 165, 166, 226, 271, 319, 360, 367

despair, 132, 133, 138, 379

destination, 65

destiny, 4, 30, 40, 52, 62, 105, 122, 148, 173, 184, 193, 195, 256, 258, 294

destroy, 25, 40, 81, 106, 132, 153, 154, 250, 258, 276, 277, 304, 376, 387

destruction, 160, 166, 177, 207, 237, 275, 278, 304, 314, 337, 357

detestable, 207

devil, 16, 64, 139, 203, 216, 230, 276, 277, 351, 399

devotion, 220

devotional, 1, 27, 402

dialogue, 160

dignity, 194

diligence, 89, 233, 321

dinner table, 330

Index

direction, 2, 3, 215, 335, 396

disagreement, 49

discern, 112, 184, 330, 343, 357

discernment, 5, 203, 289, 290

disciples, 9, 18, 309, 310, 348

discouraged, 360

discouragement, 361

disobedience, 81, 192

disobeyed, 74, 191, 369

dispensation, 375, 376

dispensations, 387

displeasure, 39

disposal, 35, 159

distort, 183

distracted, 134, 329, 377, 395

distraction, 58

distractions, 330, 332

distress, 393, 394

distresses, 138, 177, 178

distrust, 139

disturbed, 309, 310

divine, 11, 21, 33, 57, 154, 158, 211, 227, 282, 300, 347, 348, 357, 367, 380, 382, 384, 387

doctor, 21, 197

doctrines, 73

doer, 54, 175, 324

domination, 179, 372

door, 7, 8, 49, 96, 317

dormant, 123

doubt, 10, 75, 139, 152, 180, 187, 190, 191, 262, 285, 341, 361, 400

drinking, 67

duties, 73, 383

E

eagle, 140

ear gates, 313

ears, 38, 62, 113, 248

earth, 8, 13, 14, 23, 47, 55, 57, 64, 66, 68, 70, 74, 84, 87, 117, 128, 144, 145, 147, 161, 163, 186, 192, 193, 205, 214, 239, 240, 243, 260, 282, 293, 297, 309, 320, 322, 334, 343, 349, 379

earthquake, 373

east, 236

eat, 2, 7, 8, 16, 130, 191, 236, 319, 320, 338

effectively, 19, 107, 267

effectual, 188

effort, 33, 89, 192, 268, 391

embarrassments, 132, 133

emotion, 15, 37, 71

emotionally, 15, 32

emotions, 13, 30, 40, 50, 69, 84, 167, 186, 270, 362

empower, 1, 23, 123

empowered, 110, 114

empowerment, 58, 123, 232, 264, 271

encamp, 327

encounter, 21, 23, 223

encourage, 22, 23, 31, 80, 101, 190, 285, 388

encouragement, 22, 23, 31, 79, 100, 109, 350, 360, 402

Index

encourages, 100, 247
encouraging, 12, 31, 101, 266
endeavor, 345, 391
endurance, 71, 102, 255
endure, 15, 73, 136, 139, 213, 214, 225, 230, 364, 378
enemies, 21, 33, 34, 40, 49, 84, 179, 180, 206, 258, 292, 303, 304, 305, 306, 343, 346, 350, 394, 398, 399
enemy, 16, 29, 30, 36, 39, 45, 49, 58, 64, 76, 81, 82, 90, 94, 99, 106, 107, 113, 126, 127, 130, 132, 139, 159, 160, 176, 184, 189, 190, 191, 202, 203, 206, 211, 230, 238, 242, 248, 250, 253, 257, 258, 261, 276, 277, 310, 324, 325, 327, 328, 351, 352, 359, 361, 400, 401
energy, 56, 118, 391
enthusiasm, 89
entrance, 7, 192
envied, 33, 138
envy, 181, 182
epidemic disease, 337
err, 202, 275
error, 202, 258, 289, 387
escape, 57, 113, 197, 208, 367
establish, 75
Esther, 207, 208, 331
eternal life, 23, 26, 66, 161, 193, 238
Eve, 16, 178, 191, 192
everlasting, 119, 125, 128, 136, 229, 283, 292, 310, 354
evidence, 98, 189, 282
evil, 5, 29, 30, 98, 108, 138, 147, 176, 179, 181, 184, 203, 226, 235, 251, 289, 307, 317, 318, 338, 351, 352, 357, 376
exalt, 149, 150, 297, 358

excellence, 75, 323
exercise, 104
exertion, 102
exhaustion, 55
exhort, 22, 109, 185
expectation, 31, 87, 116
expected end, 51, 52, 92, 186, 344
expelled, 191
experienced, 157, 341, 356
expiration, 16
eyes, 5, 17, 29, 38, 61, 136, 184, 205, 254, 285, 297, 330, 331, 400

F

faces, 15, 25
facial expressions, 331
factor, 69, 138
failure, 175
faint, 32, 128, 141, 255
faith, 1, 9, 29, 44, 47, 52, 54, 57, 64, 65, 70, 71, 72, 78, 79, 86, 129, 133, 139, 143, 158, 159, 165, 172, 185, 189, 210, 216, 221, 222, 223, 231, 241, 242, 248, 253, 261, 266, 267, 276, 285, 287, 296, 299, 304, 308, 323, 325, 343, 344, 352, 361, 373, 376, 383, 388
faithful, 29, 74, 151, 185, 255, 263, 264, 266, 295, 302, 304, 305, 321, 324, 340, 382, 383, 391
faithfulness, 78, 149, 150, 152, 303, 335, 340, 382
Fall, 47
fallen state, 184

Index

false accuser, 277

false claims, 40

false teachings, 348

families, 30, 39, 44, 103, 110, 131, 132, 330, 337

family, 14, 16, 21, 28, 40, 41, 58, 64, 72, 79, 87, 122, 123, 131, 152, 192, 197, 203, 205, 226, 251, 258, 263, 280, 283, 287, 297, 306, 330, 331, 332, 336, 338, 352, 365, 383, 389, 390, 396, 399, 401

famous, 235

fast, 27, 29, 35, 71, 138, 308, 344, 360

fasting, 154, 174, 192

Father, 4, 6, 8, 9, 10, 12, 14, 15, 16, 18, 19, 21, 23, 25, 28, 30, 32, 34, 36, 40, 43, 45, 47, 49, 52, 54, 56, 58, 59, 60, 62, 64, 66, 68, 70, 72, 74, 76, 79, 82, 84, 87, 90, 96, 100, 103, 105, 107, 115, 121, 122, 123, 127, 129, 133, 139, 143, 148, 152, 155, 156, 160, 164, 168, 172, 176, 180, 184, 188, 192, 194, 197, 201, 206, 211, 216, 221, 223, 226, 230, 231, 234, 236, 240, 244, 248, 253, 258, 262, 267, 270, 271, 272, 273, 274, 275, 279, 283, 287, 291, 292, 296, 300, 304, 307, 308, 310, 313, 318, 322, 323, 325, 332, 334, 336, 338, 344, 347, 348, 352, 356, 361, 365, 366, 367, 368, 369, 373, 379, 383, 388, 389, 390, 392, 396, 401

Father of lights, 392

fault, 112, 175

faults, 54, 112, 113, 221

favor, 58, 93, 140, 143, 158, 164, 188, 208, 217, 244, 274, 307, 345, 358, 365

favorable, 48

fear, 5, 35, 49, 116, 134, 165, 166, 172, 189, 190, 196, 206, 241, 242, 263, 264, 310, 312, 313, 325, 352, 357, 358, 360, 361, 380, 398, 401

fearful, 242, 309, 400
fearlessly, 93
fears, 10, 14, 24, 25, 132, 264, 334, 352
feathers, 140, 303, 304
feelings, 40, 167, 201
feet, 24, 25, 50, 55, 64, 110, 124, 162, 171, 172, 262, 298, 308, 328, 335, 339, 352, 365, 392, 395
fellowship, 63, 73, 249
fervent, 19, 20, 21, 122, 393
fiber, 145, 174
fiery darts, 29
fight, 28, 127, 180, 195, 314, 338, 346, 400
fighting, 76, 89, 132
finances, 17, 87, 236, 341, 365, 396
financially, 14, 32, 46, 236
finisher, 221, 222
fire, 41, 72, 104, 105, 121, 148, 184, 216, 225, 332, 339, 362, 363, 364
Fire, 225
firm, 29, 55, 122, 126, 144, 159, 241, 248, 317, 321, 353, 398
firmness, 144
flame, 225
flawless, 72
flaws, 43, 54, 60, 72
flesh, 89, 90, 99, 113, 144, 166, 176, 183, 184, 199, 262, 346, 372, 375, 376
fleshly things, 322
fling, 37
flood, 159, 277
flow, 60, 89

flu, 381
followers, 52, 235, 237
food, 217, 307, 384
foolish, 200, 348, 356, 357
footsteps, 271, 354, 356
force, 7, 11, 63, 102, 118, 192
forfeit, 61
forgave, 81
forgetfulness, 193
forgive, 21, 33, 34, 40, 43, 66, 68, 74, 76, 82, 84, 90, 97, 129, 148, 203, 206, 214, 216, 230, 231, 232, 287, 315, 325, 369
forgiveness, 89, 158, 177, 192, 193, 198, 201, 203, 214, 215, 231, 232, 271, 273, 315, 353
forgiving, 6, 39, 77, 82, 84, 192, 231, 232, 271, 275, 292, 369
forgotten, 54, 196, 306
fornication, 67, 84
forsake, 10, 58, 132, 241, 301, 344, 349, 398, 399, 401
Fortress, 122
fortunate, 101, 278
foundation, 29, 44, 144, 146, 183, 248
fragrance, 172
framing, 286
freedom, 34, 42, 69, 154, 187, 375, 376
fresh, 110, 210
fruit, 2, 116, 117, 130, 182, 184, 191, 281, 368, 369, 370, 371
fruitful, 139, 325
fruition, 15
fulfillment, 263
future, 25, 51, 52, 92, 148, 157, 173, 174, 186, 192, 206, 255, 256, 281, 322, 332, 344, 377

G

garden, 191, 192

generation, 16, 107, 334

generations, 151

Gentiles, 156, 287, 299

gentleman, 192

gentleness, 42

gift, 45, 67, 106, 198, 233, 248, 287, 307, 308, 309, 310, 321, 344, 356, 358

gladness, 37, 71, 244, 294

glance, 54

glorifies, 98

glorify, 67, 68, 118, 149, 160, 169, 323

glory, 10, 16, 28, 57, 66, 74, 88, 94, 115, 117, 118, 119, 121, 123, 137, 140, 143, 148, 149, 156, 159, 185, 211, 244, 260, 281, 284, 294, 298, 304, 306, 308, 324, 326, 341, 359, 361, 366, 367, 385, 390, 391, 396

glowing, 20

God, 1, 2, 3, 4, 5, 6, 7, 8, 9, 10, 11, 12, 13, 14, 15, 16, 18, 19, 20, 21, 22, 23, 24, 25, 26, 27, 28, 29, 30, 31, 32, 33, 34, 35, 36, 37, 38, 39, 40, 41, 42, 43, 44, 45, 46, 47, 48, 49, 51, 52, 53, 54, 55, 56, 57, 58, 59, 60, 61, 62, 63, 64, 65, 66, 67, 68, 69, 70, 71, 72, 73, 74, 75, 76, 77, 78, 79, 81, 82, 83, 84, 86, 87, 89, 90, 91, 93, 94, 96, 97, 98, 99, 100, 101, 102, 103, 104, 105, 106, 107, 108, 109, 110, 112, 113, 114, 115, 116, 117, 118, 119, 120, 121, 122, 123, 124, 125, 126, 127, 128, 129, 130, 131, 132, 133, 134, 135, 136, 137, 138, 139, 140, 141, 142, 143, 144, 145, 146, 147, 148, 149, 150, 151, 152, 153, 154, 155, 156, 157, 158, 159, 160,

161, 163, 164, 165, 166, 167, 168, 169, 170, 171, 172, 173, 174, 175, 176, 177, 178, 179, 180, 182, 183, 184, 185, 186, 187, 188, 189, 190, 191, 192, 194, 196, 197, 198, 199, 200, 201, 202, 203, 205, 206, 207, 208, 210, 211, 213, 214, 215, 216, 217, 218, 220, 221, 222, 223, 226, 227, 228, 229, 230, 231, 232, 233, 234, 235, 236, 237, 238, 239, 240, 241, 242, 243, 244, 245, 246, 247, 248, 249, 250, 252, 253, 255, 256, 258, 259, 261, 262, 263, 264, 266, 267, 268, 269, 270, 271, 272, 273, 274, 275, 277, 278, 279, 280, 281, 282, 283, 284, 285, 286, 287, 291, 292, 293, 294, 295, 296, 297, 298, 299, 300, 302, 303, 304, 305, 306, 307, 308, 310, 311, 312, 313, 314, 315, 319, 321, 322, 323, 324, 325, 327, 328, 330, 331, 332, 333, 334, 335, 336, 337, 338, 339, 340, 341, 343, 344, 345, 346, 347, 348, 349, 350, 351, 352, 353, 354, 356, 357, 358, 359, 360, 361, 362, 363, 365, 366, 367, 368, 369, 370, 371, 373, 374, 375, 376, 377, 378, 379, 381, 382, 383, 384, 385, 387, 388, 389, 390, 391, 392, 393, 394, 395, 396, 398, 399, 400, 401, 402

Godhead, 347, 348

godly wisdom, 279, 356

gold, 72, 362, 363, 364

good, 2, 15, 17, 28, 31, 33, 37, 44, 47, 49, 51, 52, 56, 61, 71, 72, 74, 75, 80, 93, 98, 102, 104, 136, 139, 140, 142, 153, 159, 163, 164, 166, 168, 179, 181, 183, 184, 199, 203, 213, 214, 218, 220, 226, 229, 230, 243, 248, 255, 256, 270, 282, 286, 287, 289, 305, 307, 319, 320, 322, 323, 325, 330, 335, 350, 351, 357, 358, 362, 365, 369, 376, 384, 385, 393, 398

Good News, 26, 27, 28, 109, 247

goodness, 1, 136, 139, 157, 163, 282, 323

gospel, 27, 73, 78, 214, 289

gossiping, 89

government, 205, 239, 282, 292, 295, 338

grace, 26, 29, 40, 47, 54, 58, 59, 72, 84, 90, 93, 94, 105, 109, 136, 137, 140, 142, 143, 158, 163, 164, 174, 177, 183, 184, 202, 210, 214, 219, 227, 231, 234, 246, 247, 267, 271, 273, 287, 299, 307, 334, 335, 361, 363, 375, 376, 383

grandchildren, 24, 102, 107

grandparents, 106, 108

grateful, 164, 271

gratifications, 227

Great Awakening, 208

greater, 141, 229, 326, 334, 341

Greek, 1, 5, 7, 9, 11, 13, 15, 18, 20, 22, 24, 26, 29, 31, 33, 35, 37, 39, 42, 44, 46, 48, 51, 53, 55, 57, 59, 61, 63, 65, 67, 69, 71, 73, 75, 78, 81, 83, 86, 89, 91, 93, 96, 98, 100, 102, 104, 106, 109, 112, 114, 116, 118, 120, 122, 124, 126, 128, 130, 132, 134, 136, 138, 140, 142, 144, 147, 149, 151, 153, 155, 157, 159, 161, 163, 165, 167, 169, 171, 173, 175, 177, 179, 181, 183, 185, 187, 189, 191, 194, 196, 198, 200, 202, 205, 207, 210, 213, 215, 217, 220, 222, 225, 227, 229, 231, 233, 235, 237, 239, 241, 243, 245, 247, 249, 252, 255, 257, 259, 261, 266, 268, 270, 272, 274, 276, 280, 282, 284, 286, 289, 291, 293, 295, 297, 299, 301, 305, 307, 309, 312, 314, 317, 319, 321, 323, 324, 329, 333, 335, 337, 340, 343, 345, 347, 349, 351, 353, 355, 357, 360, 362, 364, 366, 368, 370, 372, 375, 378, 380, 382, 384, 387, 389, 391, 393, 395, 398, 400

green, 116, 117, 184, 210, 211

grief, 100

grieve, 67, 76, 84, 281, 313, 314

grieved, 15

grounded, 9, 55, 57, 70, 124, 151, 210, 211, 250, 253, 258

grudges, 201

Index

guard, 29, 30, 40, 70, 90, 176, 192, 203, 245, 277, 289, 329, 395

guide, 10, 23, 28, 45, 62, 64, 80, 84, 102, 145, 156, 245, 269, 318, 327, 336, 348, 355, 374, 378, 389

guilt, 26, 175, 314

guilty, 81

H

Hades, 144

Haman, 207

hammer, 225, 226

hands, 9, 27, 28, 34, 55, 87, 117, 118, 119, 152, 173, 300, 315, 362, 363, 371

happiness, 274, 307, 331, 335, 345, 358

happy, 15, 16, 33, 120, 121, 138, 169, 174, 346, 396

hardness, 159

hardships, 71, 356

harm, 36, 40, 137, 213, 230, 327, 381, 396, 398

harvest, 117, 131, 208, 229, 236, 298, 354, 368

hate, 33, 60, 107, 247, 315

hates, 43, 76, 98, 107, 277, 315

hating, 76, 84, 98

healed, 10, 112, 164, 265

healing, 35, 151, 152, 163, 192, 203, 212, 223, 338, 339, 385

health, 136, 137, 380

hear, 14, 38, 39, 53, 54, 62, 74, 76, 110, 141, 165, 215, 248, 253, 296, 324, 331, 332, 355, 358, 391, 402

hearer, 54, 175

hearts, 7, 9, 27, 34, 37, 40, 46, 69, 70, 72, 84, 86, 89, 100, 109, 110, 135, 137, 139, 145, 152, 154, 165, 166, 174, 175, 176, 183, 198, 213, 214, 235, 244, 247, 248, 249, 254, 261, 264, 291, 309, 319, 324, 329, 330, 362, 363, 373, 378, 395, 396

heaven, 8, 13, 14, 45, 65, 87, 144, 145, 154, 161, 205, 231, 238, 239, 240, 243, 260, 267, 277, 297, 300, 310, 322, 323, 343, 350

heavenly places, 240, 305

heavenly wisdom, 322

Hebrews, 11, 48, 226, 248

hedge, 29, 99, 152, 258, 294, 306, 327, 354

hell, 30, 61, 107, 177, 238, 275, 300, 399, 401

help, 1, 3, 9, 10, 12, 14, 17, 19, 21, 23, 25, 28, 32, 33, 34, 35, 36, 38, 39, 40, 43, 44, 45, 49, 52, 54, 56, 60, 64, 66, 68, 70, 72, 74, 76, 79, 82, 84, 90, 93, 94, 101, 106, 107, 108, 112, 113, 115, 117, 123, 124, 129, 133, 139, 143, 145, 148, 154, 156, 158, 160, 165, 168, 176, 177, 180, 188, 190, 193, 195, 199, 201, 205, 211, 214, 221, 223, 230, 231, 234, 236, 241, 242, 248, 253, 255, 256, 260, 264, 265, 275, 279, 290, 294, 296, 297, 298, 302, 308, 312, 313, 322, 325, 331, 332, 336, 348, 350, 352, 356, 358, 360, 361, 365, 369, 373, 381, 391, 392, 396, 398, 402

helpers, 113

heritage, 133, 203, 257

hidden treasure, 329

High Priest, 163

hinder, 90, 195, 229

hindering, 3, 148

holiness, 48, 175, 184, 290, 314, 369, 376

holy, 27, 44, 46, 48, 74, 79, 97, 146, 156, 159, 162, 166, 213, 238, 246, 270, 281, 318, 323, 325, 334, 344, 382, 399

Holy Ghost, 12, 84, 184, 216, 308, 339, 373
homosexuality, 67
honest, 9
honey, 227, 228
honor, 57, 67, 88, 118, 119, 123, 137, 148, 194, 244, 323, 367, 382, 389, 390
honorable, 75, 76
honored, 120, 137
hope, 22, 52, 92, 116, 147, 148, 159, 160, 172, 184, 185, 186, 247, 248, 327, 379
horizon, 29
house, 110, 146, 207, 210, 211, 228, 230, 280, 329, 370, 371
household, 280, 352
humbly, 21
humiliation, 366
humility, 6, 42, 43, 181, 214
hurt, 15, 84, 137, 153, 201, 230, 231, 258, 263, 264, 265, 303, 312, 351, 352, 396, 398
hymns, 109

I

illnesses, 58, 339, 381
image, 53, 54, 105, 191, 321, 347
imagination, 199
immovable, 55
imperfections, 60, 221
implant, 75
impossible, 43, 47, 79, 143, 223, 253, 267, 298, 317, 344
impurities, 72, 105, 362

incentive, 222, 375
incident, 89
incline, 215
increase, 72, 79, 143, 236, 248, 253, 308, 340, 344, 355
indulge, 2, 48, 68, 130, 376
indwelling, 54
inflexibility, 126
influence, 11, 239, 335
inform, 27
information, 201, 269
inheritance, 14, 87, 258, 273, 293, 309, 322
iniquities, 223, 274, 275, 344
iniquity, 192, 247, 250, 274
injunction, 91, 96
injure, 40, 258
injuries, 291
injustices, 69, 208
innocent, 76, 278
inspiration, 252, 378
instruction, 368
instructions, 18, 96, 154, 324, 369
integrity, 28, 84, 186, 290, 321
intelligence, 109, 357
intensity, 118, 122
intentional, 25, 220
intentions, 32, 37, 287
intercede, 85, 113, 164, 272
interceding, 9, 155, 194, 240, 306
intercessor, 272, 274
intercessory, 19

Index

intimate, 25, 90, 113, 165, 192, 223, 253, 254, 287
intimidated, 309, 310, 352
invincible army, 171, 172
iron, 113
Israel, 121, 142, 147, 191, 270, 299, 375
issue, 113, 114
issues, 34, 43, 49, 113, 176, 264

J

Jehovah Jireh, 119, 298, 385
Jehovah Rapha, 119, 152, 381, 385
Jerry Springer, 76
Jesus, 4, 6, 8, 9, 10, 12, 14, 16, 17, 18, 19, 20, 21, 23, 24, 25, 26, 27, 28, 30, 32, 34, 36, 38, 40, 41, 43, 45, 46, 47, 49, 50, 51, 52, 54, 56, 57, 58, 59, 60, 62, 63, 64, 66, 67, 68, 70, 71, 72, 73, 74, 76, 77, 79, 80, 82, 84, 85, 87, 88, 90, 92, 94, 95, 97, 99, 100, 103, 105, 107, 108, 113, 115, 118, 120, 121, 123, 127, 129, 131, 133, 134, 135, 137, 139, 143, 145, 146, 148, 150, 152, 155, 156, 157, 158, 160, 161, 162, 163, 164, 166, 168, 169, 172, 176, 177, 178, 180, 182, 184, 186, 188, 190, 191, 192, 193, 194, 195, 197, 199, 201, 203, 206, 211, 212, 216, 219, 221, 222, 223, 224, 226, 230, 232, 234, 236, 237, 238, 239, 240, 242, 243, 244, 245, 246, 247, 248, 250, 251, 253, 254, 256, 258, 260, 262, 264, 265, 267, 269, 270, 271, 272, 273, 274, 275, 279, 281, 283, 285, 286, 287, 288, 290, 292, 294, 296, 298, 299, 300, 301, 302, 304, 306, 308, 309, 310, 313, 318, 319, 320, 322, 323, 325, 326, 327, 328, 332, 334, 336, 338, 339, 343, 344, 347, 348, 350, 352, 353, 354, 356, 358, 361, 362, 364, 365, 367, 369, 372, 373, 374, 376, 378, 379,

381, 382, 383, 384, 385, 386, 387, 388, 390, 392, 394, 396, 397, 399, 401

Jew, 73, 287

job, 27, 117, 192, 197, 228, 277, 294

Joseph, 331

journey, 2, 148, 169, 233, 269, 313, 385, 392

joy, 15, 16, 17, 26, 37, 71, 120, 121, 134, 135, 140, 145, 154, 159, 161, 162, 172, 217, 222, 229, 230, 244, 260, 261, 262, 300, 318, 345, 352, 368, 382

joyful, 15, 120, 149, 229

Judge, 291, 292

judgement, 133

judgment, 114, 149, 203, 257, 289, 291, 322, 357

JUST, 78

justice, 40, 142, 257, 360

justification, 158, 257, 275

justified, 224

K

key, 25, 96

kill, 40, 106, 207, 277

kindness, 49, 136, 140, 196, 210, 214, 252, 253, 282, 284, 287, 349, 382, 383

King, 18, 37, 207, 208, 247, 259, 291, 292, 303

King Ahasuerus, 207

kingdom, 13, 16, 21, 87, 129, 151, 197, 207, 208, 281, 370, 400

Kingdom, 14, 35, 43, 55, 61, 79, 87, 168, 186, 208, 209, 221, 236, 237, 250, 281, 292, 319, 365, 371

Index

knees, 25, 154, 382
knock, 7, 8
knowingly, 20, 21, 135
knowledge, 81, 102, 142, 143, 153, 233, 234, 249, 261, 262, 300, 348, 349, 350, 355
Knowledge, 1, 349

L

labor, 55, 170, 187, 233, 293, 294, 321, 345
lamp, 110, 335
land, 16, 218, 319, 320, 341
language, 14, 44, 45, 53, 76, 83
laugh, 15, 16, 357
Law, 11, 12, 263, 291, 354, 373, 375
lead, 10, 23, 45, 52, 62, 84, 101, 145, 146, 156, 233, 237, 245, 287, 324, 336, 348, 374, 396
Leader, 222
lean, 9, 107, 117, 126, 133, 234, 252, 253, 385
learn, 32, 43, 72, 269, 369
legalistic hoops, 299
lesson, 369
lessons, 108
level, 43, 57, 58, 101, 129, 141, 148, 166, 174, 221, 290, 302
liar, 81, 242, 277, 295
liberator, 191
lies, 64, 180, 216, 258
life, 2, 4, 6, 8, 9, 11, 12, 14, 16, 18, 19, 22, 23, 25, 26, 30, 32, 36, 38, 43, 44, 45, 47, 49, 52, 54, 55, 56, 57, 59, 60, 62, 64, 65, 66, 68, 80, 87, 89, 91, 92, 95, 97, 98, 99, 103, 105, 107, 110, 111,

113, 114, 115, 117, 121, 122, 123, 125, 127, 129, 130, 131, 133, 135, 137, 138, 139, 140, 141, 145, 148, 153, 154, 155, 156, 157, 158, 161, 162, 164, 166, 167, 168, 169, 170, 174, 176, 180, 182, 184, 185, 186, 190, 192, 193, 195, 196, 199, 201, 203, 204, 206, 211, 212, 216, 217, 218, 221, 222, 223, 226, 228, 229, 230, 236, 237, 238, 240, 242, 244, 245, 248, 250, 252, 256, 261, 262, 265, 266, 267, 271, 275, 278, 279, 281, 283, 285, 286, 287, 288, 290, 292, 294, 296, 298, 300, 302, 304, 306, 308, 310, 313, 318, 320, 322, 324, 325, 327, 328, 332, 336, 340, 341, 343, 344, 345, 347, 349, 350, 351, 352, 354, 356, 357, 358, 361, 362, 365, 366, 367, 368, 371, 373, 376, 379, 381, 385, 388, 390, 391, 394, 396, 399, 401, 402

lifestyle, 1, 23, 27, 46, 61, 79, 97, 216, 246, 318, 325, 376, 399

lifetime, 125, 221, 320, 369

Light, 63, 98

limitations, 179

lives, 2, 3, 7, 10, 11, 12, 13, 14, 20, 23, 25, 28, 29, 30, 37, 38, 40, 42, 44, 46, 47, 51, 53, 54, 55, 59, 63, 64, 68, 70, 76, 79, 84, 85, 86, 87, 93, 96, 102, 103, 105, 108, 114, 116, 117, 118, 121, 131, 143, 147, 148, 152, 156, 158, 167, 169, 170, 186, 192, 195, 203, 206, 216, 223, 235, 236, 253, 254, 255, 267, 273, 278, 286, 305, 313, 323, 324, 331, 348, 351, 353, 354, 357, 370, 385, 396

longsuffering, 135

Lord, 4, 5, 6, 8, 10, 12, 14, 16, 17, 19, 21, 23, 24, 25, 26, 28, 29, 30, 31, 32, 34, 35, 36, 38, 40, 41, 43, 45, 46, 47, 48, 49, 50, 52, 54, 55, 56, 58, 60, 62, 64, 65, 66, 68, 70, 72, 74, 76, 77, 79, 80, 82, 84, 85, 87, 88, 90, 92, 94, 95, 97, 99, 100, 101, 102, 103, 104, 105, 107, 108, 110, 111, 113, 114, 115, 116, 118, 119, 120, 121, 122, 123, 124, 125, 126, 127, 128, 129, 130, 131, 133, 135,

Index

136, 137, 139, 141, 142, 143, 145, 146, 147, 148, 149, 150, 151, 152, 153, 154, 156, 157, 158, 159, 160, 162, 163, 164, 165, 166, 167, 168, 169, 170, 171, 172, 174, 176, 177, 178, 180, 184, 186, 187, 188, 190, 191, 192, 193, 194, 195, 196, 197, 198, 199, 201, 203, 204, 205, 206, 211, 212, 214, 215, 216, 218, 219, 221, 223, 224, 225, 226, 227, 228, 230, 232, 233, 234, 236, 238, 240, 241, 243, 244, 246, 248, 249, 252, 253, 254, 256, 257, 258, 259, 260, 261, 262, 264, 265, 267, 269, 271, 273, 274, 275, 279, 281, 282, 283, 284, 285, 287, 288, 290, 291, 292, 293, 294, 296, 297, 298, 299, 300, 302, 304, 306, 308, 310, 312, 313, 315, 317, 318, 319, 320, 322, 325, 326, 328, 329, 330, 331, 332, 334, 338, 339, 341, 344, 346, 348, 349, 350, 351, 352, 353, 354, 356, 361, 362, 365, 367, 369, 370, 371, 372, 373, 376, 377, 379, 383, 384, 385, 388, 389, 390, 391, 392, 393, 394, 396, 397, 398, 399, 400, 401, 402

lovable, 390

love, 2, 10, 14, 16, 20, 21, 33, 34, 42, 49, 58, 59, 60, 66, 70, 73, 84, 88, 96, 97, 99, 103, 107, 108, 119, 120, 122, 124, 125, 133, 135, 138, 145, 151, 164, 165, 166, 167, 168, 179, 190, 202, 204, 210, 217, 218, 219, 220, 221, 230, 232, 241, 242, 246, 247, 249, 250, 263, 264, 282, 283, 294, 300, 301, 302, 307, 315, 318, 320, 323, 331, 332, 334, 346, 349, 350, 352, 354, 358, 361, 362, 367, 375, 378, 379, 387

lowliness, 42

loyalty, 78

lungs, 339

lying, 60, 67, 123, 362, 393

M

mad, 74, 121

majesty, 244

malice, 181, 182, 369

manifested, 19, 211, 225, 344

marriage, 24, 122, 123, 131, 281

marriages, 30, 102, 135

marvelous light, 333, 334

masterpiece, 47

mature, 79, 185, 210, 250

maturity, 71, 178, 186, 221, 222

meaningless, 216, 309

mediator, 9, 155, 273

mediocre, 334

meditate, 1, 2, 11, 92, 175, 206, 227, 234, 318, 324, 325

meditated, 12, 176

meek, 42

melancholy, 285

melody, 109

memory, 199

mentally, 14, 15, 32, 46, 277

mentor, 113, 373

mercies, 163, 164, 170, 243

merciful, 163, 246, 247, 270, 271, 305

mercy, 47, 66, 93, 94, 100, 136, 137, 142, 143, 151, 163, 177, 184, 189, 210, 213, 214, 219, 246, 252, 253, 271, 278, 279, 282, 284, 287, 349, 383, 394

Messiah, 109, 247, 272, 293, 299, 300, 387

midnight, 196

might, 98, 102, 114, 118, 119, 126, 157, 158, 175, 255, 323, 340, 398

mighty, 162, 226, 244

milestone, 58

mind, 8, 9, 27, 28, 42, 66, 68, 69, 74, 75, 82, 83, 87, 93, 112, 127, 134, 136, 139, 164, 167, 168, 176, 178, 180, 183, 184, 190, 199, 200, 201, 203, 206, 222, 236, 242, 249, 251, 262, 270, 276, 282, 310, 314, 318, 320, 322, 331, 332, 333, 342, 361, 372, 376, 380, 386, 393, 395

minds, 70, 81, 82, 86, 109, 152, 245, 310, 348, 395

minister, 12, 28

ministries, 25, 341

ministry, 18, 20, 26, 27, 38, 87, 109, 117, 206, 211, 290, 302, 308, 341, 402

miracles, 18, 110, 137, 164

mirror, 53

misinterpret, 183

mistakes, 139, 203, 356

mistreat, 33, 304, 346

misuse, 34, 49, 304

moaning, 230

modesty, 42

mold, 47, 72, 104, 115, 127, 313

money, 84, 236, 340

moral, 112, 167, 175, 312, 321, 323, 380, 381

Mordecai, 207, 208

morning, 15, 16, 46, 136, 230

mortals, 389

Moses, 142, 402

motivation, 355

motives, 182, 235, 236

Mount Calvary, 223

Mount Moriah, 205, 297

Mount Zion, 205, 297

mountain, 95

mourning, 15, 208, 217

mouth, 11, 40, 41, 45, 66, 101, 135, 137, 140, 153, 176, 201, 206, 216, 227, 228, 233, 299, 300, 317, 318, 320

mouthpieces, 55, 186

mouths, 2, 27, 135

multiplication, 170

multitude, 20, 134, 284

muscle, 78

mustard seed, 78, 79, 285

N

narrow gate, 237, 278

nation, 13, 333, 334

nationalities, 156

nations, 274, 299, 343

natural realm, 19, 79

Nebuchadnezzar, 18

need, 2, 5, 9, 10, 12, 19, 22, 24, 25, 28, 30, 31, 35, 36, 37, 38, 40, 42, 43, 46, 47, 49, 52, 64, 66, 67, 74, 79, 82, 83, 84, 87, 89, 93, 94, 97, 100, 101, 102, 107, 108, 110, 112, 114, 117, 121, 123, 126, 136, 139, 141, 142, 145, 152, 153, 154, 162, 165, 168, 169, 173, 174, 175, 176, 180, 186, 192, 198, 199, 201, 206, 208, 215, 216, 218, 222, 232, 233, 234, 237, 242, 248, 250, 253, 254, 256, 260, 266, 269, 278, 285, 287, 291, 292, 297, 299, 306, 314, 319, 320, 324, 325, 330, 331, 332, 336, 340, 341, 348, 352, 356, 358, 364, 369, 375, 378, 382, 384, 385, 388, 389, 391, 394, 396

neglect, 53, 322

neighborhood, 21, 33, 112
neighbors, 59, 60
new ventures, 365
noble, 181, 323
north, 236
nutrients, 370

O

obedience, 5, 81, 358, 368
obedient, 33, 52, 110, 121, 168, 205, 206, 302, 320, 348, 379, 399, 401
obey, 37, 96, 273, 312, 313, 319, 320, 324, 378
obeyed, 13, 96, 273
obligation, 59
obligations, 332, 375
observation, 349
obstacles, 3, 4, 30
offense, 40, 49, 175, 330
old, 27, 60, 106, 107, 140, 149, 150, 201, 208, 250, 300, 322, 340, 341, 376
olive oil, 211
omission, 21, 66, 135
opinion, 213, 239, 279, 295
opportunity, 21, 27, 66, 375, 376
oppression, 343
ordinance, 91, 295
organism, 70
outer appearance, 362
overabundance, 370

overcome, 10, 23, 82, 171, 179, 401

overcomer, 72, 112

overflow, 16, 87, 305, 308, 319, 341

overnight, 87, 264

overpower, 144

owe, 59

ownership, 35

oxygen, 47, 136, 253

P

pain, 15, 208, 230, 264, 265, 331, 393

painful, 105, 148, 368

pandemic, 57, 151, 152, 197, 206, 208

paralyze, 401

pardon, 218, 231, 267, 272, 388

parents, 108, 254, 330

passion, 28, 39, 73, 113, 261, 294

passions, 48

path, 3, 4, 6, 30, 133, 154, 161, 237, 238, 261, 278, 300, 329, 335, 336, 374, 392

paths, 3, 4, 286, 322

patience, 42, 48, 135, 213, 214, 256, 369, 383

patiently, 31

pattern, 11, 63, 296

Paul, 27, 287, 299, 340, 373

peace, 16, 48, 49, 57, 69, 70, 71, 75, 120, 134, 135, 137, 145, 147, 154, 162, 174, 177, 180, 182, 184, 202, 203, 214, 218, 219, 230, 242, 246, 257, 259, 262, 278, 279, 285, 294, 300, 309, 310, 315, 318, 331, 344, 345, 346, 352, 358, 377, 391, 395, 396, 397

peaceful, 23, 278
peacemaker, 315, 346
penetrate, 64
perfection, 51, 140, 222, 263
perform, 73
perish, 207
permission, 132
perplexed, 132, 306
persecuted, 133, 306
persecution, 257
persuade, 51
perverse, 183
pestilence, 337, 338, 381
petition, 188, 196
petitions, 319
physically, 14, 15, 32, 46
pictures, 67
pity, 100, 213, 284
plagues, 337, 381
plaguing, 122
plans, 147, 164, 173, 202, 238, 269, 350
planted, 78, 116, 193, 195, 210, 370, 371
pleasing, 2, 14, 38, 54, 60, 85, 89, 90, 97, 107, 114, 121, 139, 157, 223, 275, 296, 308, 322, 340, 379
pleasure, 110, 134, 227, 243, 249, 261, 285, 384
pleasures, 61, 161, 235, 261, 262, 380
plenty, 16, 86
ploys, 202, 251, 350
portion, 16, 144, 230
positive, 79, 101, 130

possession, 17, 35, 289, 309, 360

possible, 79, 298, 305

potter, 28, 47, 72, 104, 313

pottery, 72

poverty, 197, 365, 367

power, 1, 2, 10, 13, 20, 27, 54, 73, 86, 102, 104, 109, 112, 113, 118, 119, 124, 130, 161, 163, 178, 179, 190, 192, 213, 214, 239, 240, 242, 255, 284, 300, 307, 333, 334, 347, 348, 351, 352, 354, 361, 367, 372, 382, 383, 384, 398

powerful, 11, 38, 226, 247, 277, 303

praise, 16, 57, 75, 118, 136, 137, 148, 149, 150, 169, 197, 243, 244, 261, 283, 323, 331, 354, 373, 382, 383

praises, 111, 137, 334

pray, 14, 18, 19, 21, 27, 30, 33, 35, 40, 44, 45, 71, 79, 84, 89, 90, 93, 112, 113, 148, 160, 173, 179, 180, 187, 192, 198, 211, 216, 226, 232, 236, 253, 266, 267, 296, 307, 308, 338, 344, 358, 378, 379, 394

prayer, 1, 18, 19, 25, 31, 32, 45, 50, 80, 112, 113, 145, 160, 171, 174, 188, 196, 226, 258, 266, 307, 308, 331, 338, 349, 350, 373, 379, 393

prayers, 18, 19, 45, 86, 93, 94, 111, 152, 160, 165, 187, 188, 215, 232, 266, 267, 296, 319, 394

preach, 185, 186

precepts, 63, 91, 142, 249, 282, 283, 295

presence, 25, 56, 71, 77, 97, 103, 129, 141, 145, 161, 162, 165, 169, 170, 194, 203, 211, 218, 241, 248, 259, 260, 261, 262, 303, 305, 306, 308, 318, 332, 344, 346, 354, 388

President, 205

price, 67, 68, 211, 299, 354

pride, 5, 6, 42, 43, 214, 226, 376

priesthood, 146, 333, 334
Prince of peace, 310
Prince of Peace, 69
principle, 29, 91, 236
principles, 182, 295
prize, 222, 391
probation, 388
problem, 7, 41, 82, 114, 201, 232, 298, 394, 396
proclaim, 185, 186
profession, 20, 84
proficient, 106
profit, 61, 191, 368
progress, 3, 28, 44, 171, 172
promise, 27, 31, 38, 121, 150, 151, 281, 349, 401
promises, 92, 142, 149, 151, 152, 199, 228, 242, 279, 285, 304, 367, 373, 392
promotes, 61
properly, 205, 384
prophesy, 203
Prophet Habakkuk, 171
prophetic, 148, 226, 228, 344
prophets, 148, 226, 280
prosper, 133, 183, 203, 257, 258, 327, 365, 370, 371, 381, 399
prosperity, 120, 124, 210, 258, 364
prosperous, 11, 14, 87, 201, 210, 345, 350
protect, 29, 30, 160, 194, 205, 303, 304, 330, 337, 395
protection, 16, 29, 99, 132, 152, 190, 194, 258, 261, 262, 277, 294, 303, 304, 306, 327, 338, 354, 357, 380, 396
protector, 338, 381, 389, 390

providence, 392

provocative, 67

psalms, 109

psyche, 167

punishment, 39, 73, 263, 264, 274, 299

purchased, 67, 239, 333

pure, 34, 43, 72, 75, 76, 84, 90, 104, 198, 199, 232, 236, 313, 315, 324, 329, 334, 362, 363

purged, 317

purified, 105, 213, 362

purity, 321

purpose, 23, 55, 67, 81, 86, 114, 126, 147, 148, 235, 272, 286, 312, 333, 341, 368

purposes, 142, 149, 150, 182, 185, 186, 199, 269

Q

qualified, 106, 400

qualities, 331, 357

quantity, 86, 173, 305

quarrel, 314

quarrelsome, 314

quiet, 81, 90, 201, 314, 316, 320, 345, 357

quietness, 69

R

ransom, 155, 157

ravage, 81

reading, 1, 27, 64, 107, 154, 184, 364, 373

Index

reap, 32, 229, 230
recognition, 61
recognize, 3, 4, 145, 151, 278, 323, 343
redeemer, 158, 191, 320
Redeemer, 119, 191, 317, 388
redemption, 157, 273
refreshes, 218
refreshment, 387, 388
refuge, 102, 122, 123, 124, 134, 159, 160, 210, 285, 303, 304, 343, 351, 352
refuse, 52, 58, 253, 254, 392, 399
regress, 90
regret, 40
reigns, 13, 185
reject, 7, 8, 253, 357
rejected, 8, 104, 149
rejoice, 72, 120, 121, 243
rejoicing, 121, 179, 394
relationships, 3, 24, 102, 135, 201, 278, 357
Reliance, 189
remembrance, 12, 53, 62, 176, 178, 325, 338
remove, 3, 49, 54, 60, 66, 75, 121, 148, 184, 199, 203, 216, 244, 250, 300, 399
removes, 3, 267
renew, 34, 60, 66, 82, 105, 111, 140, 141, 148, 176, 178, 198, 245, 363
renewed, 1, 140, 175, 176, 304, 321, 362
renewing, 164, 168, 348
renounce, 241, 251
repay, 59, 179

repent, 5, 6, 27, 40, 52, 68, 82, 117, 135, 201, 271, 307, 313, 315, 373
repentance, 76, 135, 330, 387, 399
repentant, 177
repents, 215
representative, 213
request, 187, 235, 319
rescue, 10, 145, 177, 190, 242, 266, 299, 369, 394
resentment, 231
resist, 64, 113, 126, 277
resistance, 225
respect, 68, 75, 312, 367, 382
responsibility, 42, 96, 171, 355
rest, 14, 69, 120, 195, 202, 217, 218, 240, 255, 256, 284, 313, 327, 328, 343, 344, 388, 391, 392
restoring, 6, 17
results, 19, 61, 72, 111, 188, 215, 278, 358
resuscitation, 2
retaliate, 90
revelation, 1, 269
revenge, 40
reverence, 166, 169, 312, 313, 382
reward, 293, 294, 340
Richard Richardson, 402
riches, 10, 87, 94, 118, 175, 260, 273, 298, 306, 385, 396
richness, 109
righteous, 19, 24, 27, 43, 46, 79, 103, 111, 112, 124, 152, 154, 155, 156, 188, 215, 237, 246, 247, 254, 264, 272, 295, 317, 318, 321, 322, 325, 335, 354, 381, 392, 399

righteousness, 38, 39, 42, 61, 78, 129, 142, 155, 156, 157, 158, 168, 183, 203, 217, 218, 219, 238, 247, 257, 273, 287, 290, 299, 304, 306, 314, 315, 319, 329, 335, 361, 368, 370, 371, 376, 384

rivalry, 235
roadblocks, 184
roaring lion, 277
rock, 122, 144, 145, 146, 225, 379
Rock, 122, 144, 159, 317
Roman, 66, 373
rooted, 9, 55, 57, 70, 124, 151, 210, 211, 243, 250, 253, 258
Ruth, 331

S

sacrifice, 27, 68, 155, 156, 168, 192, 222, 223, 238, 240, 246, 248, 273, 275, 281, 287, 354, 388
sacrifices, 146, 167, 375
sacrificing, 158, 192, 287, 304
safety, 58, 103, 108, 145, 207, 292, 357, 358, 380, 381
saints, 133, 140, 203, 217, 229, 243, 244, 252, 280, 289, 292, 303, 304
salvation, 27, 40, 73, 90, 122, 124, 125, 126, 159, 185, 218, 237, 243, 261, 272, 273, 275, 286, 287, 289, 292, 299, 300, 304, 345, 354
sanctification, 48
sanctuary, 145, 211
Sarah, 140
Satan, 40, 64, 81, 126, 178, 191, 217, 226, 238, 251, 276, 304, 315, 318, 324, 338, 350, 354

satisfaction, 120, 184, 218, 227, 345

satisfied, 16, 218

saturation, 348

saved, 21, 27, 28, 66, 79, 84, 135, 177, 179, 201, 214, 216, 253, 275, 287, 299, 300, 304, 353, 373, 375, 376

Savior, 4, 46, 65, 66, 73, 120, 130, 156, 157, 170, 177, 238, 254, 272, 274, 305, 306, 354, 372, 373

scamming, 84

scandal, 290

scenes, 261, 305

schemes, 36

Scriptures, 1, 67, 71, 109, 214, 216, 226, 269, 352, 353

sea, 139, 193

season, 18, 62, 101, 117, 166, 206, 208, 325, 332, 370, 371

seasoned, 107, 140, 148

secure, 75, 124, 285, 304, 328, 352, 360

security, 134, 257, 337, 381

see, 11, 16, 20, 21, 38, 41, 43, 48, 68, 72, 76, 87, 90, 96, 110, 116, 136, 145, 176, 184, 195, 206, 221, 223, 226, 230, 234, 252, 253, 258, 267, 282, 283, 294, 323, 325, 346, 357, 363, 381, 388, 394

Seek, 37, 259, 330

selfish, 235

sensitive, 28, 110

servants, 257, 332

serve, 14, 28, 40, 118, 203, 238, 258, 287, 293, 294, 312, 313, 320, 323, 375

service, 55, 110, 167, 191, 238, 270, 287

seven spirits, 333

shadow, 123, 134, 152, 177, 180, 262, 327, 328, 341, 361

shame, 16, 18, 74, 222, 331
shamelessness, 18
sharp, 7
Shekinah Glory, 110, 244
shelter, 304, 327, 328, 343, 352
shield, 99, 132, 190, 194, 303, 304, 306, 321, 327, 328, 331
shine, 70, 99, 323, 325, 332
shortcomings, 60, 112, 221, 231
sickness, 65, 161, 255, 338
Sickness, 333, 334, 386
sicknesses, 57, 337, 381, 385
sight, 2, 56, 60, 85, 90, 114, 139, 152, 210, 220, 317, 320, 322, 388
significant, 18, 54
signs, 110
silence, 239
sin, 12, 14, 26, 27, 48, 54, 63, 65, 66, 70, 76, 77, 82, 84, 98, 99, 107, 113, 124, 135, 143, 154, 157, 158, 160, 164, 168, 175, 176, 178, 187, 192, 193, 202, 203, 215, 217, 223, 238, 240, 245, 246, 248, 249, 250, 252, 269, 271, 272, 273, 274, 284, 287, 290, 292, 299, 315, 317, 318, 330, 335, 354, 366, 376, 377, 379, 387
sincerity, 165
sinful, 23, 67, 149, 238
singing, 109, 120, 121, 149, 229
sinner, 8, 27, 177, 215, 218, 253, 280
sinners, 93, 163, 247, 252, 253
sinning, 82, 84, 250
sins, 20, 21, 27, 67, 82, 97, 112, 113, 118, 120, 157, 192, 215, 216, 229, 230, 267, 273, 274, 275, 292, 299, 300, 304, 354, 373, 375, 376, 387, 388

sisters, 39, 55, 71, 220, 221, 345

situation, 2, 11, 32, 44, 49, 64, 89, 90, 92, 93, 110, 112, 117, 131, 140, 173, 180, 182, 186, 226, 296, 297, 322, 379, 384, 394, 396

situations, 9, 24, 30, 79, 90, 91, 226, 262

skill, 233, 286, 355, 357

skillful, 157, 233, 278

slandered, 33

slavery, 354

small beginnings, 342

snare, 82, 249, 250

soaring, 140

social media, 67, 76

Solomon, 233, 355

solution, 19, 41, 396

solve, 10

Sons, 152

sorrow, 16, 153, 161, 229, 252

sorrowful, 217, 218

soul, 12, 28, 30, 61, 109, 127, 134, 144, 145, 167, 168, 169, 172, 179, 214, 216, 217, 218, 226, 251, 256, 284, 285, 293, 320, 328, 332, 354, 363, 372

souls, 21, 28, 57, 126, 159, 163, 183, 185, 208, 217, 276, 303, 343, 368, 383

south, 236

sow, 229, 230, 236, 345, 365

sower, 236, 365

speak, 2, 13, 23, 27, 39, 40, 41, 45, 49, 79, 80, 86, 91, 92, 130, 131, 160, 169, 176, 182, 186, 191, 204, 208, 213, 220, 221, 226, 296, 302, 330

speech, 53, 64
spirit man, 1
spirit of fear, 401
Spirit of Holiness, 333
Spirit of Might, 333
Spirit-led, 45
spiritual death, 299
spiritual eyes, 184
spiritual growth, 259, 376
spiritual realm, 79, 89, 206, 226
spiritually, 14, 15, 46, 71, 277, 345
spite, 149, 401
spouses, 39, 331
Spring, 47
stagnant, 203
standing, 5, 7, 28, 52, 97, 158, 192, 199, 213, 216, 223, 237, 242, 271, 283, 313, 321, 322, 368
stature, 104, 347
statutes, 175, 282
steadfast, 55, 151, 194, 249, 276
steadfastness, 159
steal, 40, 106, 174, 277, 324, 325, 358
stealing, 40, 84
steps, 4, 80, 101, 112
steward, 17, 28, 365
stewards, 2
storehouse, 236
storms, 2, 57, 78, 103, 108, 160, 190, 195, 196, 197, 211, 223, 260, 262, 304, 310, 327, 328, 343, 352, 362, 383
streams of income, 14, 87, 341

strength, 22, 25, 29, 30, 56, 62, 66, 74, 82, 84, 94, 102, 103, 107, 114, 115, 118, 119, 122, 123, 125, 126, 137, 138, 140, 141, 144, 145, 153, 159, 164, 167, 170, 172, 183, 190, 195, 211, 217, 253, 255, 259, 260, 264, 300, 317, 318, 320, 328, 331, 343, 361, 369, 383, 385

strengthens, 45, 47, 58, 101, 160, 195, 383

stressed, 137

stressing, 69, 352

strife, 48, 182, 314, 315

strive, 129, 199, 314, 391

strong, 39, 58, 78, 79, 92, 102, 114, 131, 132, 140, 144, 171, 210, 214, 241, 256, 261, 360, 361, 388, 398, 399

Stronghold, 102, 124

studied, 12

study, 2, 11, 64, 79, 91, 154, 156, 160, 168, 201, 206, 227, 234, 249, 255, 268, 269, 289, 316, 325, 335, 336, 344, 361, 379

studying, 1, 192, 324, 373

stumble, 107, 146, 158, 202, 313, 325

submission, 187

submit, 28, 73, 110, 368

substitute, 145

success, 37, 61, 71, 258, 302

successful, 11, 61, 171, 241, 330, 365

suffered, 20

suffering, 57, 73, 135, 161, 171, 208, 213, 214, 240, 270, 367, 393

sufficient, 86, 138, 145, 173, 247, 360, 361, 383

sugar daddy, 37

Summer, 47

Sunday, 70

superabundantly, 86
superficial, 54
superior, 179
supernatural, 174, 186, 195, 203, 260, 308, 318, 328, 358, 382
supplications, 187, 215
supply, 10, 86, 94, 260, 298, 319, 385, 396
support, 9, 144, 205, 252
surrender, 8, 49, 54, 68, 121, 180, 199, 230, 265, 319
sustaining, 115, 197, 344, 383
swarming locust, 16
sword, 12, 38, 92, 192, 226, 257
symptoms, 6, 74, 338, 339

T

tasks, 94, 114, 124, 230, 241
taste, 227
teach, 49, 106, 107, 108, 109, 114, 153, 175, 186, 221, 269, 282, 365, 373
teachable, 42
teacher, 84
teaches, 13, 142, 191, 247, 252
teaching, 21, 106, 154, 160, 221, 267, 268, 365, 373, 378
tear, 17
tears, 229, 230
temperance, 181, 276, 380
temperatures, 47
temple, 67, 68, 83, 84, 280, 382
temples, 83, 84, 281

tempt, 82, 90, 113, 176

temptation, 82, 126, 138, 304

temptations, 217, 383

tenderhearted, 213, 214

tenderness, 259

terminate, 222

terrified, 58

terror, 171, 241, 263, 360, 398

terrors, 261

test, 30, 72, 138, 139, 225

testament, 151

testify, 26, 98, 190

testimonies, 22, 23, 28, 79, 209, 388

thankful, 69, 70, 383

thankfully, 187

thanksgiving, 18, 19, 57, 188, 344

thinking, 127, 206, 396, 398

thoughts, 12, 69, 81, 82, 134, 147, 198, 199, 226, 284, 285, 378

thousand, 151, 380, 381

throne, 47, 93, 94, 222, 267

time, 16, 18, 21, 26, 32, 37, 38, 39, 40, 43, 51, 58, 64, 68, 72, 84, 93, 94, 96, 101, 102, 107, 110, 115, 117, 124, 126, 128, 134, 140, 145, 147, 151, 155, 160, 161, 165, 173, 174, 178, 189, 192, 199, 206, 207, 208, 223, 226, 248, 253, 258, 264, 273, 286, 293, 294, 319, 320, 330, 349, 350, 356, 361, 364, 368, 369, 389, 396

timid, 400

timidity, 401

timing, 31, 234, 248, 255, 256, 266, 344, 394

tongue, 2, 41, 44, 130, 133, 136, 201, 203, 257, 314, 393

Index

tongues, 44, 45, 220, 221, 393, 394
torment, 8
tough, 90, 356
track, 4, 21, 68, 161, 202, 203, 283, 313, 332
train, 2, 106, 109, 153, 356
tranquility, 69, 358
transform, 201
transformed, 54, 82, 154, 324
transgression, 175, 314
translated, 54
trauma, 59, 330
traumas, 265
traveled, 3
tread, 64
trembling, 172, 247
trials, 2, 22, 24, 25, 57, 64, 71, 72, 115, 138, 139, 149, 153, 177, 185, 197, 223, 225, 242, 248, 253, 254, 260, 262, 341, 383, 398
tribulation, 149
tribulations, 2, 25, 101, 138, 149, 153, 197, 223, 303, 341
tricks, 36, 184, 202, 203, 277, 310
triumph, 122, 159, 172, 257
trouble, 61, 74, 100, 102, 103, 124, 145, 160, 171, 173, 177, 253, 258, 284, 340, 346, 349, 350, 351, 361, 393
troubled, 9, 101, 132, 309, 310
troubles, 7, 24, 25, 64, 115, 124, 134, 147, 162, 171, 173, 177, 223, 253, 262, 392, 396, 397
true, 9, 37, 38, 59, 63, 75, 76, 81, 84, 116, 120, 123, 135, 151, 181, 221, 226, 253, 264, 269, 295, 296, 335, 348, 358, 366, 380, 391, 401

trust, 5, 9, 15, 29, 38, 52, 78, 87, 98, 101, 102, 103, 116, 117, 122, 123, 126, 128, 133, 138, 141, 145, 149, 150, 153, 168, 174, 183, 188, 189, 190, 196, 198, 200, 205, 206, 210, 223, 236, 241, 248, 253, 255, 261, 263, 266, 267, 299, 301, 303, 310, 338, 357, 360, 372, 396, 401

truth, 53, 64, 84, 102, 113, 149, 150, 156, 162, 165, 166, 169, 188, 216, 242, 249, 253, 258, 269, 277, 283, 292, 295, 299, 303, 304, 313, 332, 335, 336, 344, 348, 353, 354, 372, 373, 376, 382, 383, 384, 387

truths, 45

TV, 67, 76, 77

U

umbrella, 184, 277, 327

unafraid, 7

unbelief, 10, 79, 143, 285, 361

uncomfortable, 293

unconditional, 60, 66, 164, 283

understanding, 5, 14, 44, 52, 70, 83, 103, 117, 128, 129, 167, 182, 203, 220, 233, 234, 262, 268, 269, 270, 278, 285, 289, 318, 344, 348, 355, 397

uneasiness, 134, 202

unforgiveness, 89, 232, 362

ungodliness, 126, 149

ungodly, 376

unholy, 84

union, 114, 367

Universe, 360

unknowingly, 21, 135

unknown, 189, 208
unrighteous, 153, 217
unrighteousness, 77, 317, 318
unsaved, 113, 254
unseemly, 84
unyielding, 126, 127, 159
uplift, 149, 297
uplifting, 101
upper room, 45
UPRIGHT, 78
uproot, 176
uprooted, 78
upset, 39, 40
utterances, 44, 226

V

vain, 170, 187
validity, 75
vengeance, 40, 179
verse, 3, 5, 38, 53, 343
vessel, 28
victorious, 1, 271, 310, 327, 328, 360
victory, 12, 32, 174, 178, 240, 243, 258, 327, 399
vindicate, 180, 257, 292, 315
vindication, 257, 258
vindicator, 90, 179, 394
virgin, 192
virtue, 152, 227, 323, 339, 380, 381
virtues, 333

virus, 339
vision, 104
voice, 7, 8, 28, 52, 206, 215, 239, 312, 313, 324, 374
voices, 52, 149, 209

W

wait, 8, 15, 31, 32, 117, 141, 159, 194, 266, 341, 344, 378, 383
wandering, 23
warfare, 58, 171, 195, 391
warning, 149, 185
wars, 48
waste, 81, 218, 337
wasted, 55, 56, 72, 341
water, 92, 117, 195, 253, 370
way, 2, 3, 4, 11, 23, 24, 25, 27, 28, 39, 46, 49, 52, 54, 57, 59, 60, 62, 64, 78, 83, 84, 90, 104, 106, 110, 113, 121, 126, 129, 130, 132, 135, 143, 153, 154, 156, 159, 161, 165, 171, 188, 189, 191, 195, 197, 201, 205, 214, 215, 237, 244, 252, 264, 271, 278, 289, 300, 314, 315, 328, 335, 336, 338, 354, 358, 369, 379, 392, 396, 400, 401
weak, 64, 131, 142, 172, 217, 256, 303, 361
weakness, 112, 113, 361
weaknesses, 39, 82, 383
wealthy, 87
weapon, 45, 133, 203, 257, 258, 327, 381, 399
weary, 32, 103, 128, 129, 141, 190, 217, 218, 255, 256, 261, 328
week, 90, 94, 97, 119, 330, 361

weeping, 15, 230

weight, 54, 252

welfare, 147, 235

west, 236

West Nile Virus, 381

whisper, 145

wholesome, 75, 76, 291

wicked, 166, 183, 239, 252, 254, 274, 380

wilderness, 64, 209, 344

wiles, 113, 127

win, 133, 235, 296

windows, 87

winds, 78

winepress, 208

Winter, 47

wisdom, 5, 89, 109, 147, 154, 163, 181, 182, 185, 186, 203, 233, 234, 248, 268, 278, 279, 290, 314, 321, 322, 349, 355, 356, 357, 358, 383

wise, 5, 163, 174, 181, 191, 200, 268, 278, 279, 289, 355, 356, 357, 369

wish, 46, 309, 350

withhold, 245, 320

witness, 28, 98, 376, 382

witnessing, 22

witty inventions, 14, 365

womb, 52, 74, 124, 148, 152

wonderful, 19, 87, 111, 149, 150, 188, 215, 269, 333, 348, 376

wonders, 110

Word, 1, 2, 8, 9, 10, 11, 12, 13, 14, 16, 19, 22, 23, 30, 37, 38, 40, 47, 48, 49, 52, 53, 54, 55, 56, 60, 61, 64, 65, 72, 76, 79, 81, 82, 84, 85, 90, 91, 92, 96, 98, 99, 101, 102, 107, 109, 110, 111, 113, 114, 121, 129, 130, 131, 133, 143, 146, 149, 150, 153, 154, 156, 158, 159, 160, 168, 170, 175, 176, 178, 180, 184, 186, 187, 193, 197, 198, 199, 202, 206, 214, 215, 221, 226, 227, 228, 233, 234, 244, 246, 248, 249, 250, 252, 253, 254, 256, 258, 260, 262, 263, 265, 266, 268, 269, 278, 281, 282, 283, 289, 290, 293, 295, 296, 304, 306, 308, 315, 324, 325, 330, 332, 333, 334, 335, 336, 341, 344, 348, 358, 360, 361, 364, 365, 372, 373, 378, 379, 381, 382, 383, 384, 388, 398, 399, 401

world, 7, 10, 13, 20, 22, 23, 55, 57, 59, 61, 66, 68, 70, 74, 76, 90, 106, 107, 128, 134, 135, 149, 152, 153, 160, 163, 168, 170, 186, 190, 195, 208, 217, 232, 238, 239, 245, 253, 262, 264, 271, 273, 275, 285, 287, 294, 298, 301, 307, 309, 310, 323, 326, 334, 348, 350, 362, 366, 367, 382, 383, 385, 388, 392, 395, 396, 399, 401

worldliness, 174

worldly wisdom, 279, 356

worry, 9, 66, 173, 174, 263, 338, 344, 379, 395, 396, 401

worrying, 64, 352, 396

worship, 1, 3, 27, 110, 149, 150, 162, 196, 197, 308, 312, 313, 332, 344, 354, 373, 382, 383

worshiping, 154

worth, 90, 175, 221

worthy, 57, 73, 75, 105, 119, 123, 137, 150, 162, 173, 295, 336, 401

wound, 172, 330

wounded, 273, 331

wounds, 59, 122, 265, 330

wrath, 39, 73, 149, 182
writers, 295

Y

year, 2, 116, 184, 336, 360, 375, 402
yielding, 116, 184, 378
YouTube, 67, 76

Z

zealous, 122, 33

The 180-Days of Communing with God Daily Devotional